T0270869

Trademarks, Brands, and Competitiveness

Routledge International Studies in Business History

EDITED BY RAY STOKES AND MATTHIAS KIPPING

Trademarks, Brands, and Competitiveness

Edited by
Teresa da Silva Lopes
and Paul Duguid

Routledge
Taylor & Francis Group
New York   London

First published 2010
by Routledge
711 Third Avenue, New York, NY 10017

Simultaneously published in the UK
by Routledge
2 Park Square, Milton Park, Abingdon, Oxon OX14 4RN

Routledge is an imprint of the Taylor & Francis Group, an informa business

First issued in paperback 2013

Typeset in Sabon by IBT Global.

Library of Congress Cataloging-in-Publication Data
 Trademarks, brands and competitiveness / edited by Teresa da Silva Lopes and Paul Duguid.
   p. cm.—(Routledge international studies in business history ; 19)
   Includes bibliographical references and index.
   1. Brand name products—History. 2. Trademarks—History. 3. Commerce—
History. 4. Competition. I. Lopes, Teresa da Silva, 1968– II. Duguid, Paul, 1954–
   HD69.B7T693 2010
   658.8'27—dc22
   2009026702

ISBN13: 978-0-415-77693-6 (hbk)
ISBN13: 978-0-415-63573-8 (pbk)

Contents

PART II
Trademarks and the Law

PART III
Building Brands

Tables

x   *Tables*

Figures

Preface

What a wonderful book Lopes and Duguid have compiled on trademarks, brands, and their role in a competitive business world. The chapters, when taken as a whole, allow one to understand the power, the possible longevity, and the need for legal care of brands and trademarks over time.

Since commerce commenced, merchants found ways to stamp their "mark" on their very best goods. However, Lopes and Duguid begin this journey with the explosion in and, importantly, the registration of trademarks in nineteenth-century France, Britain, and the United States.

Several authors underscore the importance of a brand with a registered trademark from the standpoint of innovation. The key here is one of protection. With a protected trademark, a brand owner can begin to invest in unique product quality, in marketing, in innovation, and also in export. Thus begins the virtuous circle of better margins and returns as share of a specific market is increased by the superior brand. Both business historians and economists will be interested in the development of higher economic returns from brand leaders in a product category.

As product quality is improved and marketing investment and share of market increased, a brand begins to build a reputation for both objective qualities (e.g. smoother taste) and subjective ("I feel more confident when I am seen with Johnnie Walker Whisky").

In the past, under UK accounting principles, these brand reputations have been quantified and put on the balance sheet.

Several chapters explore how a group of brands from one country can actually provide a sector reputation for the country as a whole (Denmark and the UK cases are utilized). I remember, well, in the 60's/70's when UK hi-fi components were considered the best in the world, and exports boomed.

The second section, "Trademarks and the Law", is immensely valuable, as once a brand owner has invested in building a preeminent reputation, trademark infringement or "passing-off" can be quite economically damaging to the rightful trademark owner. Higgins' chapter reminded me of the common use of geometric forms on beer and other alcoholic beverages, including, of course, Bass Ale's famous red triangle, which makes an appearance in Joyce's *Ulysses*. More up-to-date was the battle between Sir

Stelios Haji-Ioannou's "Easy" colour orange on his fledgling mobile phone business and France Telecom's Orange brand.

The chapter by Davis and Maniatis raises the spectre of well-known trademarks creating barriers to entry by new brands. However, it is the share of a market that represents the barrier to a new brand wishing to obtain economic scale. As long as the well-known/high-share brand continues to provide innovation with unique and desirable qualities, advertises effectively, and does not price too high, that brand should be able to defend its market share, not because the brand is well known but because the reputation for quality and value remains intact.

The same article quotes one authority as arguing,

> A brand has the unique ability to transfer consumer loyalty between products, services and categories over time.

Well, not necessarily, as the case of Nescafé illustrates. Nestlé, in about 1940, created a new process for making "instant" (soluble) coffee. It became extremely popular, especially in tea cultures where the kettle was always at the ready. On numerous occasions, in several countries, Nestlé attempted to introduce a roast- and ground-coffee line extension. These attempts failed as roast and ground users saw an instant coffee brand as inferior to the "real" coffee. It was not until Nestlé, years later, innovated with the Nespresso trademark and preparation system that they could obtain a meaningful share of the value in the roast and ground coffee market.

Duguid's attention to the supply chain aspect of trademarks/brands is quite welcome. More than ever before in business, a complete analysis of the economic profit or cost in each element of the "value chain", from raw material through to consumer purchase price, is necessary for brands to gain economic advantage.

Stefan Schwarzkopf turns to the role of advertising agencies in creating brands with "unique selling propositions" and "emotional selling" propositions from registered trademarks; I have seen advertising, inspired by insightful consumer research, accelerate consumer sales by remarkable percentages in a brief period of time.

The case study on Shell Oil and corporate advertising is interesting. Shell is an example where the corporate name is also the brand name seen by the consumer. Corporate advertising is wasted for companies like Procter & Gamble, where the consumer brand names are quite different. Kraft Foods is an interesting example, where Kraft means cheese to the consumer, but cheese is a small part of total revenue, hence corporate advertising would serve little purpose.

Peter Miskell provides a great coda to the book with his chapter that explores the "wars" between advertised brands and the retailers' private labels. This is especially relevant as we see today's budget-conscious consumers trading down to lower-priced options. I have always found that the best strategy for the advertised brand is to build in more demonstrable product quality benefits and to fine tune the emotional links using sound consumer research.

I have been blessed in business with having worked with stable and very strong international brands, both at Kraft/General Foods and at Diageo. I presided over either the leading brand in a category or at least a very strong number two. My job was then to strengthen the consumer perception of these brands by improving or maintaining high quality, providing appropriate marketing spending behind well researched campaigns, and, in many cases, creating line extensions consistent with the individual brand's consumer values.

Lopes and Duguid's book contributes to a better understanding of how careful management of trademarks and brands can contribute to economic advantage in the marketplace.

Jack Keenan
London, 2008

Introduction
Brands and Competitiveness[1]

Teresa da Silva Lopes and Paul Duguid

It is widely accepted that competitiveness—the comparative strength of nations, regions, and firms in providing goods or services—is a critical factor in modern economic development (Porter 1985). Brands, and by extension trademarks, provide one particularly important weapon in the arsenal of competition, yet their role is less well understood than it should be (Lopes 2007). The chapters in this book set out from several directions to understand how brands promote competitiveness at a variety of levels, from the nation and the region to the firm and the supply chain.

Throughout, the authors provide their own distinctive accounts of brands and marks and use them to analyse aspects of competitiveness at the level of the nation, the region, the firm, or the supply chain. All agree, however, on the general definition of a brand as a name, term, symbol, or design (or combination of these) used by a firm to identify its goods or services and differentiate them from the competition. A trademark is then that aspect of the brand that can gain legal protection through registration. These broad definitions do not ignore the different tasks that brands perform. As the following chapters show, brands play different, though related, parts to support different aspects of buying and selling. For consumers, for instance, they can make it easier to find and recognize particular products and, by acting as an indicator of quality, they can help to reduce the risks and uncertainty inherent in the purchase of a product. For producers, on the other hand, they have the capacity to shape consumers' interests and tastes and to develop loyalty. Consequently, brands tend to be generally looked at in this book, and elsewhere, as economically beneficial. Nevertheless, it is important to consider, as some of the following chapters do, the extent to which brands, as a kind of monopoly, can distort markets, inhibit innovation, provide unreasonable barriers to entry, and promote rent-seeking behaviour. This book attempts to give a rounded view of brands and their part in promoting competitiveness, without being blind to their limitations. To do this, it has drawn on new work from scholars in a variety of disciplines that, together, set brands and trademarks in economic, social, cultural, and historical context.

Overall, the book addresses some of the enduring questions concerning brands, trademarks, and competeness. How do brands and trademarks work? What are they good for? What kinds of competitive advantage can they promote? How do they differ in practice? What are the strengths and deficiencies of contemporary trademark laws? Does trademarking promote or discourage innovation? What does national trademarking activity tell us about the evolution of business? How are successful brands created and how do they embody reputation? How important have public relations and advertising been to the modern conception of the brand? And how do brands differ among our different levels of analysis—the country, the region, the firm, and the supply chain?

Thematically, the book is divided into three sections. The first addresses the relation of brands and marks to national competitiveness. The second looks at the law, and thus focuses more on trademarks in particular than brands in general. The third then turns back to brands and examines how they transcend the limits of the mark to be built into robust competitive tools. Each section draws on the disciplinary strengths of the different authors, who have backgrounds in business, economics, history, law, and marketing. Inevitably, the different chapters are not always in complete agreement with one another, but collectively we hope they build, together, to provide a useful, multiperspectival, and complementary overview of brands in theory and brands in practice.

Although the theoretical perspective is broad, the empirical cases discussed focus primarily on the United Kingdom and UK regions. This focus in part reflects the background of the authors and the origin of this book in a workshop organized by the School of Business and Management at Queen Mary, University of London. But this focus is also theoretically advantageous. The United Kingdom has historically been strong in consumer goods (Chandler 1990). And consumer goods, for their part, are particularly helpful for analysing the role of brands: Firms in the consumer goods sector tend to rely heavily on brands for their competitive advantage. The book does, though, discuss other countries and other sectors. Among the other countries discussed to varying extents are France, Portugal, and the United States, and one chapter (Hansen's) analyses, in detail, the national brand of Denmark in order to make a broader point about how and why nations create brands. And besides consumer goods, individual chapters discuss service marks and high-tech brands.

Part I raises many of the key issues of the volume, defining concepts and providing historical and contemporary accounts of the contribution of brands and trademarks to economic growth. Chapter 1 opens the discussion with a historical view of the subject. Paul Duguid, Teresa da Silva Lopes, and John Mercer examine a century of national rates of trademark registration. This long-term perspective allows them to contrast the evolution of marking and of business in three major trade marking countries: France, the United Kingdom, and the United States. The results are surprising. Many who work on this area assume that 'Anglo-Saxon' countries in general, and the United States in particular, led the transition to the modern trademark. Registration data tell a different story. Instead of the United States standing out as historically on the leading edge, France stands out, and France and Britain both appear to have had both an earlier and more enduring interest in trademarking than the United States, where rates of registration are, by contrast, comparatively low. If, and it is a large 'if', rates of marking can be taken as a proxy for innovation in branding, then these results are surprising.

Although chapter 1 establishes an empirical datum for much that follows, in chapter 2, Mark Casson and Nigel Wadeson lay down a series of central theoretical concepts. In the context of the book as a whole, other chapters can then be read as addressing a selection of these concepts, providing empirical detail, and expanding on or adjusting the theory from different directions. A central notion for Casson and Wadeson concerns reputation, which they see working at a number of distinct levels: the reputation of goods, of suppliers, regions, of sectors, and of nations. Although Casson and Wadeson take primarily an economic approach, they acknowledge the failure of economics to account for such things as self-esteem, social identity, group membership, and the display of membership, all of which are well known to marketing theorists and all of which play a critical role in reputation and its network effects. Consequently, they combine the rigour of economic theory with some of the insights of historical, sociological, and management analysis, before then turning these powerful tools on the analysis of export performance and the extent to which it can be improved through government intervention or support.

In chapter 3, Christian Helmers and Mark Rogers return to trademarking activity and registration data. In contrast to chapter 1, however, they look at more recent years (1996–2000), UK and European marks, and a different and highly intriguing question: To what extent do trademarks provide a proxy for innovation? Adding firm- and sector-performance data to registration data, the chapter paints a rich and complex picture of the relation between trademark activity and performance. (The authors are careful not to imply a direct causal relationship between the former and the later.) Using Schumpeter's notion of creative destruction, Helmers and Rogers then investigate the extent to which other firms' trademarking within an industry exerts competitive pressure on a firm's performance, or whether this static competitive effect is offset by rising overall productivity within the industry.

Chapter 4 combines issues discussed in the preceding chapters with an extended study of national reputation and the effects this can have on particular sectors. With 'Danish Modern' as his subject, Per Hansen develops a conceptual framework for analysing the relationship between nation brands, country image, and product brands. He looks in detail at the construction from the 1940s to the 1970s of the concept of 'Danish Modern' and the ways in which, in the United States in particular, this was closely related to the emerging image of Denmark, an image that had strong appeal in certain sectors of society but which was distasteful in others. Hansen argues that economists and marketing theorists lack the tools to address these issues adequately and leans more heavily on cultural theorists and anthropologists, thus broadening further the multidisciplinary perspective reflected by this book as a whole. Refusing to essentialize brands and their meaning, Hansen instead traces the narrative process by which national and product images are developed.

In all, then, the first section attempts to present a novel mix of historical perspective, empirical data, and theoretical insight. Collectively, the chapters present a picture of the evolution of brands. It suggests that, although these were once primarily the concern of individual firms, over time they have developed to become important tools for advancing regional and national competitiveness. In the process, of course, this evolution has introduced complex tensions among the demands and interests of the firm, the region, and the nation: interests that at times cohere and at times compete.

Part II takes as its particular topic the relationship between brands and the law, considering both the influence of the law on brand strategy and, reciprocally, the influence of strategy on the law. Combining economic theory with legal and administrative history in chapter 5, David Higgins looks at the way regulation and adjudication shaped the landscape in which businesses still compete with the help of trademarks, noting how strategy affects the law, as well as how the law affects strategy. Higgins explores how the law evolved, both through legislation and through litigation, to provide insight into why trademark law and practice have taken the shape they have. Taking the years following the landmark Trade Mark Registration Act [1875] and examining the contribution of the Lancashire textile industry, which was the dominant industrial sector among early registrants, Higgins argues that the law advanced towards an idea that trademarks could simultaneously secure the property rights for producers while protecting the consumer from fraud.

Although Higgins looks at the influence of historical (and historic) trademark decisions, in chapter 6, Jennifer Davis and Spyros Maniatis bring us up to the present, looking at contemporary court decisions and their likely future effects. The authors of this chapter, like those who precede them, note the positive contribution marks can make, but they turn our attention to brands' darker side, noting that this is increasingly becoming an issue for the courts. On the one hand, as is widely acknowledged, brands deserve the courts' protection because they can promote competition. On the other, they merit the courts suspicion because they can lead to monopolistic behaviour and inhibit innovation by diverting entrepreneurial activity into extracting and protecting rents. Capital that might have flowed to product innovation, for instance, has, of late, increasingly been spent on buying existing brands. Concern about the monopolistic character of brands has grown as trademark owners have sought to extend the reach of their brand by advancing the concept of trademark 'dilution', claiming that trademark rights may be infringed even where there is no danger of confusion or fraud. Recently, as the chapter shows with an illuminating sampling of recent court decisions from the United Kingdom, Europe, and the United States, owners have also sought to use their trademarks to supplement and extend patent monopolies. As the value of trademarks continues to grow, the authors suggest, the courts will increasingly face dilemmas over protecting the rights of the trademark holder and protecting the rights of the consumer.

Part II, then, builds on part I by exploring the law that has allowed brands to evolve and flourish over the past century or more. The achievements and economic advantages of brands have been widely celebrated, but as these two chapters together indicate, brands may have evolved beyond the characteristics we tend to applaud. Higgins carefully plots the way in which the law managed, over time, to knit together the interests of businesses and consumers by the beginning of the twentieth century. Davis and Maniatis, however, indicate the way in which this historic compromise is currently being pulled apart and the two interests, of business and consumer, are increasingly coming into conflict and confrontation. Furthermore, Higgins adds that the narrow definition of trademark has encouraged producers to prefer to the broader concept of brand. As a consequence, Higgins concludes, consumer legislation is superseding trademark law. In all, what had been for a long time 'settled' law seems likely to become increasingly unsettled. The confident assumptions of Landes and Posner (1987), which have been so influential in economics, law, and marketing are now looking more dubious.

Part III of the book looks at the building and repositioning of individual brands, providing historical example of the interplay of law and firm strategy and a test for economic theory. In chapter 7, Paul Duguid turns attention away from the competition between firms, regions, and nations, which tends to emphasize the way in which brands are weapons in the fights between similar entities, such as, for example, Nike and Adidas. Duguid explores, instead, the ways in which complementary firms, cooperating with one another in supply chains, are also in competition with one another to brand the chain as a whole. Here, successful branding seems to lead to the extraction of rents and control of the chain. Thus, these internal competitive battles can be as fierce as, and sometimes fiercer than, the external, horizontal competition that draws most of our attention. Such fights, he suggests, with examples of the seventeenth-century book trade and the nineteenth-century wine trade, preceded modern branding and were a critical part of the formation of modern branding case law. But with the rise of modern disaggregated supply chains, he argues, using the example of the personal computer supply chain, such struggles may be returning to prominence.

6   *Teresa da Silva Lopes and Paul Duguid*

In chapter 8, Stefan Schwarzkopf examines developments in the conceptual understanding of brands during the past century. Schwarzkopf looks at Lever, using their experience with advertising agencies to identify forms of shared knowledge and practice that developed between producer and marketing firms in the inter-war years. By the Second World War, Schwarzkopf argues, the advertising profession had come to understand that the narrow view of trademarks needed to be expanded to encompass the broader concepts of brands and branding. This evolution, he argues, was so successful that it called for new legislation, reminding us, once again, that strategy can drive law as much as law can shape strategy. Schwarzkopf concludes that the role of the advertising agency changed. As he points out, this transformation is usually seen as a product of the 1950s. His data show, by contrast, that advertisers very consciously transformed conventional trademarks into new kinds of cultural signifiers from the 1920s.

In chapter 9, Michael Heller presents another historical case study that, by being richly informed with contemporary marketing theory, again suggests that a better understanding of the past will help us to interpret brand practices we see today, many of which are not quite as novel as is sometimes believed. Like Schwarzkopf focusing on the inter-war period, Heller follows the internationalization and marketing strategy of Royal Dutch Shell between 1921 and 1938. He explores the numerous strategies—internal marketing, sponsorship, indirect product branding, and corporate social responsibility—Shell deployed to develop and project its corporate identity within the British Isles. Many of these strategies were highly innovative. In particular, Heller notes, where other oil companies sought to brand their products, Shell preferred to brand the company first, and let its image indirectly cast its products in a favourable light.

Finally, in chapter 10, which brings us once again close to the present, Peter Miskell provides more detailed evidence with which to explore and test theoretical claims. He examines the development of marketing and branding strategies at Unilever, one of the world's leading consumer goods companies over the second half of the twentieth century. The 1960s, Miskell shows, marked a challenging period for producers like Unilever, for a shrinking number of outlets accounted for an increasing share of sales in Western Europe. The chapter shows business history at its best, allowing us to understand, in detail, Unilever's differing and occasionally dithering attempts to respond tactically and strategically to the challenge that the growing power of supermarkets presented to the company's brands. Francis Bacon reminded us of the link between knowledge and power, and Miskell shows how part of the new power of the retailers came from their growing knowledge of consumer patterns. Gathered through point-of-sale technology, this knowledge was readily available to retailers but not to Unilever, and it allowed retailers to develop new products under their own brand and to promote these over similar products branded by Unilever. Like Duguid, Miskell is interested in the role that brands play in vertical, as well as horizontal, competition, and in how, in the modern marketplace, these two kinds of competition interact. Miskell analyses the several strategies Unilever contemplated to deal with its diminishing power in the supply chain, and concludes that its most successful response was to push more and more of its products up the value chain.

The last section of the book, then, provides valuable case studies, set in their historical context, with which to explore the theories developed across the book as a whole. In particular, they show not only the development of particular brands, but also the development of the concept of brands, which now extends well beyond the limited confines of the trademark, however many brands may be dependent on the law of marks that underpins them. Schwarzkopf and Heller note the growing arsenal of original weapons deployed in the conventional 'horizontal' brand wars between like firms and products, and Duguid and Miskell turn our attention by 90 degrees to consider the emerging 'horizontal' brand skirmishes that are demanding new tactics and strategies and putting constantly evolving pressure on the law. Looking back over the book as a whole, we see how the changing demands of the marketplace put constant demands on the strategy not only of firms but of regions and nations, which manage both to take part in and to supervise the struggles among branders, and who at times want to take advantage of, and at times want to restrict, the growing monopolies of certain marks.

Despite some healthily contrasting views between authors about the function and consequences of brands, their one message is clear throughout: brands and trademarks are critical to understanding, to promoting, and, occasionally, to restricting the competitiveness of firms, industries, regions, and countries. The book also seeks to indicate, both directly and indirectly, how the legal system works as a 'referee' in the complex game of competition (North 1990). For economists, it provides a survey of contemporary theory and a clutch of empirical data to interrogate the adequacy of that theory. For business historians, it provides examples of rich empirical research at work. For marketing scholars, it revises not only the theory, but also the chronology of many conventional accounts, while again providing useful case studies and underlining the case specificity of successful brand development. And for other social sciences, it provides empirically informed critiques of the role of brands in society.

NOTE

1. We are very grateful to Routledge and the series editors for the chance to publish this collection; to the authors, not only for their contributions, but also for their prompt and enthusiastic responses to our intermittent demands. We are particularly grateful to Jack Keenan for attending the conference and providing the preface. The Economic and Social Research Council (ESRC) sponsored the conference and the Centre for Globalisation Research at Queen

Mary, University of London, hosted the conference that led to this book. We would also like to thank John Mercer, research assistant on the ESRC grant for helping with the editing. Tim Ambler, Giuliano Maielli, Stefanie Decker, Sushanta Mallick, and Brigitte Granville also contributed to the success of the original meeting. Although the chapters in this book began their lives at the conference, some have been extensively rewritten for publication.

BIBLIOGRAPHY

Chandler, A. (1990) *Scale and Scope: The Dynamics of Industrial Capitalism*, Cambridge, MA: Harvard University Press.

Landes, W. and Posner, R. (1987) 'Trademark law: An economic perspective' *Journal of Law & Economics*, 30(2): 265–309.

Lopes, T. (2007) *Global Brands: The Evolution of Multinationals in Alcoholic Beverages*, New York: Cambridge University Press.

North, D. (1981) *Structure and Change in Economic History*, New York: W. W. Norton.

Porter, M. (1985) *The Competitive Advantage of Nations*, New York: Free Press.

Part I

Trademarks and National Competitiveness

1 Reading Registrations

An Overview of 100 Years of Trademark Registrations in France, the United Kingdom, and the United States

Paul Duguid, Teresa da Silva Lopes, and John Mercer

Trademarks as we know them today are essentially a nineteenth-century creation. Undoubtedly, marks have antecedents stretching back millennia, but as nineteenth-century commentators (Upton 1860), legal historians (Schechter 1925; Sherman and Bently 1999), and business historians (Chandler 1990; Wilkins 1992) generally agree, it is only in the nineteenth century that a defensible property right in marks sufficient for the task of modern marketing emerges. Most commentators also agree that the affirmation of this property right resulted in part from legal decisions made in courts and in part from statutory law, though they differ on the significance of each. The contribution of registration is less usually noted. In an argument that should gain a sympathetic hearing from institutional economists, however, the legal historians Sherman and Bently (1999: 72) have recently helped to dismiss the conventional view that registration is of 'little conceptual interest,' insisting rather, on 'the important role played by registration in determining the scope of intangible property' more generally. Indeed, it is widely assumed that the United Kingdom had no trademark law *per se* until it instituted a system of registration in 1876.

In other areas of intellectual property, work on registrations, from the analyses of the early Stationers' Register for copyright (Arber 1950) to more recent analyses of patent registrations (Khan and Sokoloff 2001; Moser 2005), has been highly productive. Among other things, such studies have yielded insightful analyses of intellectual property-related activities within individual countries and of the differences in these activities between countries (Khan 2005). To date, despite their importance to modern business practices, nothing of the kind has been done for trademarks. This omission may reflect a more general neglect of trademarks in histories of intellectual property. Yet for business historians, as scholars since Chandler (1990) have recognized, it is impossible to understand large tranches of modern business activity without acknowledging the evolving contribution of trademarks and modern branding. And we would add that it seems difficult to understand the evolution of trademarks and branding practices without having some grasp of the patterns of registrations accompanying that evolution. Indeed, as we argue in the following, ignorance of cumulative registration data may have led analysts to underestimate major forces in the development of trademarking.

As it is the aim of this collection to advance the history of marks and brands, so it is the aim of this chapter to begin a very preliminary analysis of registration data and, in so doing, to indicate the potential (and the pitfalls) they hold. Although we accept that, in the long term, much of the interest in the various national and international registers will come from detailed analysis (see, for example, Helmers and Rogers, this volume), it is our goal in this chapter to present an overview, painting with a broad statistical brush a comparative picture of registration in three countries important to the history of marks: France, the United States, and the United Kingdom.

Our focus is primarily business–historical. The information collated and published by trademark agencies provides a vast yet intricate record of the ways in which firms invented, protected, and deployed their trademarks to find customers, to open markets, to gain competitive advantage, and to protect that advantage once gained. Thus, the registration data give insight not merely into trademarking itself, but also into the development of national and international competitiveness in branded goods and services. Beyond these business–historical matters, the registration data undoubtedly offer an important resource for understanding intellectual property regimes more generally. This topic, however, lies beyond the ambition of this chapter.

Of the three countries chosen, France needs little justification. Starting in 1803, it is perhaps the earliest country to have instituted a national (as opposed to a guild-based) system of trade mark registration. It was only with a law of 1857, as we note below however, that reliable registration data began to emerge. France remained, as we shall see, the dominant register of marks for another century or more, as well as a major influence on national and transnational marking practices around the world. By contrast, the United States only began registering in 1870 and the United Kingdom in 1876.[1] Although these two are, to a significant degree, laggards, the size of their economies and the range of their marking, as well as the accessibility and relative reliability of their data, make them worthy foils for historical analysis of the French data.[2]

Before advancing, we need to offer a caution. Neglect of trademark history aside, the registers have no doubt been ignored because of their unwieldy and often impenetrable nature. The data present anyone attempting to use them with daunting challenges. The numbers can be very large, the details very small. By the end of the nineteenth century, France, for example, was regularly registering more than 10,000 marks each year. 50 years later, it was registering 20,000 marks a year. So too, a little while after, was the United States. Much of this data, however, comprises individual and frequently one-off registrations by small firms whose ambitions outstripped their capabilities and who, for one reason or another, disappear from historical records after this brief appearance. The gross numbers, the minutiae they are built up from, and the evanescence of the vast majority of registrants can easily overwhelm the historian. Indeed, occasionally they seem to have overwhelmed the registrars themselves. The latter grappled continuously with intricate questions concerning who could register and what could be registered. In the process, and faced with unexpected deluges of registrations, they changed their practices almost without explanation and abandoned certain kinds of reporting without apology. The French, for example, published nothing until 1884, then published reliable and insightful distillations of their data until 1906, after which these useful digests disappear. The British, for their part, floundered initially under the pent up demand for marks. They did produce apparently robust reports on registration quite regularly, but these turn out to be hard to reconcile with one another. The US Patent and Trademark Office, for its part, took years to introduce a reliable system of categorization for marks, so for a long time it produced fairly reliable gross numbers (though these, too, can be hard to reconcile with one another), but very little by way of further analysis. As a consequence, in this preliminary look at these data, we have not always managed to resolve, or even explain, many discrepancies. We view the data reported here as usefully illustrative or indicative of trends, but far from dispositive or probative.[3]

Given the scale of the data and the growing number of national and international systems that developed almost simultaneously, this chapter is, of necessity, limited to an overview of the development of the three national systems mentioned. With some glances back and forward, we look primarily at the period years from 1860 to 1970, arguing that, within this period, a multilateral system of trademark registration developed that shaped the national and international systems in place today. We begin with a quick look at the relevant law for each country. From there, we give an account of the annual totals for each country over the period under review. The gross numbers are limited in what they can show. They, nonetheless, offer the chance to compare different countries and their appetite for marks with, as we shall see, some unexpected results.

Next, to get a little closer to the data, we look at one particular subset of the whole, the registrations for nondurable consumer goods in a set of benchmark years. We have picked this area because, as we shall show, it was the dominant sector in each of these three countries as they embarked on registration. Although its dominance diminished over time, this sector has remained highly important.[4] Very briefly, we turn to look at some international aspects of national trademark registers before finally concluding with some comments on what our analysis shows and what further investigation might reveal.

AN OVERVIEW OF THE LAW

For the Anglo-Saxon tradition that shaped the law of the United States and the United Kingdom, rights in names were restricted until the nineteenth century by the limitations of the Statute of Monopolies (1624), cases such as Blanchard *v.* Hill (1742), and the decline of guilds. Systems of marking that did endure from earlier periods, such as the cutlers' (Higgins and Tweedale 1996a) and the silversmiths', are best understood as part of vestigial guild systems that declined in the United Kingdom from the seventeenth century. Thus, it is not surprising that in France, where the guild system survived until the revolution dissolved them in 1791, the tradition of protecting marked goods had greater continuity. So strong was that tradition that many rights dissolved in 1791 were reinstated quite quickly: cutlers and jewellers regained many of their rights in years VI and VII (1797–1799), while the law of 22 germinal year XI (1803) attacked the counterfeiting and usurpation of marks of artisans more generally. This law made registration with the local *Tribunal de Commerce* a precondition for prosecution, and thus established a tradition of regional registration in France. A law of April 24, 1824 extended protection from artisans to the names of businesses and places as well. Finally, French trademark law underwent a thorough revision with the law of June 23, 1857. Among other things, the new law sought the protection of French-owned names in foreign countries by establishing a principle of reciprocity to be guaranteed by treaty. Consequently, France embarked on a round of bilateral agreements, beginning with Russia in 1857, and taking in the United Kingdom in 1860 and the United States in 1869, so helping precipitate related legislation being passed soon after in the last two countries. Following the law of 1857, registration in France was still organized regionally, but a summary of all registrations was gathered annually and made available for inspection in Paris. Here, too, a register for foreign marks was opened in 1860 at the Tribunal de Commerce of the Seine. It was, however, only in 1884, with the launch of the *Bulletin Officiel de la Propriété Industrielle*, that the registrations and registration data were published.[5] The law of 1857 proved as stable as it was influential. As one commentary argues, 'although modified in 1874, 1890, and 1920, it was a law destined to last 100 years' (Beltran, Chauveau and Galvez-Behar 2001: 91).

In the United States, trademark law first developed in individual states. New York led in 1845.[6] But it was only with a California law of 1863 that state registration began.[7] In 1870, federal trademark law passed, bringing with it federal registration.[8] This was overseen by the US Patent Office, in Washington, DC, which published registered marks weekly in the *Official Gazette of the United States Patent Office*, and annually in its annual report from 1873.[9]

Nine years after it was passed, however, the Supreme Court declared the federal law unconstitutional.[10] Attempts to amend the law or the constitution failed, but under its treaty obligations, the United States enacted law to allow registration by foreign citizens from countries with reciprocal agreements and Indian tribes, who remained the primary focus of US federal law until 1905, when new federal law embracing US citizens was enacted. In the interim, however, the Patent Office continued to register marks from US firms. The 1905 law proved more robust than its predecessor, and lead to a spike in trademark registrations (see figure 1.1), after which registrations continued at a significantly higher rate than during the legal 'interregnum' of 1880–1904. This law held sway until US trademark law was consolidated in the Lanham Act of 1946.[11]

The United Kingdom, as noted, was the last of the three to enact trademark law. Registration only began in 1876, following the Trade Marks Registration Act of the previous year. Legend has it that the brewers Bass parked a dray outside the door for the week before the register opened on January 1, 1876, to ensure that its was the first name on the list.[12] Bass was not the only enthusiastic company. In its first year, the register was overwhelmed and the deadline for existing marks to be registered was twice extended. At the same time, the registration of marks from the cotton sector, which had a tradition of shared marks that had to be reconciled with the register's purpose of recording unique marks (Higgins and Tweedale 1996b), was postponed, causing a delayed surge when these were eventually admitted to the register. Although—indeed, perhaps because—it was the last of our three countries to introduce registration, and because it had a particularly strict process for examining registrations, the registration scheme in the United Kingdom—and particularly its published data—came to enjoy greater stability than those in France or the United States. The

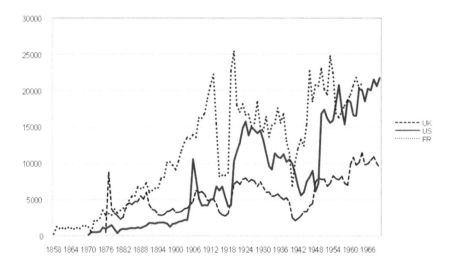

Figure 1.1 Annual trademark registrations in France, the United States, and the United Kingdom, 1858–1970. Source: Annual registration data for France come from Empotz and Marchal (2002), p.225; for the United Kingdom from the *Annual Report of the Patent Office* for the relevant years; and for the United States from *Index of Patents* (later the *Index of Trade Marks*) and the *Official Gazette of the US Patent Office*, again for the relevant years.

same cannot be said of the related law. In the period under review, UK trademark and merchandize marks law had to be amended or substantially revised in 1876, 1877, 1883, 1887, 1888, 1905, 1919, 1926, and 1938.[13]

AN OVERVIEW OF REGISTRATION

Table 1.1 shows the number of marks registered by each country before 1960. France, the table reveals, recorded more marks than the other two countries put together. This has little to do with France's earlier beginning. The predominance of France was maintained for a century, as table 1.1, which plots the number of marks registered in each country by year, shows.

With few exceptions, more marks were registered in France each year than in either of the other two countries. The early exceptions are easily understood. As noted, in the United Kingdom, pent up demand for marks was remarkably strong when the firms were allowed to register in 1876—so strong, indeed, that most applications made in 1876 were not included in the register until the following year, a delay that had a further knock-on effect on 1878. Hence, the clear initial spike in the UK line in figure 1.1. The United Kingdom surpasses France once more, in 1883, after the UK law was broadened and a surge of cotton marks flooded the register (Higgins and Tweedale 1996b). These exceptions aside, France maintains its lead over both countries until 1940, when, under pressure of war and occupation, its annual registrations dip below those of the United States, but only briefly. The brevity is noteworthy, given the different effects the Second World War had on the economies of the two countries. Finally, French registrations dip below US registrations for three years in the late 1950s, though quite why is not immediately clear. By 1960, it has taken the lead again.

Figure 1.1 represents the absolute number of registrations. A more accurate sense of France's dominance in this area is provided by figure 1.2, which adjusts the registration data to allow for the relative differences in population in the three countries. As this chart shows, allowing for population differences, the only time when France is not the leading per capita registrant is during the surge in UK marks in 1877–1878 and the adjustments of UK law in 1883–1884. During these two two-year periods, the United Kingdom takes the lead. In all but a handful of years, the United

Table 1.1   Number of Trademark Registrations to 1960, in France, the United States, and the United Kingdom

Country	First Year	Trademarks to 1960
France	1856	1,142,367
United States	1870	639,849
United Kingdom	1876	436,744

States trails both countries. Some of France's numerical dominance must, in part, be attributed to the comparative openness with which it accepted marks for registration. Yet this alone does not explain its lead. After 1945, for example, the Lanham Act introduced a supplemental register, making their overall data reflect a permissiveness as generous as France's, yet still France maintained its lead. Furthermore, the UK registrar was historically particularly severe, winnowing down applicants to a lesser number, who were allowed to advertise a claim to a mark and winnowing again before accepting the mark for registration.

These annual figures are, undoubtedly, limited in what they can reveal. Nonetheless, what little they do reveal is intriguing. Business–historical interest in trademarks is fairly recent. A key moment comes with Chandler's (1990) *Scale and Scope*. He identifies a sequence of changes in business practice—first in production, then in packaging, then in branding, and finally in advertising—that prompted a revolution in the way goods, and particularly consumer goods, were sold. This change, in Chandler's view, is part and parcel of the 'second industrial revolution,' a revolution led by the United States. Here Chandler reflects the contemporary commentator, Arthur Greeley, who wrote in 1889 that 'the growth of trade-marks and increase of trade-mark litigation in the United States during the past few decades have been commensurate with the marvelous growth of American commerce' (Greeley 1889: 18–19).[14] Taking up Chandler's argument, Wilkins's (1992; 1994) much cited articles echo the importance of modern trademarking in this process, identifying 'modern brands' with changes in

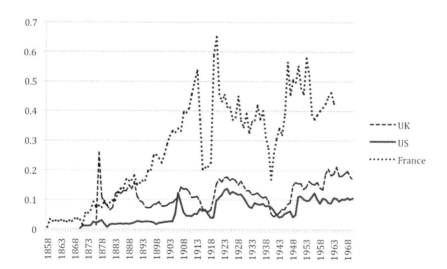

Figure 1.2   Annual trademark registrations per 1,000 population in France, the United States, and the United Kingdom, 1858–1960. Source: as for figure 1.1; population data from Maddsion (2003).

the law of the United States. This perspective is echoed in numerous essays and books, such as Koehn's (2001) *Brand New*, which is almost wholly Anglo-Saxon in its outlook. In general, it seems fair to say that, in the burgeoning literature on trademark history, when it is not assumed that the United States led the transition to modern marks, then it is at least taken for granted that that the story of this remarkable transformation can be told from the US point of view. Figures 1.1 and 1.2 throw some doubt on that assumption. They show, after all, not only that the United States did not lead, either chronologically or in the number of marks registered, but also that of the three nations under discussion, in terms of per capita registrations, it seems to have come in last.

Business historians are not alone in their narrowness of focus. The economic historian Kahn (2005) suggests that the US democratic system made the country inherently superior in protecting and developing intellectual property systems. Her argument, moreover, emphasizes that qualitative conclusions about these systems can be reached from quantitative registration data. That the United States registered more patents than the United Kingdom, Kahn suggests, is evidence of the superiority of the system. If we accept this problematic transition from quantity to quality, it is quite clear that, in regard to one particular kind of intellectual property at least, on Kahn's own terms, the US, for all the strengths of its democratic system, was not superior. Finally, it seems worth noting that legal historians seem equally unwilling to take the French into account. Schechter's (1925) ground-breaking study of trademark history has almost no place for the French. The more recent work by Sherman and Bently simply asserts that 'the primary source of inspiration' for the international spread of trademarks was the United States (Sherman and Bently 1999: 212).

We should also add that the difference between France and the other two countries shown in figure 1.2 seems particularly to be a feature of trademarks. The data for per capita patent registration show the three countries moving more or less in step. If, then, France was uniquely influential and dominant in this particular area of trademarks, not only in the nineteenth century—when they both forged path-breaking law and foisted it onto often reluctant trading partners—but well into the second half of the twentieth—when they continued to register more marks than either the United Kingdom or the United States—the history not only of marks and marketing, but also of the law and even of the second industrial revolution may need to be reassessed.

Differences in national registration data suggest other avenues for research. The different appetites of the three countries discussed here may reflect the relative levels of competition and concentration within particular countries. Heavily concentrated industries are likely to have less interest in marks than heavily competitive ones, and the rise and fall of monopolies and 'trusts' are suggested in the rise and fall of sectoral data (discussed in the following). On the other hand, some sectors have long-established, innovative traditions. In France, for example, champagne registered large numbers of marks from the 1820s on, and in the case of Sosthène Thomas *v.* Lovie (1855) won from the courts the right to register fictitious marks two years before the law was changed. Moreover, France's permissive attitude to registration reduced the monopolistic potential in marks. As noted, Helmers and Rogers (this volume) have suggested, too, that the level of marking may reflect levels of innovation, not only in marketing but in economic activity more generally. The data we present here cannot resolve these questions, but they do suggest that they need further and closer comparative analysis.

These issues aside, undulations in the data suggest that a national rate of trademarking is responsive to a number of stimuli. One is clearly legislation and regulation. As figure 1.1 shows, there is a noticeable decline in US registrations after the Supreme Court ruling of 1879 and a countervailing surge after 1905, at which point it briefly outpaces the annual rate of registrations in the United Kingdom. In the United Kingdom, registrations climb noticeably after adjustments to the law in 1883, 1888, 1906, and again in 1919. That last surge, however, is hard to separate from the effects of war and its aftermath, pointing to another set of influential factors on rates of registration. War's contribution can be seen early on in the French data, where the Franco-Prussian war of 1870–1 causes a brief but steep decline. It is yet more noticeable in the data for all three countries between 1914 and 1918 and between 1939 and 1945, with the later entry of the United States into both wars postponing the fall in its annual registrations, while all three countries experience the post-war surge at about the same time.

Another contribution to the rates of registration comes, of course, from economic cycles. French gross domestic product (GDP) shrank in the late 1870s and between 1899 and 1904. Registration figures seem to reflect the initial downturn, dropping in 1878 and in 1899 and 1901, but in both cases they turn around more quickly than the general economy, yet the figures fail to reflect smaller declines over the period. The UK economy contracted between 1891 and 1894, and again from 1899 to 1902, and it is noticeable that UK annual registrations peak in 1890 and do not achieve the same level again until 1907, when the rate of registration may have been helped by a relaxation of certain registration restrictions in 1906. Given the anomalous state of its law, it is harder to read the economy into the US data in this period. If the data are less clear cut in the 'depression' of the 1890s, the effect of the business cycle on registration can be read more directly in the steady fall across the 1930s in the UK, in the US, and, to a lesser extent, in French registrations.

Although economic cycles have clear effects, economic growth is less easy to trace. Even though increases in GDP have been associated with increases in the number of annual registrations, our attempt to track trademarking in the United States and the United Kingdom with growth in GDP in the post-war years found the relation between the two variables is not statistically significant.[15] Another influence on registration may be global-ization. The constant rise in the rate of registration up to 1914 took place against a background of increasing globalization. Similarly, the decline in marks in the 1920s accompanies the retreat from internationalization dur-ing that period, and the steady rise in the 1950s again follows the recovery of international trade after the Second World War.[16] In all these cases, the rate of registration is more of a lagging than a leading indicator.

CONSUMER GOODS

The trademark data make possible the analysis of annual registrations by various categories. For the business historian, analysis by firm is a tempt-ing possibility, though, as we have noted, this involves dealing with a vast array of company names, many of which are hard to trace outside the register. The data also allow analysis of registration by sector. The task, although easier than analysis by firm, is not quite as easy as it may seem. Although France and the United Kingdom obliged applicants to iden-tify their sector from a set list of categories, the United States provided no such list until 1923. Consequently, though US applicants do declare their sector, there is no consistency in the data. Furthermore, the French changed their categories intermittently, and the British changed theirs once in the period under review.[17] In order to allow the comparisons that follow, we have tagged the US registrations for a set of benchmark years with the categories found in the initial UK list, and identified equivalent categories in the French lists. Inevitably, this has led to some subjective judgments. Again, we must acknowledge that, given the inevitable vari-ability, our argument attempts primarily to be indicative of trends rather than definitive.

As we noted earlier, we have chosen to focus on the category of 'nondu-rable consumer goods' (hereafter, 'consumer goods'). Our groups, some of which merge multiple categories in the French and UK lists, are paper and stationery, food including tea and coffee, alcoholic and nonalcoholic bever-ages, tobacco and tobacco products, household goods and toiletries, and medicines. The last category is not usually recognized in the class of con-sumer nondurables today, as advertising for medicine is subject to its own set of regulations (Corley 2005) and sales are also highly controlled. Nev-ertheless, our inclusion seems appropriate for the early years of the register, when products such as bitters were sold both as alcohol and as medicine and many medicines were little more than rebranded food. For consistency, we have kept the category in our consumables group throughout.

Figure 1.3 compares the rate at which each of the three countries reg-istered these kinds of goods. The table indicates that in the early registers of France and the United States, consumables made up more than 60 per cent of the register. Their dominance, in part, justifies our focus on consumables. In France, the proportion of consumables stays above 50 per cent for all but the last two of the benchmark years, when it is still a little over 46 per cent. In the United Kingdom, by contrast, consumables only once surpass 50 per cent, reaching 55.85 per cent in 1900. Having climbed to this point, the proportion of consumables in the UK register declines significantly to 1910, and the UK proportion of consumables hovers at around one-third of total registrations in each of the succeeding benchmark years, suggesting that the sector was, at best, able to hold its own against the new technologies that presumably account for much of its decline in the register. On the other hand, it is clear that goods other than consumables have always held a significant part of UK trademarks.

The United States presents an interesting contrast to the other two countries. The portion of the register taken by consumer goods begins almost as high as in France, a much higher point than the United Kingdom, but this is the high point, and from here it begins a steep and steady decline, as other goods take up more and more of the register, until, in 1970, the proportion of consumables in the US register is just over a quarter (27.21 per cent). In sum, the French, in general, maintain their enthusiasm for this category across the century, the United States loses its early enthusiasm, and (1900 aside) the British can barely be said to be enthusiastic at all.

Tables 1.2 to 1.4 break the category of consumables down into its constituents, showing again some variance among countries. In France, as table

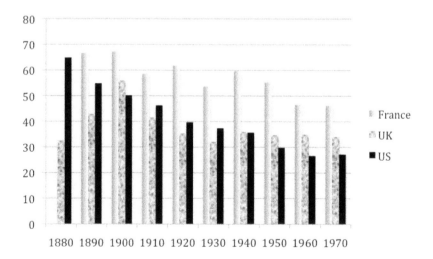

Figure 1.3 Proportion (%) of nondurable consumer marks in the registrations in France, the United States, and the United Kingdom during benchmark years 1880–1970.

1.2 indicates, in the benchmark years the dominant category in the register as a whole and not just among consumables is usually either food or drink, with the exception of 1920, when the category of household goods and toiletries briefly dominates (before dropping almost 50 per cent by the next benchmark year). Food, drink, and cosmetics are, of course, categories for which French leadership is well recognized and the data do little more than reflect that. Tobacco, subject to a monopoly in France, is a relatively insignificant category, while stationery plays a larger part in France than in either of the other countries. The final row in the table shows the leading overall category for the benchmark years. In France, this is always a consumer category.

Table 1.3 looks at the same categories in the UK data. Apart from the UK's relative indifference to the consumables sector, already noticed, it is interesting to see that, as in France, food and drink dominate the consumer category in the early benchmark years, though drink slips away fairly dramatically after 1890, and medicine rises to dominate three of the last four years selected. In general, the UK consumable marks are spread more evenly across the six categories (with the later exception of tobacco, which falls under 2 per cent in each benchmark year, and under 1 in France) than in either of the other two countries, though this results in the individual categories holding a lower proportion of overall registrations than in the other countries. The final row of table 1.3 shows that the registers for the benchmark years were not always led by a consumer category. The early dominance of cotton piece goods (1880 and 1890) is partly attributable to the way these were added to the registry.

The early dominance of tobacco in the early benchmark years for the United States make these noticeably distinct from the other initial years for the other two countries. The dramatic fall in tobacco no doubt reflects the formation of the tobacco trusts (Hannah 1976), though there is no noticeable rebound when the trusts were broken under the Sherman Act. Similarly, the portion of drink registrations, on the other hand, had shrunk into insignificance well before the Volstead Act of 1919. In the United States, the proportion of drink marks falls more steeply and further than in the United Kingdom. The effects of legislation are probably more recognizable in the diminishing portion of medicine marks. This can probably be traced to the Wiley Act of 1906, whose section 8 was directed specifically at 'misbranding', though it must be acknowledged that food, also subject to the act, evidently overcame the restrictions and dominates the selected years from 1900 to 1960.

Looking across the years and across the countries, we can see that drink (predominantly alcohol) has predominated in French trademarking, with food close behind, which is not surprising, yet food is the dominant category in both the United Kingdom and the United States, which is, perhaps, a little surprising. The appearance of clothing in both the United Kingdom and United States in 1950 also merits further explanation.

Table 1.2 Proportion of Nondurable Consumer Goods in Trademark Register by Category: France, 1858–1970

Category	1858–1873*	1886	1890	1900	1905	1910	1920	1930	1940	1950	1960	1970
Stationery	7.83	3.12	2.94	3.38	2.34	2.28	2.57	3.19	2.13	8.92	4.06	9.04
Food	14.86	13.33	10.27	13.61	14.88	13.79	13.09	13.59	16.13	14.05	11.42	9.26
Drink	14.44	25.29	28.01	18.19	16.61	13.44	14.11	15.00	15.15	12.68	11.21	13.18
Tobacco	—	2.46	2.64	1.81	1.70	1.53	1.64	0.97	0.93	0.64	0.80	0.43
Household and toiletries	11.73	15.85	15.40	14.71	13.79	15.42	18.29	9.58	12.01	10.57	9.00	6.55
Medicine	3.35	7.08	7.25	15.51	14.75	12.10	12.05	11.33	13.46	8.40	10.18	7.75
	52.21	67.14	66.51	67.20	64.08	58.57	61.76	53.65	59.80	55.27	46.66	46.21
Leading category† (all categories)	food	drink	drink	drink	drink	food	house-hold	drink	food	food	food	drink

*Before 1884, the French did not publish their trademark data and the registration data were kept in manuscript. In 1874, however, the *Annales de la Propriété Industrielle, Artistique et Littéraire* (vol. 19, pp. 19–20) published an analysis of the first 15 years of registration, from which the numbers for this column are compiled. Data have not been found for all years.
†This is the category (not necessarily a nondurable consumer good) that has most marks in the register for that year.

Table 1.3 Proportion of Nondurable Consumer Goods in Trademark Register by Category: United Kingdom, 1876–1970

Category	1876	1880	1890	1900	1905	1910	1920	1930	1940	1950	1960	1970
Stationery	5.95	4.94	2.98	2.14	3.97	3.62	3.43	4.18	3.68	5.04	4.22	4.98
Food	15.42	5.49	10.08	15.33	15.61	13.89	10.33	11.94	9.41	8.77	10.10	7.07
Drink	9.47	6.29	10.84	6.67	5.20	5.28	3.00	3.73	3.84	5.07	4.14	5.26
Tobacco	5.07	5.27	7.62	14.71	6.77	3.25	4.17	1.46	1.82	1.22	1.57	1.84
Household and toiletries	2.86	5.41	7.57	9.18	10.04	7.69	8.99	5.11	5.46	5.53	4.92	6.56
Medicine	6.17	4.87	3.79	7.82	7.21	7.65	5.25	5.53	11.74	8.98	9.95	8.30
	44.93	32.27	42.87	55.85	48.80	41.38	35.17	31.94	35.94	34.60	34.90	34.02
Leading category (all categories)	food	cotton*	cotton	food	food	food	food	food	medicine	clothing	food	medicine

*The precise category in the register is 'cotton piece goods.' These were in all three cotton categories.

Table 1.4 Proportion of Nondurable Consumer Goods in Trademark Register by Category: United States, 1870–1970

Category	1870	1880	1890	1900	1905	1910	1920	1930	1940	1950	1960	1970
Stationery	2.48	1.43	1.99	0.87	3.40	4.21	3.66	4.17	3.94	3.61	3.09	2.51
Food	7.44	15.71	15.32	17.49	14.71	20.92	17.19	15.36	13.64	13.12	7.53	8.39
Drink	12.40	6.86	7.16	6.53	13.41	3.69	2.90	2.22	4.28	2.29	2.22	2.20
Tobacco	19.01	20.57	3.33	2.45	3.20	2.19	1.32	1.13	1.15	1.26	0.73	1.65
Household and toiletries	7.44	6.29	11.49	7.76	4.84	6.84	7.84	7.42	7.49	4.92	5.73	8.97
Medicine	9.09	14.00	15.53	15.04	8.79	8.46	6.81	7.08	5.21	4.59	7.35	3.49
	57.85	64.86	54.82	50.15	48.36	46.31	39.72	37.38	35.72	29.79	26.65	27.21
Leading category (all categories)	tobacco	tobacco	medicine	food	food	food	food	food	food	clothing	food	food

INTERNATIONAL MARKING

We suggested earlier that the initial UK and US trademark laws arose in response to international pressure, particularly from the French. Given the international origins of the law, it is interesting to see to what extent registrations were, themselves, international, that is, to what extent did non-nationals register in national registers? The registers provide some geographical data (usually city and country) for each registrant, though if the registrant is established in the country of registration, that local address will usually be given, whatever the firm's national origin. Nevertheless, this aspect of the register does offer one way to gauge the internationalization of trade, though here, as elsewhere, our data are preliminary and, at the moment, only address the early years of registration.

The French Napoleonic Code had guaranteed foreign firms with a base in France access to registers open to natives, but the law of 1857 also allowed nondomiciled firms that came from countries with a reciprocal agreement to register marks and gain protection. By the end of 1879, 20 years after the register opened, approximately 6.6 per cent of all marks registered over those two decades (2,263 out of 34,421) were foreign owned. The first countries with reciprocal access were Russia, the United Kingdom, and Belgium. UK firms were quick to take advantage. (The Russians were not.) Of the foreign firms to register in the first 20 years, the British account for more than 75 per cent. US firms, which could only start registering after the convention of 1870, account for less than 3 per cent.[18]

The French reliably published data on the number of marks registered by foreign firms from 1886 to 1906 (after which they, unfortunately, seem to have stopped). These indicate that the number of foreign registrants rises steadily across this period. British firms remain dominant, though the register becomes increasingly international, and the number of US registrants is rising in the first years of the twentieth century.

Though we do not yet have a comparably robust series for foreign registrations in the United Kingdom or United States, the UK register also had early appeal for foreign firms. Among the first year's applicants (many of whom were only registered in the following year), 9 per cent are foreign firms. They come from seven countries, with the French providing more than 6 per cent of total applications, and states that now make up Germany accounting for five of the countries and just under 2 per cent of the marks. The 14 US applications account for less than 1 per cent of the total. A decade later, foreign registrations account for about 7.6 per cent of total marks registered in the United Kingdom, with Germany accounting for just over 1.5 per cent of all marks registered, France for just under 1.5 percent, and the United States for just over 1.25 per cent. These are the three major countries of origin. More remarkable, perhaps, is that the foreign marks come from a total of 36 countries, suggesting the extent to which the British market presented a large magnet to trademarked goods from around the world in 1886.

In the first year of registrations in the United States, by contrast, it is noteworthy that no foreign firms register. The following year (1871), seven UK marks and two Canadian marks make up the foreign contingent, accounting for a little over 2 per cent of the total. Nine years later, just before the Supreme Court decision against the federal law, foreign marks had crept up to just over 6 per cent, with Britain accounting for more than half the foreign registrations, trailed by France, then Germany, out of a total of seven countries. International interest would seem to have continued climbing: In 1890, foreign firms hold 8.6 per cent of the marks registered that year, with the United Kingdom holding just over 4 per cent and the French close behind. These figures come fairly close to the proportion of foreign marks in the French register. They cannot be taken at face value, however: As a result of the Supreme Court's decision in 1979, federal law, written primarily to fulfill international treaty obligations, heavily favoured foreign firms. In the 1905, when the law once again protected US firms engaged in domestic commerce, foreign firms' registrations shrink dramatically to a mere 1.5 per cent of registrations as US firms flood the register (see the spike in registrations in figure 1.1). The year 1910 might, then, be a more reasonable benchmark for measuring the international character of the early US register. That year, foreign firms from 21 countries account for almost 10 per cent of registrations.

At this point, after a slow start, the US market seems to have been approaching a high point of internationalization, albeit a little more slowly than the European ones. The trend was curtailed by the war, and the contrast with the post-war data from 1920 is particularly dramatic, reflecting, among other things, the sharp turn against globalization. Foreign marks have shrunk to just over 4 per cent of the US total. UK firms still lead, with 1.9 per cent of all marks, though this is almost as low as in 1871. The French are in second place, but Germany, in the aftermath of the war, has fallen behind Canada, Bohemia, Norway, Spain, and Switzerland.[19].

These data are partial and as hard to interpret as to gather, so we do not want to read too much into them. If we use international registrations as our evidence, in the years before the First World War, France, the United Kingdom, and (though here our evidence is less direct) Germany stand out as highly international in their commerce; the United States, until the immediate prewar period, significantly less so. In the case of the first two, the registers suggests that this international character is evident both in the degree to which firms from these countries operated (and registered marks) in foreign markets and to the extent to which they were open to foreign firms operating (and registering marks) in their national markets. The United States clearly went through a transition in this period, from one with relatively few firms selling in foreign markets and relatively few foreign firms working in the United States towards a position in the early twentieth century, more like the other three.

The data also hint at the notion of a healthy 'balance of trademarks,' whereby countries with robust economies both attract foreign firms and trade in foreign markets with comparable vigour. It is illuminating in this regard to look at preliminary data for Portugal between 1884 and 1905; however, because of Portugal's historical relationship with the United Kingdom, the data need treating with special caution.[20] The figures for registration in Portugal suggest that country had a very high level of foreign activity. By 1885, two years after the Portuguese began registering marks, foreign firms account for almost two-thirds of marks registered. Although the figure falls to 13 per cent in 1905, over the 20 years in between, foreign firms account for one-third of all marks, a far higher proportion of foreign firms than is found in the registers of the three countries at the centre of this discussion. From 1885 to 1895, the United Kingdom contributes more than one-fifth of the applicants and almost the same proportion of the marks registered. France contributes one-sixth of registrants, but almost one-fifth of the marks. (French firms, in general, tend to register multiple marks more than firms from other countries.) Germany accounts for just under 4 per cent of the applicants and under 5 per cent of the marks.

As the Portuguese share of the marks increases over the next decade (1896–1905), a period, it must be noted, of significant political tension between the United Kingdom and Portugal, the British share falls to just under 14 per cent of marks; by contrast, Germans account for a little over 10 per cent. The French shrink to around 3 per cent in both categories, but, of course, over this decade, the French and the Portuguese were both able to register marks internationally under the Madrid convention, so French figures from this period deserve caution. The United States, without such alternatives, nonetheless accounts for less than the French. From the perspective of Portugal, in comparison to the large, trading economies of France, the United States, and the United Kingdom, these figures reveal a significant imbalance of trademarking, for although foreign firms make up a large part of registrations in Portugal, Portuguese marks are rare in the foreign registers we have looked at.[21] In all, the Portuguese case suggests the extent to which foreign marks could dominate an economy, keeping local firms not only out of foreign markets, but even out of their own domestic markets.

CONCLUSION

This chapter has given a very preliminary reading of trademark registrations in three countries: France, the United Kingdom, and the United States. Its overall goal has been less to report on the contents of the registers than to indicate ways in which they offer fertile ground for further research, providing a little-used vantage point to throw light on many questions concerning national and international trade in marked goods.

One of the major advantages of these resources is that they allow direct international comparisons of trademark regimes. Debates about the intrinsic superiority of different countries' laws and regulations are legion (Kahn 2005; Stone 1936), but they are more likely to reach a conclusion when comparable data are used. Yet in the area of trademarks, conventional accounts have tended to stay within one country. As we have shown, the conventional picture changes a good deal when international comparisons are made. Instead of the United States standing out as historically on the leading edge of innovation in the law and practice of trademarking, it appears, from several directions, to have been on the trailing edge.

The data allow us not only to compare the overall appetite for marks in different countries; they also allow us to compare the appetite of different sectors. Thus, we have shown France's enduring interest in marks for consumer goods, which may, to some extent, account for its overall enthusiasm for marks in general. By contrast, we have seen that the British appetite for these marks was always rather restrained. For its part, the United States went from early enthusiasm to continually diminishing interest. Unsurprisingly, food is a dominant sector in all three countries, though in France drinks (in particular alcohol) are almost as important. The overall decline in consumer goods over the first century of marking is, no doubt, a reflection of the growth in new sectors in nonconsumer and durable goods, where change has been much more dynamic across the twentieth century. It also reflects the 'first mover' status of consumer goods.

Such results indicate that registration data can address questions beyond the interests of marketing and the history of marketing, taking in topics relevant to the development of national economies more generally. Furthermore, as our glance at the international aspects of national registers suggests, the registers also help trace the extent to which nations were receptive to foreign goods and firms and to which national firms were willing to venture into foreign markets. Here, as we have shown, the French and the British were early to internationalize, but both US firms and US registers were slower. A sideways glance at the case of Portugal, in this context, leads us to suggest the concept of a balance of trademarking, whereby a healthy economy has a manageable proportion of foreign marks in its own registers and a significant proportion of its domestic firms in foreign registers.

Although our purpose is primarily business historical, for the purposes of this chapter, we have not ventured down to the level of individual firms, which demands a more painstaking and rigorous analysis of the data than we have so far achieved. This omission leads us to our final conclusion, which is that, although the registers are remarkably rich resources, there is a great deal more work to be done.

NOTES

1. It has been suggested (Rosen 2008) that the United States may have begun registering some marks before 1870. As noted in the following, some US states had begun registering marks in the decade before 1870.
2. It was noted in 1862 that trademark registration was functioning in Austria, Bavaria, Belgium, France, Hanover, the Netherlands, Portugal, Prussia, Russia, Sardinia, Saxony, Spain, Sweden, Norway, and Württemberg (Select Committee on Trade Marks 1862: paragraph 72).
3. Our primary sources for registration data are as follows. In France, the *Bulletin Officiel de la Propriété Industrielle*. This was published from 1884 onwards and, as noted, provided reliable digests of data until 1906. In the United Kingdom, *Annual Reports of the Patent Office* and the *Trade Marks Journal*. And in the United States, the *Official Gazette of the US Patent Office* and related indexes published in the Patent and Trade-Mark Office's annual reports. Other sources will be indicated where relevant. Where these publications did not produce digests, we have counted individual marks. As noted, it has often been impossible to reconcile inconsistencies between our counts and those of the various official publications.
4. One reason we look at the dominant sector is that dominant players tend to get their way when law is made. To consider not only the effects that law has on business but also that business has on law, it is useful to know what were the dominant businesses. If we take North's (1981) image that if businesses are the players, then national institutions, such as trademark regimes, are the referees; we need to recognize that dominant players often play the referee with great success.
5. Consequently, our data for France before 1884 is limited.
6. Connecticut and Pennsylvania followed in 1847, Massachusetts and Iowa in1850, Ohio in 1859, California and Michigan in 1863, Oregon and Kansas in 1864, Nevada in 1865 and Maine and Missouri in 1866.
7. Along with California, Oregon, Kansas, Missouri, and Nevada instituted systems of registration.
8. However, see note 1.
9. Before the trademark repository was established, however, some companies registered marks as designs, as, indeed, was the case in the United Kingdom, where marks had occasionally been registered under copyright provisions. This tradition of registering designs under copyright law in the United States led to label registrations, which begin in 1874 (Hopkins 1905).
10. The court ruled that trademarks did not fall under the 'progress' clause of the US Constitution, the grounds on which the congress had claimed the right to legislate.
11. The Lanham Act added a 'supplemental register' in which applicants could register marks that were not currently registrable, but might become so in the future. This register, although not guaranteeing protection, served to provide evidence of usage and ownership. The federal registers were kept open during the interregnum of 1879–1905 on the same principle. We have not used data from the supplementary register in this chapter.
12. True or not, the story reflects the position of the alcoholic beverage business in particular, and consumer nondurables more generally, among the more influential sectors that shaped the law directly and indirectly.
13. Rather as the Lanham Act would do later in the United States, the UK act of 1919 separated the register into two parts. Owners were now able to record in 'part B' of the register some marks that did not satisfy the existing criteria for distinctiveness. This was an attempt to enable registration of *de facto*

trademarks, and, as with the laws of 1862 and 1875, to help UK firms register their marks overseas by making registration of overseas marks in the United Kingdom easier. The 1938 law retained this division in the register, but introduced a new list of categories under which marks had to be classified. This law remained in place until 1984.

14. Greeley was well aware that the limited protection offered by the law limited the number of marks likely to be registered. He estimated that the law of 1881 reduced the number of marks to about one-quarter of what they might otherwise have been (Greeley 1889: 156). But even if we multiply the number of marks registered in the United States between 1880 and 1904 by four, the total is still about 75 per cent of the number of marks registered in France over the same period. Moreover, it is quite clear from the registrations after the changes of 1905 that Wise's estimate was an exaggeration. US marks do not increase four-fold.

15. Linear regression between the size of annual increases in GDP at constant prices and the number of trademark registrations in each year show that the relation is not statistically significant. Higgins argues that the rate of growth of GDP is 'negatively correlated with the trends in registration' (Higgins 2008: note 41).

16. These waves of globalization are probably better traced in the international registration of marks following the Madrid conference of 1891. As France was initially far more active in the international register than either the United Kingdom or the United States, it is quite likely that figure 1.1 actually underestimates the French appetite for marks.

17. The French had introduced three lists in the nineteenth century alone, beginning with 57 categories and climbing to 74 in 1886. In 1920, it introduced a list of 80 categories. The British used 50 categories in 1876 and stuck resolutely by them for 60 years, although the growth in registrations under the category 'miscellaneous' indicated that the system was increasingly under strain. In 1938, they changed to a system of 34 classes.

18. These data come from the registers for foreign marks in the Archives de Paris.

19. Our category of Germany here includes firms from Prussia, though these were registered separately at the time.

20. These data come from the archives of the INPI Portugal.

21. These proportions are not a function of international registration under the Madrid convention. Between 1903 and 1906, the final years of the decade under consideration, that international register recorded 1,064 marks, but only 41 of these are Portuguese.

BIBLIOGRAPHY

Arber, E., ed. (1950) *A Transcript of the Registers of the Company of Stationers of London, 1554–1640*, 5 vols, New York: Peter Smith.

Beltran, A., Chauveau, S. and Galvez-Behar, G. (2001) *Des Brevets et des Marques: Une Histoire de la Propriété Industrielle*, Paris: Fayard.

Chandler, A. D. (1990) *Scale and Scope: The Dynamics of Industrial Capitalism*, Cambridge, MA: Harvard University Press.

Corley, T. A. B. (2005) 'UK government regulation of medicinal drugs, 1890–2000', *Business History*, 47(3): 337–351.

Empotz, G. and Marchal, V. (2002) *Aux Sources de la Propriété Industrielle: Guide des Archives de l'INPI*, Paris: Institut National de la Propriété Industrielle.

Greeley, A. (1899) *Foreign Patent and Trademark Laws: A Comparative Study with Tabular Statements of Essential Features of Such Laws*, Washington, DC: John Byrne & Co.

Hannah, L. (1976) *The Rise of the Corporate Economy*, London: Methuen.

Higgins, D. (2008) 'The making of modern trade mark law: The UK, 1860–1914, a business history perspective' in L. Bently, J. Davis and J. Ginsburg, eds., *Trade Marks and Brands: An Interdisciplinary Critique*, Cambridge, UK: Cambridge University Press, pp: 42–62.

Higgins, D. and Tweedale, G. (1996a) 'Asset or liability?: Trade marks in the Sheffield cutlery and tool trades', *Business History*, 37(3): 1–27.

Higgins, D. and Tweedale, G. (1996b) 'The trade marks question and the Lancashire cotton textile industry', *Textile History*, 27(2): 207–228.

Hopkins, J. L. (1905) *The Law of Trademarks, Tradenames, and Unfair Competition*, 2d ed., Chicago: Callahan and Company.

Khan, B. Z. (2005) *The Democratization of Invention: Patents and Copyrights in American Economic Development, 1790–1920*, New York: NBER/Cambridge University Press.

Khan, B. Z. and Sokoloff, K. L. (2001) 'The early development of intellectual property institutions in the United States', *Journal of Economic Perspectives*, 15(3): 233–46.

Koehn, N. (2001) *Brand New: How Entrepreneurs Earned Consumers' Trust from Wedgwood to Dell*, Boston, MA: Harvard Business School.

Maddison, A. (2003) *The World Economy: Historical Statistics*, Paris: Organization for Economic Development and Co-operation.

Moser, P. (2005) 'How do patent laws influence innovation? Evidence from nineteenth-century world fairs', *American Economic Review*, 95(4): 1214–36.

North, D. C. (1981) *Structure and Change in Economic History*, New York: W.W. Norton & Co.

Rosen, Z. S. (2008) In search of the *Trade-Mark Cases* Social Science Research Network Report 1268558. Available online at http://papers.ssrn.com/sol3/papers.cfm?abstract_id=1268558

Schechter, F. I. (1925) *The Historical Foundations of the Law Relating to Trade-Marks*, New York: Columbia University Press.

Select Committee on Trade Marks (1862) *Report from the Select Committee on Trade Marks Bill and Merchandize Marks Bill*, London: House of Commons.

Sherman, B. and Bently, L. (1999) *The Making of Modern Intellectual Property Law: The British Experience, 1760–1911*, New York: Cambridge University Press.

Stone, H. F. (1936) 'The common law in the United States', *Harvard Law Review*, 50(1): 4–26.

Upton, F. H. (1860) *A Treatise on the Law of Trade Marks with a Digest and Review of the English and American Authorities*, Albany, New York: Weare C. Little.

Wilkins, M. (1994) 'When and why brand names in food and drink' in Jones, G. and N. Morgan (eds.), *Adding Value: Brands and Marketing in Food and Drink*, London: Routledge, pp: 15–40.

———. (1992) 'The neglected intangible asset: The influence of the trade mark on the rise of the modern corporation', *Business History*, 34: 66–99.

2 Export Performance and Reputation

Mark Casson and Nigel Wadeson

This chapter considers the relationships between reputation, brands, trademarks, and export performance. The study of brands and trademarks has traditionally been regarded as an aspect of research in marketing, but recently economists have taken an increasing interest in the subject (for a survey of the links between marketing and economics, see Carter, Casson and Suneja 1998). In economic theory, brands are regarded as an important mechanism for overcoming 'market failures' caused by 'information asymmetries' (Balasubranyam and Salisu 1994). An important difference between the economic and marketing approaches to brands is that the former operates with an explicit 'rational action' model of human behaviour, whereas the latter adopts a more pluralistic and interdisciplinary approach. It is the economic approach that is the basis of this chapter.

According to the economic theory of brands, consumers regularly encounter the problem that they are uncertain about the quality of a product. The observable qualities of a product are often only superficial. A rational consumer needs to acquire credible information about products. Obtaining this can be costly, however. Although obtaining information second-hand is normally cheaper than through direct observation, there is a risk that the source of the second-hand information may misrepresent the situation, either through incompetence or, if they are the supplier, by deliberate intent.

Not all suppliers are dishonest, however. Under certain conditions, the owners of a brand have an incentive to supply truthful information. One reason is that their reputation is at stake. Once this is lost, the brand owners will have to incur the cost of rebuilding it, or risk losing their ability to charge a premium price. Indeed, in many cases it would not have paid for them to invest in this reputation to start with, had they not intended to be honest in their claims for their product.

A potential weakness of the economic approach is that the qualities of a product about which consumers care the most are often highly subjective. Economists tend to assume that most important qualities are objective, such as the freshness of food or the mechanical reliability of a machine. In practice, however, subjectivity is important. For example, a consumer may simply want other people to be impressed by the fact that they can afford to buy a particular type of product, and can make a wise decision to select a particular brand. In this case, the reputation of the brand helps to boost the reputation of the consumer who purchases the brand. This enhancement of personal reputation may well be of intrinsic value to the consumer (as well as having instrumental value by impressing influential people, for example helping the consumer to obtain a bank loan or get a better job). In this context, a brand provides value to the consumer independently of objective qualities such as product reliability. A brand that achieves the status of a fashion icon provides value even though the fashion may have no lasting objective value.

The key to modelling the 'social psychology' of such intrinsic demand for reputation is to recognize that the 'utility' that economic agents maximize is not just the traditional materialistic utility of hedonistic utility theory, but a form of utility that includes the socially oriented satisfactions of peer-group status and self-esteem. By allowing utility to encompass status and self-esteem, it is possible to analyse the way in which the demand for branded goods derive not only from the need for reassurance about the objective qualities of goods, but also from a socially-embedded need for personal reputation too.

The remainder of this chapter is organized in three parts. The first part sets out the economic approach in a systematic way. It reviews key concepts and provides simple definitions. These definitions highlight some important distinctions between related concepts that are often ignored in the literature.

The second part discusses the interdependence that exists between the reputations of different agents within an economy. The economic effects of reputation are complex. An agent's reputation may be either positively or negatively affected by interrelationships with other agents' reputations. Agents may collaborate to invest in collective reputations, such as a national reputation for excellence in a particular industry that boosts the reputations of individual brands in that industry. Sometimes there will be conflicts of interest about the types of collective reputations that should be built.

All of these issues are relevant to export performance. Evidence concerning the promotion of exports from the UK is presented in the third and final part. This evidence supports the view that national sectoral reputations are important in directing the search and experience decisions of foreign customers. It also demonstrates the need for careful targeting and quality control in trade promotion activities.

KEY CONCEPTS IN THE STUDY OF REPUTATION, BRANDS AND TRADE MARKS

This section begins by defining some of the key concepts on which the following analysis depends. The clarity provided by explicit definitions is extremely valuable when the complexities of reputational interdependence come to be explored later in the chapter.

An agent (individual, organization, or product) has a *reputation* for possessing a certain quality or characteristic (good or bad) if many other agents (individuals or organizations) believe that the agent possesses this quality. Such qualities can be termed 'defining' qualities. A reputation is *warranted* when the belief is true. An agent might have a reputation with just one other agent, in which case the reputation is embedded in a single dyadic relationship. At the other extreme, all agents might share the same belief about the agent concerned, in which case the reputation is universal. The term 'reputation' normally connotes an intermediate case, in which the belief is shared by a large number of agents, but not by all of them; this is the way in which the term is construed in this chapter.

A *reputation-owner* is an individual or organization that controls the qualities on which a reputation depends and can appropriate rewards from the reputation, e.g. a firm that owns the right to market a branded product. A rational reputation-owner will pursue a strategy designed to maximize its rewards. These rewards are defined relative to the objectives of the reputation-owner (which may be materialistic or social, as explained previously). A rational strategy normally involves selecting particular qualities to which a reputation should relate, and implementing controls to ensure that its reputation for the chosen qualities is warranted.

Reputation is fundamental to market operations. When selling a product, reputation has a dual effect involving both *adverse selection* and *moral hazard* (Mailath and Samuelson 2006; Weigelt and Camerer 1988). If the purchasers of the product are unable to properly distinguish the qualities offered by different suppliers, then high quality suppliers will not be able to reap the full rewards of their quality in terms of being able to charge higher prices, which may result in a lack of higher quality suppliers in the market (Akerlof 1970). This is the problem of adverse selection caused by asymmetric information: customers do not know the characteristics of products or services offered by different suppliers, and so are unable to compare them properly. Thus, crucial differences that differentiate high quality goods from low quality goods go unnoticed.

The second effect of reputation involves moral hazard, and it relates to the actions of suppliers. A supplier with a good reputation has an incentive to maintain high quality. So long as a reputation-owner values its reputation, it is unlikely to cut its quality in order to increase profits for a short period of time, selling at a premium while delivering lower quality at lower cost. Such behaviour would cause a reputational loss, which would be costly to reverse, and could lead to a significant loss of profit in the long run.

There is an important difference between search goods and experience goods (Nelson 1970). The qualities of a search good can be evaluated prior to purchase, but the qualities of an experience good cannot. Reputation is particularly important in creating efficient markets for experience goods. When a consumer is choosing between different varieties of a search good, he/she can examine a large number of alternative varieties and select the one that offers the best value for money. If the consumer has examined all of the relevant qualities prior to purchase, then he/she will not be disappointed when it finally comes to consuming the product.

By contrast, the qualities of an experience good cannot be evaluated in this way—these are only revealed once the product is used. This reduces the incentive for the customer to evaluate goods carefully beforehand, since what he/she perceives, in terms of observable qualities, is no guide to the true, but hidden, qualities of the product. Being aware of the potential risks, a rational consumer of an experience good will rely heavily on the reputation of the producer or retailer. When reputation mechanisms work well, the reputation of the good will, indeed, be correlated with the hidden qualities that matter. Rational consumers will take steps to assure themselves that reputation mechanisms are working properly so that they can rely on this correlation at the time they purchase the good.

Purchasing a search good is not totally risk-free, however. The evaluation of a search good may be costly. Thus, in order to evaluate different varieties of a good, a consumer may have to visit different retail outlets that stock different varieties, or spend longer in a store that sells a full range. Although a certain amount of 'comparison shopping' may be enjoyable, it becomes irksome beyond a certain point. At this stage, the consumer must trade off the risk of missing out on the ideal variety against the cost of continuing to search for it.

The distinction between a search good and an experience good is not an absolute dichotomy. A good may have qualities that, though not immediately visible, can be assessed through deliberate investigation. In self-service grocery stores, for example, consumers can examine each item of fresh produce individually prior to purchase, or they can just 'grab and go'. Income-rich time-poor consumers will tend to grab and go and then discard the inferior quality items later; income-poor time-rich consumers are likely to make a careful selection. Under these circumstances, it pays the income-rich time-poor consumers to shop at the same store as others of their type, because otherwise the income-poor time-rich customers are likely to have selected the best items and left mainly poor quality items for the grab-and-go customers.

A solution to this problem is for the income-rich consumers to pay the supplier to resolve the problem for them. The supplier may sort and grade the goods using quality-control procedures, based upon its specialist knowledge of the hard-to-observe qualities. The suppliers recover their additional cost by charging a premium price for the highly graded items. Effective grading requires both competence and integrity on the part of the supplier; it is, therefore, only viable if the supplier has a good reputation.

As a result, investing in a reputation allows a supplier to attract customers who are willing to pay a premium price. Although neoclassical economic theories, such as perfect competition, assume perfect information, so eliminating reputational issues, the imperfect knowledge present in the real world gives reputation a key role in allowing markets to function effectively. Reputation helps to align the interests of suppliers with those of their customers so that customers are better able to obtain high-quality supplies. Reputation can also reduce the informational costs involved in making transactions. Instead of investigating a product and its supplier, a customer can choose to rely on their reputations instead, particularly where the consumer already has relevant knowledge of them. Alternatively, the consumer may have reputational knowledge of an intermediator that can be relied on instead.

There is, however, an issue regarding the competitive nature of the premium price. If there are many reputable suppliers, then competition between suppliers will tend to drive down price to a level where reputable suppliers just break even. As a result, the price premium reflects the incremental cost of maintaining the level of quality that the reputation guarantees. Where there are only a few reputable suppliers, an element of monopoly may well enter the price premium. In this case, consumers of high quality items pay a greater premium than is warranted by the costs of achieving the guaranteed level of quality. The high price is a disincentive for consumers to purchase high-quality items. A monopoly of reputation is, therefore, likely to reduce consumption of high-quality items. Consumption of low-quality items will tend to increase, but by not so much as consumption of high-quality items has fallen, and, as a result, overall consumption of the product will fall as well. These consumption effects are socially wasteful, as they stem from an artificial scarcity of high quality caused by the monopoly of reputation.

The strength of reputational effects can vary. Within a small, tight-knit community, reputational information may spread very quickly. Within a larger community, high-reputation intermediators may be important in assessing quality. Suppliers may also use various means, such as advertising, to signal quality (Kirmani and Rao 2000).

A firm may also seek to build a common reputation across a range of different products. Where it is an existing exporter, for example, its brand will help it to export a new product. A *brand* is essentially an identity that can be conferred on an individual item of product. Items that share the same brand are expected to share the same mixture of *defining qualities*. Some entities may have more than one defining quality. A valuable brand is one that potential customers associate with desirable qualities; one with a good reputation. The use of a known brand name is a signal of quality for a good, and so it may be particularly useful to extend a brand name to a new experience good (Smith and Park 1992).

To substantiate the claims made about a product, a marketing strategy may also involve the use of a *supporting myth*. A supporting myth is a story that explains (maybe only superficially) why a product possesses the quality or characteristic that it claims to possess. The supporting myth may contain significant elements of truth, interpreted in a way that maximizes its credibility. An image may also be used. The *image* of an entity is a visual representation of it that associates it with the defining qualities with which it claims to be associated. It may also illustrate the supporting myth. The image may be expressed through pictures or performances, or a combination of the two, and disseminated through a variety of media.

In order to have a reputation, a product must be identifiable. A *name* or *logo* is, therefore, normally used to carry reputation, differentiating a product from other similar products. A logo is a visual symbol, often typographic, which represents a product. It may involve an abbreviation of a name (e.g. an acronym). Attaching a logo to a communication provides the intended recipient with a simple means of identifying the source of the message.

However, the use of names and logos to carry reputation involves the danger that different entities will happen to choose similar names and logos, so making high-reputation products less easily identifiable. It also carries the danger that some low-reputation entities will deliberately assume the names and logos of high reputation entities in order to gain the advantages of their reputations, so damaging them in the process if they deliver poor quality. These problems create a need for a legal remedy.

Trademarks are just such a remedy and are used to protect products or brand identities. A trademark is a legally protected name and logo associated with a product or brand. The owner of the trademark has the exclusive right to affix the trademark to units of product, and the exclusive right to employ the trademark in advertising and other forms of communication. This exclusive right is designed to protect the owner against competition from imitators. The trademark may be designed in such a way as to deter forgers and fraudsters from offering products marked is a similar way—irrespective of whether the actual quality of their products is inferior. Ramello and Silva (2006) provide a review of the economics of trademarks, stressing the links with branding and persuasion. The effectiveness of a trademark depends on how well known and how good the reputation of the product brand is and how well the trademark is recognized by potential customers.

REPUTATION-BUILDING AS A BUSINESS STRATEGY

Reputation need not relate simply to the general level of quality. A customer may be interested in many different aspects of a service or product. For instance, an importer of coffee may be interested in the taste and quality of the coffee, the efficiency and reliability of the service offered by the exporter, and perhaps whether the coffee is sourced in what the importer considers to be a demonstrably ethical manner. This complicates matters for the reputation owner significantly. As the relevant dimensions of reputation increase in number, it becomes more difficult to establish a good reputation across all of them. This also complicates the entrepreneurial decision over exactly what type of reputation to build, and how to go about building it. If there is a need to economize on conveying information to potential customers, then suppliers will wish to convey the information likely to lead potential customers, most cost effectively, to try out their products in preference to others, while also making it likely that a good proportion of customers will buy again on the basis of past experience.

Investment in reputation is an entrepreneurial action aimed at taking advantage of a perceived opportunity to profit from supplying a product and supporting services that are known for particular defining qualities. Such an investment may, for example, involve advertising, and involve earning low profits or making losses early on during the process of building reputation. Indeed, discount price promotions or free samples may have to be offered initially in order to tempt potential customers to experience a product.

Although reputation can be built, at least to some extent, through customer experiences, suppliers will normally want to take further measures in order to enhance the growth of reputation. A consumer needs to be convinced that it is worthwhile incurring the costs involved in investigating the product and the supplier, or of trying out a product where it is an experience good. Beyond this, there may also be relevant product features that cannot be observed simply through experience of consumption. Product qualities such as ethical sourcing and good treatment of the firm's staff may also need to be communicated. The reputation-owner has to decide how much to spend on marketing and what messages to try to communicate. A heavy expenditure on sales and marketing can, in itself, help to lend credibility to the product (Klein and Leffler 1981; Milgrom and Roberts 1986). Suppliers may have little chance of recouping their investments in customers if, once they have tried products and had their expectations confounded, they fail to purchase again. Hence, such expenditure itself can act as a signal of quality. According to Nelson (1974), the main information conveyed by advertising for an experience good is simply the fact that the good has been advertised, whereas for a search good advertising mainly conveys direct information about the qualities of the product. Evidence has supported the view that consumers evaluate the experience and search qualities of a product differently (Jain and Posavac 2001).

INTERMEDIATION BY REPUTATION-BROKERS

Once agents acquire a reputation, they can leverage this reputation by endorsing other people's reputations (Spulber 1996). Thus, a celebrity may endorse a fashionable product; a firm with a good reputation may take over another firm without a reputation so that the output of this firm can be sold at a higher price; or a firm producing a well-known brand may 'extend' the product to another field in order to compete with reputable producers who are already established there.

The greater an agent's reputation, the greater is the incentive for that agent to specialize in exploiting it. In some cases, agents may be able to sell their good name, as in the case of the certifying organizations discussed in the following paragraph. In other cases, agents need to 'internalize' the exploitation of their reputations by taking ownership and control of the activities that they propose to endorse, as when a reputable firm takes over a less reputable one. Internalization of this kind generally occurs in cases when taking full responsibility for the production of a product is the only way of guaranteeing its quality in a credible manner—either because it is the only way to be sure that the quality is good, or because it is the only arrangement that customers believe can guarantee that the quality is good.

An important aspect of reputational intermediation is certification. Certifiers typically charge a fee for endorsing the quality of other people's output. By being certified by an independent agent, a supplier is able to gain from the reputation of the certifier. This helps to redirect the investigation of a producer and its products through a single channel. Rather than investigating each supplier, a customer investigates whether a supplier is certified, and whether the certifier is reliable. If many suppliers use the same certifier, then the customer needs to investigate the certifier only once. This effects a considerable economy for the customer, since the only information the customers require on an individual supplier is whether they are certified or not.

Some trademarks are owned by independent certifying organizations, rather than by suppliers themselves. Additional credibility can sometimes be gained for a certifier if it is a nonprofit organization. A nonprofit organization may have less incentive to 'sell' certification without proper quality control in order to maximize its licence fee income. However, nonprofit organizations may be susceptible to similar incentives if salaried managers employed by such organizations can increase their pay and perks as a result.

Once a supplier has built a good reputation in its home market, it may then face a challenge in exporting high quality supplies. Although it has a track record to support its reputation in its home market, potential customers in other countries may not have knowledge of it. However, where local suppliers have poor reputations, a customer may welcome the chance to buy from abroad. If the purchase is of sufficient value and the cost of experiencing supply is high, then the customer may invest some effort in evaluating the reputations of foreign goods or suppliers. Alternatively, the reputations of intermediaries may be relied upon instead. Although the main body of literature on exporting pays little attention to the role of intermediaries in exporting, they are, in reality, of major importance (Peng and Ilinitch 1998; Trabold 2002).

The use of a high-reputation intermediator can allow low-reputation foreign suppliers to supply high quality products where reliance on their own reputations alone would not allow this. An entrepreneurial intermediator may, therefore, seek out such low-cost foreign suppliers and work with them to ensure that they then achieve high quality. This allows a form of arbitrage from foreign suppliers with inherent advantages over home suppliers, such as cheaper labour.

In this context, both industry trade associations and the government (including constituent public bodies such as industry regulators) can play a certifying role. Certification has become increasingly global. Most global industries are regulated, to some degree, by international standards institutions, which define standards and publish procedures for auditing compliance with them. Some of these organizations report to intergovernmental bodies or treaty organizations; others are federal organizations accountable to national trade associations or other local bodies.

Certification applies not only to firms, but to individuals, too. For example, a reputable firm may be perceived as 'certifying' its employees, in the sense that by working for the firm, and having the firm sell the products of their labour, employees are able to obtain a premium on what they could earn if they were simply self-employed. The employees are 'certified' by being recruited by the firm, and become more valuable as a result. Part of the gain accrues to the individual, but most of it accrues to the firm, in terms of the profit that it makes on the product generated by employees.

Individuals can also benefit from certification by professional associations. Professional associations often certify using formal procedures, based on examinations or approved work experience. Many professional associations are international in their scope—like the international standards organizations mentioned previously. However, many professional associations still retain their national origins; in some sectors each profession still has its own system of national accreditation, whereas in other sectors the national organizations of certain countries, like the United States or United Kingdom, provide accreditation that is recognized in other countries too.

COLLECTIVE REPUTATIONS AND THE
FORMATION OF SOCIAL GROUPS

Leveraging an existing reputation is not the only way in which a reputation can be shared. People may associate together for the specific purpose of creating a collective reputation. In other cases, collective reputation may be a by-product of association for some other purpose. Most groups have some sort of collective reputation, which is shared by all their members, even though it may be rather weak. For example, individuals may gain in terms of reputation by being members of particular religions or social groups. Financiers in the City of London historically traded on the principle of 'my word is my bond', and could face social and business ostracism if they cheated on this. Individuals gain reputationally by serving successfully as employees of high-reputation organizations, as noted, and organizations can gain reputationally by having high-reputation individuals closely associated with them, such as when they serve as directors.

Conversely, a group of agents who share a common reputation may be thought of as belonging to a social group. If a group has a reputation, then any 'badge of affiliation' may be regarded as a 'trademark' of the group.

In many cases, agents have a choice as to whether they belong to a group, but in other cases, they do not. Thus, an individual cannot easily change citizenship; the individual is born as a citizen of a particular country, and is 'branded' with whatever characteristics are associated with it. Similarly, with firms, although large multinationals may be able to change the country in which they are headquartered, small firms cannot normally afford to relocate just to maximize the benefits from the reputation of the country in which they are based.

When reputation is ascribed, rather than acquired, agents may be dissatisfied with the reputation they possess. They may be tempted to disown the group to which they belong. In particular, they may try to disguise their origin by acquiring a trademark very different from the one that they have been ascribed. Thus, a British firm in an industry dominated by German technology might give itself a German-sounding name. For similar reasons, food companies in many countries often choose French- and Italian-sounding brand names, rather than indigenous names, as do firms in the design and fashion sector.

Conversely, groups with good reputations may be inundated by agents who wish to join in order to benefit from this reputation. There is a serious risk of dilution; as the size of the group expands, the average calibre of recruit is likely to diminish, and reputation may decline as an increasing proportion of the membership fails to live up to the traditional standards associated with the group. The natural way of addressing the dilution issue is to regulate membership of the group. This requires a mechanism for registering members. It is also necessary to establish the conditions of membership (perhaps through a formal constitution) and to implement an admissions process.

Fraud is also an increasing risk for the successful group. To 'free ride' on the reputation of an established group, it may not be necessary to formally join the group. When dealing with people who have no knowledge of the group other than its reputation and its trademark, use of the trademark may be sufficient for an impostor to benefit from the reputation of the group. Hence, the trademark is quite likely to be imitated. Policing of the trademark then becomes a further task that must be carried out to protect the interests of legitimate members, and a further cost that the membership must bear. The importance of controlling the use of marks has long been recognized. In medieval times, the forgery of personal seals and of makers' and merchandise marks on cloth were widely recognized as potentially serious problems.

Highly reputable groups may be able to borrow funds by issuing credit notes that carry their mark. The mark gives the creditor confidence that the debt will be repaid. Political units such as principalities and nation-states have been quick to exploit this potential by borrowing to finance projects of either a civil or military nature. The issue of coinage was an early manifestation of this process. Coinage carried the image of the ruler, whose personal reputation, coupled with the reputation of the political unit he/she controlled, reassured the holder of the coinage about its quality; this reassurance of quality gave the holder a degree of confidence that allowed the issuer to profit from seignorage—in other words, the value of the coin exceeded the value of the precious metal from which it was made. Reputable coinage has the additional advantage that its reputation makes it widely acceptable as a means of payment, and thereby allows the holder to reduce the cost of transactions. Indeed, rulers have traditionally designed coinage to be easily portable, easy to conceal (for security in transit) and have made it available in conveniently small denominations, in order to maximize the seignorage. The converse of this is that counterfeiting has generally been regarded by political leaders as a most serious offence, to be treated as seriously as murder and treason.

If a membership of a group is represented by a brand, then a brand may be said to implicitly define a group. When people observe other people dressing in a particular way, for example, they may decide that these people form a group. The dress they wear becomes the brand of the group. This brand identifies people who share a reputation for behaving in the way that people who dress that way are believed to behave. This raises the possibility that ordinary objects—such as clothes or other possessions—can become brands of particular groups. Once the object in question is recognized as a brand, people can decide whether they wish to identify with the group. If they do so, they know that they will be able to share in the reputation of the group. Such a group could, in principle, emerge spontaneously, although it is most likely, in practice, to emerge through emulation of a successful role model, whereby people attempt to free-ride on the reputation of a highly-reputable person by dressing in a similar way or acquiring similar possessions.

A highly-reputable person has the option of either encouraging emulation of this kind or discouraging it. If the person wished to encourage it, then he/she would dress in a manner that others could afford to imitate, and acquire possessions that others could afford to buy. To maintain the reputation of the group, however, the person would tend to display fairly expensive clothes and other possessions in order to prevent the reputation of the group becoming devalued by the fact that absolutely anyone could join it.

This social process can be exploited by entrepreneurs who innovate branded goods endorsed by highly reputable celebrities. Display of their branded product then becomes the mark of membership, and entitles the member to share in the reputation that accompanies this display. The profit from group formation is shared by the entrepreneur and the celebrity (who will normally receive an endorsement fee). The extent to which the consumers benefit will depend upon how much competition there is in the supply of such celebrity goods, as discussed earlier. This, in turn, may reflect the number of celebrities who are available to endorse rival brands.

It is tempting to suggest that this mechanism, based on a self-defining group, lies behind the proliferation of brands in sectors such as clothing and alcoholic drinks. A feature of the 'spontaneous' group is that it is joined by simply purchasing a branded product and its subsequent display. In the case of clothing, the important thing is to display the product and its trademark, either publicly in the street or privately at a social function, and in the case of alcohol the important thing is to order the drink when going out with friends. Two consequences follow from the simplicity of the spontaneous group: First, anyone can join, provided they can afford the purchase price, and, second, there is no commitment or obligation entailed other than the financial sacrifice involved in the purchase itself. In this respect, the spontaneous group is quite unlike most formal groups, where admission is regulated and membership involves a commitment that makes it difficult to leave. These characteristics suggest that spontaneous groups will appeal most to those who are excluded from other groups because they cannot satisfy the entry requirements; and by those who do not want to make a long-term commitment because their lives are unsettled. Both the characteristics are shared by the young and often poorly-educated consumers who constitute a large portion of the market for heavily branded clothing and drink products.

INTERNAL VERSUS EXTERNAL REPUTATION

An apparent anomaly indicated by this analysis, however, is that some of the spontaneous groups associated with the mass consumption of branded products have a bad reputation, rather than a good one. This anomaly is also reflected in the lifestyles of some of the celebrities who endorse these brands. 'Hoodies' wearing distinctive branded clothing and teenagers consuming branded alco-pops both enjoy a bad reputation with the public. To understand this anomaly, it is necessary to appreciate the difference between the internal reputation and the external reputation of a group. The analysis so far has focused mainly on the external reputation of a group. For many purposes, however, it is the internal reputation that is most important to a member. It is internal reputation that allows a member of a group to win the respect and trust of other members of the group. Thus, if the primary economic and social objective of the group is to promote links between members, rather than links between members and nonmembers, then it is the internal reputation acquired by joining the group that is of paramount importance when deciding whether to join.

The anomaly just noted related to the bad *external* reputation of the group. By encouraging animosity from other groups, a bad external reputation can be valuable in promoting bonding within the group. Each member appreciates that other members, like themselves, are cutting their links with nonmembers, through joining a disreputable group, and are thereby increasing their dependency on fellow members; thus, personal allegiance is focused very much upon the group itself—at least for a time. Young people may wish to join groups of this nature because it allows them to advertise the fact that they are freeing themselves from parental control and are seeking to make alliances with people of their own age. These alliances include peer-group alliances and alliances of a romantic or sexual nature. The role of branded products in facilitating such alliances among young people is well illustrated in the choice of celebrity endorsement, the messages used to advertise the relevant products, and the places in which these advertisements are displayed.

DESIGNING AN EFFECTIVE TRADEMARK

A person's reputation within a social group is closely related to considerations of status. It is often supposed that people who belong to the same group share the same status. This class-based view of society supposes that differentiation of status is effected through a hierarchy of social groups, with members of elite groups taking precedence over members of ordinary groups. In practice, however, there is substantial differentiation of status within groups. Formal groups, in particular, tend to adopt organizational structures in which council members, officers, and fellows take precedence over ordinary members, and full members take precedence over associates.

The display of a product, as we have seen, can act as a signal not only externally, but also internally, i.e. to members of the group to which the person belongs. Display of a product can signal a number of relevant characteristics of the owner, such as wealth, where conspicuously expensive goods are concerned, and power, where special influence is required to procure a good that mere money cannot buy. Display may also signal the owner's discrimination and taste. Discrimination is often judged against the norms of the prevailing fashion, so that high-status is ascribed to someone who displays the very latest fashion. Signals of wealth, power, and discrimination may often point in the same direction, as people with wealth can afford to keep their possessions continually up-to-date with the latest fashions, yet people who are good at anticipating fashions may become wealthy because of their business acumen. Although these signals may be of external relevance, they are mainly directed internally to peers within the same social group.

The provenance of a possession, in terms of where it was purchased and who produced it, is also of potential significance in status terms. This has important implications for the design of trademarks, because it means that, when applied to status-related goods, trademarks must be recognized readily not only by prospective customers but also by the people to whom the goods are meant to be displayed while in the customer's possession. A status-conscious customer may only purchase a good when he/she is confident not only that the brand is reputable, but that its reputation is appreciated by others and that its provenance is conspicuous. Trademarks for status-related products, therefore, need to be durable, as well as highly recognizable.

EXPORT PROMOTION: THE NATION STATE AS AN INTERMEDIARY

As already noted, the way that a firm or product is viewed from outside its own country may have a lot to do with the reputation of the nation with which it is associated (Al-Sulaiti and Baker 1998; Papadopoulos and Heslop 2002; Jaworski and Fosher 2003; Usunier and Cestre 2007; Hanson, this volume). Such reputational effects are known as 'country-of-origin' effects. A firm from a country viewed as having low corruption and strong institutions may be viewed as more likely to conduct itself with probity. Similarly, a firm from a nation with a strong education system, expertise in a particular industry, and discerning customers may be viewed as being relatively likely to deliver high-quality products. According to recent Anholt Nation Brands Index figures, only German or Japanese products are rated more highly by foreigners than UK products, but UK arts and culture are also ranked highly.

Such effects can also exist at an international level. For instance, much regulation is common across EU countries, and there is a degree of shared cultural heritage, and so member states might, to some extent, share a collective reputation. However, the general commonality is weaker than at the national level, particularly due to the strong diversity across EU member nations, though this has to be traded off against the possibility that a common EU reputation could be better known in some parts of the world than the reputations of some of the individual EU nations. Some evidence is offered by the Anholt Nation Brands Index Q2 2006, which included the EU and put it in first place, with the United Kingdom in second place. To some extent, however, the EU reputation may simply be viewed as a composite of individual member nations' reputations.

Shared signs of quality also exist at the international level. For instance, trademarks such as the Woolmark and Fairtrade are used by many firms in many different countries. The International Standards Organization is another example of an international brand, providing standards against which organizations can be certified. Some multinational companies endorse other firms in the countries where they operate. For instance, Microsoft not only certifies individual IT professionals, but also certifies other firms as 'Certified Microsoft Partners'.

There has been increasing interest in the idea of 'nation branding' in recent years, in which governments actively seek to manage their countries' reputations (Olins 2002). Nation branding may aim to change negative or false stereotypes, although there may be problems in carrying this out, such as a lack of coordination across relevant bodies, a lack of continuity between governments, and the use of nation branding for party political aims (Szondi 2007). National brand can be used as a tool for general diplomacy, and for promoting exports and inward investment. It has also been generalized as a marketing concept in the form of place branding (Kavaratzis 2005). Nation branding can be problematic because a country's image is highly multifaceted (Roth and Romeo 1992). Different industries may also prefer different types of images.

The interrelationships of reputations within a country form a complex matrix with strong hierarchical elements. The identity of the home nation determines many of the conditions under which the organization operates; this can have significant implications for how it is viewed. This effect can be particularly strong where the organization is regulated by a national regulator, such as in the financial, food, and pharmaceutical industries.

Collective reputations (Tirole 1996; Winfree and McClusky 2005) can also exist for regions and industrial sectors within a nation. Agglomeration externalities, local traditions, and other factors common to firms within a region or sector, together with positive experiences of the region's or sector's products, give credibility to the reputations of firms from within the sector or region. Sometimes this gives rise to the use of collective trademarks (Cuccia, Marrelli and Santagata 2007). Where a region's name is given to a type of product, such as Parma ham or Champagne, there may sometimes be legal exclusivity for production within the region, and hence this will act as a special type of trademark, known as a 'geographical indication'. Such legal protection has been backed by the European Union in world trade talks, although countries such as the United States, Canada, and Australia have resisted this, arguing that it infringes the rights of those who have brought expertise from relevant regions with them as immigrants, and those onto whom they have passed their knowledge, and that such protection would have to apply equally to regions outside the EU. In EU law, the types of geographical indications for food products are known as Protected Designation of Origin, Protected Geographical Indication, and Traditional Speciality Guaranteed.

There are many other ways in which different organizations within a nation can share in collective reputations. By using auditors with a high reputation, an organization is able to improve its reputation for financial probity. The auditors, in turn, depend partly for their reputation on that of the professional association to which they belong.

A product brand may share the reputation of the producing firm, and, to some extent, directly also shares in the reputation of its home country. A product brand may also apply to a range of different product items. A product can thus be seen as lending a collective reputation to its compo-nents or ingredients, and an organization lends a collective reputation to the work of its employees and subcontractors. These effects also work in the opposite direction, so that, for instance, the use of a high reputation component may help to give credibility to a product.

Supply chains may involve the sharing of reputation. By using certain high reputation suppliers, firms are able to improve the reputation of their own products. This, however, raises the issue of competition for reputa-tion within supply chains (Duguid, this volume). The branding and trade-marking of Intel computer processors ('Intel inside') is an example of this. A high-reputation computer supplier might lose out from reputational enhancements further back in the supply chain that improve the reputa-tions of its competitors' products. Similarly, a supermarket chain might prefer to use its own brand on some products (Miskell, this volume). Some-times, a supplier may also gain in reputation by supplying customers who give the right sort of image to its product, or who provide the right sort of supporting services when selling it on.

Collective reputations owned and managed by independent intermedi-ators can be particularly important for small organizations, which lack the resources and market presence to build strong reputations and brands across large numbers of potential customers.[1] The ability to access the col-lective reputation of a respected intermediary is often crucial for first-time exporters who lack reputations of their own. The most vulnerable firms in this category are firms that have only recently been founded, and whose owners have had no previous work experience with a reputable larger firm. These firms do not even have an existing reputation on which they can build. A less vulnerable group comprises firms that have already suc-cessfully launched their products in their national market, but have yet to export. They have graduated from serving a purely local or regional market to serving a national market, and have therefore already gained some expe-rience in entering new areas, if only within the same country. One 'step up the ladder' from these firms are firms that have already exported to easy markets, such as neighbouring countries, to which transport costs are low, or to culturally similar countries, which share a language or have a similar legal system. In some cases, however, these firms may only be exporting to certain groups within these foreign countries, such as emigrant com-munities that are being supplied with ethnic foods. Finally, there are firms that are already experienced exporters, but that have never exported to a particular country before. In the 1980s and '90s, the rise of new indus-trial powers in Asia, and the liberalization of post-Communist countries, opened up markets to many established firms. Lacking reputation in these new markets, national reputation was often very important, even to firms that, in their own domestic markets, were 'household names'.

Collective reputations can have a key influence in directing the search activities of foreign customers towards particular countries. For instance, a customer may feel that a particular region of a country has a good reputation, and so undertake search activities such as visiting a trade fair there instead of in another country. In this way, search is first directed at a particular country or region, and then moves on to identifying particular suppliers within the country. The costs of search mean that a good reputation can exclude others from the search, at least until the reputation has been refuted. Evidence has demonstrated that importer search activity is often quite limited and may often rely on known contacts for recommendations (Liang and Parkhe 1997; Subramanian 2000). Hence, the ways in which reputations are embedded within social networks are important in leading to the establishment of trading relationships.

Local suppliers with poor reputations may lack incentives to build improved reputations due to the problem of having to overcome the effect of existing expectations, and due to the competition from foreign firms that already have better reputations. In addition, if initial exporters from a country gain poor reputations, they will make things more difficult for other firms that try to export from the same country (Das and DeLoach 2003). Hence, country-of-origin expectations may become self-fulfilling (Chisik 2003). This self-fulfilling aspect is perhaps reflected by the fact that most trademarks registered in developing countries have been registered by firms from industrialized countries, according to Baroncelli et al. (2005), though this might also be explained by a range of other factors.

It is often difficult for reputation brokers to extract all the benefits that they provide to their clients through the fees that they charge. Customers do not always check carefully whether producers are properly accredited or not, and so people who do not belong to accrediting organizations can sometimes still benefit from their activities. This suggests that accreditation may be undersupplied in a market economy because it is difficult for those private organizations that supply such services to extract all their benefits as profit. This is a special case of the 'free rider' problem in the provision of 'public goods'.

Undersupply of private reputation brokerage provides a potential rationale for state bodies that support trade development, such as UK Trade and Investment. In trying to promote an industry's exports to a country where it has not yet achieved much export penetration, the state body will want to be careful to involve high quality firms so that the initial collective reputation that is built is positive. This also helps to enhance the brand of a body such as UK Trade and Investment itself, which is important in maintaining the interest of overseas organizations in their initiatives. Since UK Trade and Investment is an intermediator, it must defend its high reputation.

The principle of intermediation as applied to export promotion is illustrated in figure 2.1. The two key elements in the diagram are the light grey circles representing a high-quality producer in the exporting country (e.g. the UK) and a prospective customer for UK products in a foreign country. The thick black line indicates the desired outcome—namely a successful export deal. The other lines in the figure indicate channels of communication between the agents involved.

A problem for the high-quality producer is that there may also be a low-quality producer whose output is liable to be confused with its own. This low-quality exporter is illustrated by the white circle. Although the exporting country's government may wish that this low-quality exporter were based in some foreign country, in reality it may be based in the exporting country itself. However, the low-quality producer may not be able to communicate with customers as effectively as other agents, because it lacks credibility; this is illustrated in the figure by the fact that the relevant lines of communication are in grey, rather than black.

The high-quality firm may endeavour to create a brand that differentiates its product from the low-quality product. Investing in a new brand is very expensive, however, and so the high-quality exporter may decide to share a reputation with other exporters of the same type. One solution is to

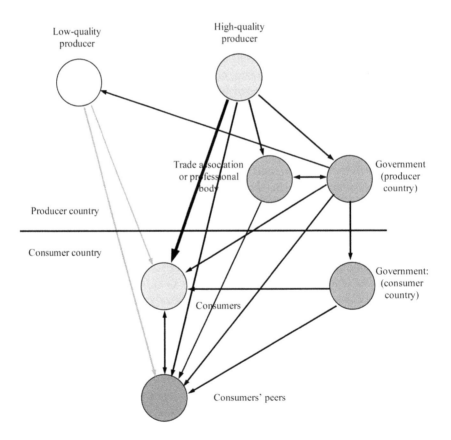

Figure 2.1   Typical network of communication in national trade development support.

join a trade association, indicated by a darker grey circle, which accredits its members and which will refuse membership to low-quality firms. The 'free rider' problem may, however, result in weak or nonexistent trade associations in certain sectors. This provides an opportunity for government to step in. Government will coordinate its activities with those of the trade associations where they exist, and otherwise pursue an independent line. Government may communicate with the low-quality firm in order to exhort it to improve its quality and to join the trade association; it is sometimes difficult, however, for government to actively discriminate against low-quality firms, particularly if they are concentrated in some of the poorer regions of the country.

The government in the producing country can also confer with the government in the consuming country, and so indirectly influence consumers through its political links. Government can also target the customers' peers, as when it attempts to persuade influential people in the foreign country that buying from its country is a good decision. This means that foreign customers who are susceptible to peer-group pressure and are aware of this opinion will purchase exports irrespective of whether they believe that these exports are objectively superior or not.

A SURVEY OF EXPORTER REPUTATION

The remainder of this chapter reports the results of a research project funded by UK Trade and Investment (the department of government responsible for promoting UK exports and attracting inward foreign direct investment). It investigates (among other things) the role of national reputation in supporting UK exports, and the role of national government in building such reputation (the role of regional government in export promotion is excluded from the study). The research involved nine industry case studies: two in the oil and gas sector, and one in each of airports, sport and leisure, power, creative/media, financial services, life sciences, and information and communication technology. Each case study examined a mixture of trade development activities—inward missions, outward missions, seminars promoting UK competencies, representation at trade fairs and exhibitions, receptions with customers, foreign journalists, foreign government officials and opinion leaders, and so on.[2]

Almost all of the firms interviewed believed that the reputation of the United Kingdom in their particular sector was of considerable value to them. Most firms also believed that UK Trade and Investment leadership was of considerable value to them. Except in a few cases, the firm's reputation, by itself, was not enough to ensure business success. Once the firm had made contact with overseas customers, and had done business with them, it could rely on its own reputation to secure future business. But to secure this business to begin with, it was a great advantage for the United

Kingdom to have a strong reputation in the sector. The role of UK Trade and Investment, our interviewees were clear, was not merely to support them as individual firms, but to boost the reputation of the United Kingdom so that foreign customers would take them seriously. A number of interviewees commented that once an event had raised UK reputation in a given country, a repeat event would attract a lot more interest, and potential customers would investigate the firm's offering more seriously. Persuading foreign customers to carry out a detailed appraisal of the firm's offering was crucial to winning new business, and this was most likely to happen if the foreign customer had acquired a good impression of the United Kingdom as a source of supply in his or her sector.

NATIONAL REPUTATION

The simplest way of thinking about reputation as a 'public good' to be shared by firms is to postulate that all UK firms will benefit from a positive image of the UK economy overseas. Although this view has some validity, matters are not quite so simple as this, as our results revealed. There are some national characteristics that genuinely benefit all sectors and, therefore, all firms. A reputation for honesty and integrity in business dealing is useful everywhere, for example. Although it may be particularly relevant in sectors such as banking and insurance, it also applies to other sectors.

Other characteristics may benefit some sectors at the expense of others, however. Political concerns over national reputation may lead to certain sectors being favoured, e.g. life sciences, sport and leisure, creative and media, and financial services. Other sectors may have an 'image problem', such as chemicals and oil and gas. Some sectors may be high-profile but in the wrong way, such as security.

There is no economic law showing that positive-image sectors contribute most to the economy. A government report on sector priorities used a 2 × 2 table based on 'attractiveness' and 'fit'. It placed almost all positive-image sectors in the high-fit category and almost all negative-image sectors in the low-fit category. It has been said that this further damaged the reputation of the negative-image sectors—directly, by creating a false impression that they made little contribution to the economy (even though this was not the implication and is not true), and indirectly, through inducing cuts in support that adversely affected the quality of business support available to them.

The logical way to address this issue is to identify some universally desirable qualities and then not only to promote the industries that already have these qualities but to encourage other industries to adapt in order to acquire these qualities too. If it is believed, for example, that the chemical industry is dirty and polluting, but the pharmaceutical industry is clean and good for health—which is typical of the superficial stereotypes that some of our interviewees alleged permeated government thinking—then instead of promoting pharmaceuticals and not chemicals, it may be better to promote UK pharmaceuticals as the cleanest of the clean, and UK chemicals as the cleanest of the relatively dirty. Managing national reputation is not simply a matter of highlighting the good and disguising the bad, but of being seen to be addressing the bad in a constructive manner.

SECTOR REPUTATION

When asked about reputation, almost every firm in our study emphasized that it was more concerned with the reputation of its sector than with the reputation of the UK economy as a whole. Firms wanted the customers with whom they dealt to believe that the United Kingdom was good at producing the particular products that their firm supplied. They wanted a national reputation in the sector that was based on explaining to foreign customers why the United Kingdom was a particularly good location for producing the product and why the quality achieved was likely to be high relative to the price charged (i.e. providing a supporting myth).

This concern of sector reputation was related to the firms' concern that UK Trade and Investment should be responsive to their lobbying. There was a common view that the UK government was inherently distrustful of lobbying by firms and that, as a result, individual sectors such as their own were quite likely to be handicapped by the unintended adverse consequences of new government legislation. They, therefore, considered that an effective dialogue with government and government promotion of a sector's reputation went hand-in-hand.

Our evidence suggests that globalizing the reputation of a sector that already has a good regional, national, or European reputation seems to be more effective than trying to create a reputation for a sector from scratch. For example, airport ground service suppliers have achieved only limited success in capitalizing on UK architectural and engineering success in terminal design; their knowledge-base is quite different to that of the successful professional consultancies. This example suggests that support should be targeted at firms that have already demonstrated their capacity to be one of the best producers in their sector in the United Kingdom.

However, this strategy should not be taken to extremes. Supporting sectors and firms that are already highly successful may add little value because the reputation of the sector concerned is already as high as it is likely to get. Although supporting sectors that already have strong global reputation may be useful in helping them to overcome barriers to market access, indiscriminate support for such sectors may offer little return in terms of further enhancement of reputation.

REGIONAL REPUTATION

Few people argued that regional reputation is more significant than national reputation, except in the context of the food and drink sector, and for some 'heritage' products. In the oil and gas sector, a 'North Sea story' with a regional dimension had been promoted, but this was set in the context of lessons that regions in other countries could learn from. It did not suggest that the region concerned was the only UK region capable of supplying the products concerned.

With the exception of London, few regions seemed to have acquired a distinctive international reputation for their 'clusters'. Our interviewees expressed little enthusiasm for the idea that national benefit could be derived from promoting specific regional clusters through UK Trade and Investment. It was widely argued that the promotion of regional reputation detracted from more important messages about the United Kingdom, and that, if carried to extremes, the effect on foreign buyers could be sufficiently confusing that it might put them off buying from the United Kingdom altogether.

There was particular concern that the promotion of regional reputation at trade fairs was wasteful and damaging to the national interest. It was claimed that UK Trade and Investment had been unable to fully address this issue. Our results on regional delivery suggested that organizing the delivery of UK Trade and Investment support with the advice of a federation of regional bodies might help to overcome this problem.

CONCLUSION

Brands carry reputation, and reputation is a crucial aspect of economic relations. However, in studying brands, the complexity of reputational issues should be recognized, including the interrelationships of the reputations of different entities both within nations and internationally. Understanding the role of reputation helps us to understand how markets really work, and involves issues such as the gaining of market power through reputation, the roles of intermediaries, issues of shared reputations, and the problems of building and then maintaining reputations. Such issues are also crucial in understanding the export process.

NOTES

1. This is one reason for franchising, where different firms have a contract with the franchisor to use its brand. Franchising is also an important method of internationalization, in which a brand is shared with foreign firms.
2. Each case study involved a programme of interviews with 12 to 18 organizations. Interviews were conducted face-to-face wherever possible, and

otherwise by telephone or email. Interviewees were asked about the pattern of 'networking' in their sector. They were also asked about their own place in the network, and the place of UK Trade and Investment. The value of reputation in developing export business was then examined in some detail, together with other issues that lie outside the scope of this chapter.

BIBLIOGRAPHY

Akerlof, G. A. (1970) 'The market for "lemons": Quality uncertainty and the market mechanism', *Quarterly Journal of Economics*, 84 (3): 488–500.

Al-Sulaiti, K. I. and M. J. Baker (1998) 'Country of origin effects: A literature review', *Marketing Intelligence & Planning*, 16 (3): 150–199.

Balasubramanyam, V. N. and M. A. Salisu (1994) 'Brands and the alcoholic drinks industry', G. G. Jones and N. J. Morgan (eds) *Adding Value: Brands and Marketing in Food and Drink*, London: Routledge, 59–75.

Baroncelli, E., C. Fink and B. S. Javorcik (2005) 'The global distribution of trade marks: Some stylised facts', *World Economy*, 28 (6): 765–782.

Carter, M. J., M. C. Casson and V. Suneja (eds.) (1998) *The Economics of Marketing*, Cheltenham: Edward Elgar.

Chisik, R. (2003) 'Export industry policy and reputational comparative advantage', *Journal of International Economics*, 59 (2): 423–451.

Cuccia, T., M. Marrelli and W. Santagata (2007) 'Collective trade marks and cultural districts: The case of San Gregorio Armeno–Naples', *EBLA Working Papers* 200701, University of Turin.

Das, J. and S. B. DeLoach (2003) 'Strategic trade policy in the presence of reputation spillovers', *Journal of International Trade & Economic Development*, 12 (2): 101–116.

Duguid, P. (2008) 'Brands in chains', this volume.

Jain, S. P. and S. S. Posavac (2001) 'Pre-purchase attribute verifiability, source credibility, and persuasion', *Journal of Consumer Psychology*, 11: 169–180.

Jaworski, S. P. and D. Fosher (2003) 'National brand identity and its effect on corporate brands: The nation brand effect (NBE)', *Multinational Business Review*, 11 (2): 99–113.

Kavaratzis, M. (2005) 'Place branding: A review of trends and conceptual models', *Marketing Review*, 5 (4): 329–342.

Kirmani, A. and A. R. Rao (2000) 'No pain, no gain: A critical review of the literature on signaling unobservable product quality', *Journal of Marketing*, 64: 66–79.

Klein, B. and K. B. Leffler (1981) 'The role of market forces in assuring contractual performance', *Journal of Political Economy*, 89: 615–41.

Liang N. and A. Parkhe (1997) 'Importer vendor choice behavior: A comparative study', *Journal of International Business Studies*, 28 (3): 495–530.

Mailath, G. J. and L. Samuelson (2006) *Repeated Games and Reputation*, New York: Oxford University Press.

Milgrom, P. R. and J. Roberts (1986) 'Price and advertising signals of product quality', *Journal of Political Economy*, 94 (4): 796–821.

Nelson, P. (1970) 'Information and consumer behavior', *Journal of Political Economy* 78 (2): 311–329.

Nelson, P. (1974) 'Advertising as information', *The Journal of Political Economy*, 82 (4): 729–754.

Olins, W. (2002) 'Branding the nation: The historical context', *Journal of Brand Management*, 9 (4–5): 241–248.

54   *Mark Casson and Nigel Wadeson*

Papadopoulos, N. and L. Heslop (2002) 'Country equity and country branding: Problems and prospects', *Journal of Brand Management*, 9 (4–5) 294–314.
Peng, M. W. and A. Y. Ilinitch (1998). 'Export intermediary firms: A note on export development research', *Journal of International Business Studies*, 2 (3): 609–620.
Ramello, G. B. and F. Silva (2006) 'Appropriating signs and meaning: The elusive economics of trade mark', *Industrial and Corporate Change*, 15 (6): 937–963.
Roth, M. S. and J. B. Romeo (1992) 'Matching product category and country image perceptions: A framework for managing country-of-origin effects', *Journal of International Business Studies*, 23 (3): 477–497.
Smith, D. C. and C. W. Park (1992) 'The effects of brand extensions on market share and advertising efficiency', *Journal of Marketing Research*, 29 (3): 296–313.
Spulber, D. F. (1996) 'Market microstructure and intermediation', *Journal of Economic Perspectives*, 10 (3): 135–152.
Subramanian, R. (2000) 'Search and deliberation in international exchange: Micro-foundations to some macro patterns', *Journal of International Business Studies*, 31 (2): 205–222.
Szondi, G. (2007) 'The role and challenges of country branding in transition countries: The Central and Eastern European experience', *Place Branding and Public Diplomacy*, 3: 8–20.
Tirole, J. (1996) 'A theory of collective reputations (with applications to the persistence of corruption and to firm quality)', *Review of Economic Studies*, 63, (214): 1–22.
Trabold, D. B. (2002) 'Export intermediation: An empirical test of Peng and Ilinitch', *Journal of International Business Studies*, 33 (2): 327–344.
Usunier, J.-C. and G. Cestre (2007) 'Product ethnicity: Revisiting the match between products and countries', *Journal of International Marketing*, 15 (3): 32–72.
Weigelt, K. and C. Camerer (1988) 'Reputation and corporate strategy: A review of recent theory and applications', *Strategic Management Journal*, 9: 443–454.
Winfree, J. A. and J. J. McCluskey (2005) 'Collective reputation and quality', *American Journal of Agricultural Economics*, 87 (1): 206–213.

3 Trademarks and Performance in UK Firms

Christian Helmers and Mark Rogers

This chapter provides a synopsis of recent research on firm-level data on UK and Community-wide trademarking. The role of trademarks in the innovation system has been greatly neglected in economic and, to a lesser extent, management research. The specific contribution of this chapter is to ask what quantitative evidence there is that trademarking and performance are positively associated in firms (both directly and via spill-overs to other firms in the industry). We are in the unique position of being able to provide such evidence because of the endeavours of the authors and other researchers in matching trademark data to large firm-level data sets.

Before reviewing the empirical results, let us place the role of trademarks in the appropriate economic context. In some industrial countries, the number of applications (and grants) of trademarks are around twice that of patents. Trademarks are also used extensively by service sector firms, whereas patents are not. Since the service sector in modern economies, such as the United Kingdom, is far larger than the manufacturing sector (the high patent-using sector), this provides a very strong reason for further investigation of the role of trademarks.[1] Furthermore, trademark activity has increased rapidly in recent years, with a particular boom in the late 1990s.

In this chapter, we first review the characteristics of trademarks and the existing economic theories that attribute to them an important role in firm performance. We then briefly discuss the data sets used for our analysis, outline their basic features with regard to trademarks, and provide an overview of how the economic impact of trademarks can be assessed. Next, we analyse, in detail, the effect of trademarking on a range of economic performance measures both for large-, as well as small- and medium-sized, enterprises. Then we provide some evidence on so called Schumpeterian effects evoked by trademarks. More specifically, we investigate whether other firms' trademarking within an industry only exerts competitive pressure on a firm's performance or whether this static competitive effect is offset by Schumpeterian effects, i.e. rising overall productivity within the industry through a generally high degree of trademarking in the industry.

The conclusion sums up the main insights derived from the empirical analysis presented in this chapter.

BACKGROUND

A trademark is a legally protected 'sign' that is used to distinguish a product or service. The 'sign' can be any word(s), graphics, figures, images, or similar that acts as a distinguishing feature. Trademarks can also be distinctive shapes, colours, or sounds, although few applications to register such marks have been accepted. Trademarks, from a legal perspective, are intended to help prevent 'unfair competition'. The registration of a trademark makes it easier to stop a business from imitating its rivals or their products. Unlike a patent, a trademark does not indicate an inventive step, hence, perhaps unfairly, trademarks are often thought to be less significant. A firm has two ways of obtaining trademark protection in the United Kingdom. The cheapest method is to apply for a UK trademark (UKTM) from the UK Intellectual Property Office; this costs around £200 (€215). An alternative route is to apply for a Community trademark (CTM). The CTM was introduced in 1996; at around £1,500 (€1,606), applying and registering a CTM is more expensive, but it covers all countries in the European Union. In both cases the initial registration lasts for ten years, at which time a renewal fee is payable (£200 for UKTMs and €1,500 for CTMs).[2] Applications for trademarks are examined and then published, allowing a period of time for others to object, before full registration.[3] Each trademark application has to specify a class in which the trademark is to be used.[4] Both kinds of mark can be renewed indefinitely.

Trademark activity increased substantially in the 1990s in many major economies. The most notable increase in trademark applications occurred in the United States, where applications rose from 127,294 in 1990 to 354,775 in 2006.[5] In contrast, European economies experienced significant, but less pronounced, increases. Applications for trademarks with the German Patent Office, for example, doubled from 31,675 in 1990 to 72,321 in 2006.[6] In the United Kingdom, applications increased from 32,513 in 1990 to 63,276 in 2005. In Japan, however, trademark applications fell during the same period (probably a reflection of the low growth in Japan's economy). Although the number of applications in Japan amounted to 167,906 in 1991, it fell by nearly 24 per cent to 135,777 in 2006.[7] The numbers of applications for the new CTM was high at 43,000 in its first year (1996), as firms were allowed to convert existing national trademarks into CTMs. By 2005, CTM applications were 77,000.

Patent applications make an interesting comparison. In 2003 in the United Kingdom, there were 16,923 trademark registrations but only 3,646 patent grants.[8] The numbers of applications for trademarks and patents were roughly the same, at around 20,000, but a far higher proportion of patent applications are rejected on examination, whereas most trademark applications become full intellectual property rights.

The Economics of Trademarks

In this section, we outline four canonical views of trademarking. The first is that trademarks help to solve the information asymmetry between seller and buyer: firms use trademarks to signal to consumers that the product is of a certain, consistent quality. In this way, the 'search costs' of customers are reduced, the firm can charge a higher price, and the firm's profits increase.[9] These assumptions imply that there should be a positive association between the stock of trademarks that a firm has and profitability. Furthermore, this view suggests that the rapid growth in trademark activity in the late 1990s originated in a worsening of the informational asymmetry faced by consumers. To our knowledge, there is no literature that is concerned with trends in the extent of information asymmetry, but the discussion surrounding the economics of information and the Internet suggests that the extent of asymmetry could change (see Varian, Farrell and Shapiro 2004).

The search cost view is, then, static but we can easily see how it could be extended to innovation. If a firm cannot trademark a new product, it may be deterred from pursuing the innovation by fear of rivals immediately imitating their product. Hence, the second view assumes that trademarks provide a similar function to patents and can be viewed as an element in the process of innovation. Mendonça, Pereira and Godinho (2004) support this view and suggest that trademark applications can—like R&D or patents—be a proxy for innovative activity. Clearly, in this case it is the current trademark activity (i.e. a 'flow'), rather than the stock of trademarks held by a firm, that is the relevant proxy.

The third view of trademarks stems from the theoretical industrial organization literature on brands, entry, and barriers to entry (see Davis and Maniatis, this volume). There is a traditional argument that incumbent firms may use product or brand differentiation as a strategic barrier to entry.[10] Theorists are interested in whether there is over- or underprovision of brands and products in terms of societal welfare, with the result tending to depend on specific demand and (fixed) cost assumptions (e.g. Perry and Groff 1986). From this perspective, the rapid rise in trademark activity in the late 1990s, although potentially beneficial to incumbent firms, is unlikely to be beneficial for society.

The final view of trademarking is that it has little inherent value but reflects how management practices, and fashions, change. We think of this as the 'management fad' view, as the increased use of trademarks may only be due to changing management practices and, specifically, a rush by managers to copy rivals' activities, rather than any inherent value relevance for trademarks per se. Such a view also raises concerns over the possibility of reverse causation: managers of high productivity firms may have more discretionary funds and allocate some of these to copying the latest management fad. The empirical analysis can use lagged values of trademark activity as a method of control for such endogeneity.

Data on Trademarking Activity of Firms

In order to assess the role of trademarks on firm performance, we need data that map the trademark activity of firms. The Oxford Intellectual Property Research Centre has spent a number of years developing such databases. In this chapter, we draw on two of them. The first is a database of 1,600 large UK firms for the period 1996 to 2000. The second is a database of 232,490 small- and medium-sized enterprises (SMEs)[11] for the period 2001 to 2004.[12] For most of our analysis presented in the following, we have used only the subset of 130,082 SMEs active in 2001. Both databases have information on two types of trademarks: UKTMs and CTMs.

Table 3.1 shows the average percentage of large UK firms that trademark in each year (1996–2000). Note that the propensity to trademark varies substantially across sectors. The retail sector has the highest propensity to apply for UKTMs (55 per cent of firm-year observations), whereas only 12.5 per cent of firms in real estate do so. Service firms in several sectors are as active as manufacturing firms in UKTMs. The propensity to apply for a CTM is lower than that for a UKTM in all sectors and somewhat lower in services than in manufacturing. The last two columns of the table show the average trademarks per year per 1,000 employees. Again there are some very large differences in mean values across sectors.[13] The table is based on 5,283 observations (i.e. firm-year observations) and the results for large firms reported in this chapter are based on this sample.

Table 3.2 shows a similar set of summary statistics for the SME data set. The full data set contains information for 232,490 SMEs over a later five-year period (2001–2005) than in table 3.1. Trademark intensities are much lower for SMEs, varying between little more than 0.1 per cent (real estate) and 2.4 per cent for the manufacturing and wholesale sectors. In general, the number of SMEs taking out a CTM is significantly lower relative to UKTMs across all sectors. This reflects the fact that SMEs do business mostly on the domestic market and have less interest in international intellectual property (IP) protection.

How Can We Test any Impact of Trademarks on Firm Performance?

In this section, we outline a number of techniques that assess the association between trademarking and firm performance. All of these techniques have been used in studies of the role of R&D, patenting, or other aspects of innovation. Indeed, it is important to use established techniques when looking at the role of new data on trademarks.

- Share-market value studies. Where data on the share- or stock-market value are available, we can assess the association of trademark activity on the share-market value of firms. Generally, it is only large firms that are listed on share markets, so this method is often only applicable to databases of large firms. The market value of a firm should reflect the expected future flow of profits, hence a strength of this technique is that it looks at an association between trademarking now and expected future profits. Hall (2000) provides an excellent overview of these studies.
- Productivity studies. If there are data on the value added of the firm, as well as data on labour and capital inputs, it is possible to analyse the association between productivity and trademarking. Since trademarking might be expected to influence future productivity there is a need to lag the trademark variables. See Griliches and Mairesse (1995) for an overview of problems in estimating firm-level productivity.
- Growth studies. A particular area of interest for micro or small firms concerns their ability to grow. The seminal discussion of this issue is Penrose (1959), and Macpherson and Holt (2007) review recent papers. In summary, the firm's entrepreneurial and learning capabilities are

Table 3.1   Trademark Propensity and Intensity for 1,600 Large UK Firms, 1996–2000

Sector	Percentage of firms trademarking		Trademarks per 1,000 employees	
	UKTM	CTM	UKTM	CTM
Agriculture, mining	9.46	7.43	1.17	2.09
Manufacturing	41.64	33.18	33.57	10.46
Electricity, gas, water	51.4	27.1	6.92	1.99
Construction	25.52	6.77	1.88	1.03
Service sectors				
Finance	27.6	12.5	42.79	14.4
Real estate	12.5	5.47	2.32	28.1
Wholesale	35.94	22.92	12.84	15.47
Retail	54.71	24.14	10.29	6.76
Hotels/catering	44.74	13.68	23.25	268.51
Transport/communications	49.24	34.47	21.14	13.41
Business services	29.17	19.68	52.14	43.42
Other services	31.56	16.1	82.67	81.49

Note: Trademark data refer to 'publications'. A publication occurs if an application passes an examination for distinctiveness.

Table 3.2   IP-Active SMEs (Trademark Publications—by Sector, 2001–2005)

Sector	Percentage of firms trademarking		No. of trade-marking SMEs	
	UKTM	CTM	UKTM	CTM
Agric., Mining	0.47	0.17	74	27
Manufacturing	2.42	1.34	2,572	1,428
Electricity, Gas, Water	0.47	0.47	5	5
Construction	0.37	0.05	199	28
Service sectors				
Finance	0.89	0.35	279	110
Real Estate	0.13	0.03	137	34
Wholesale	2.40	1.00	1940	809
Retail	1.68	0.63	376	141
Hotels/catering	0.93	0.26	191	54
Transport/ communications.	1.07	0.56	292	154
Business services	1.33	0.90	2116	1,428
Other services	1.33	0.53	1073	428

thought critical. Empirical papers on large databases tend to follow Hart and Oulton (1996; 1999) by analysing how the growth of sales revenue, employment, or assets evolves across hundreds of thousands of firms. In the following, we report on whether trademarking SMEs have higher growth rates.

- Survival studies. Firm survival or equivalently firm failure is the most fundamental measure of firm performance. Given the importance commonly attributed to IP in determining firm performance and shaping industry dynamics, it is important to assess the role of IP, and specifically trademarks, as a determinant of firm survival. See Helmers and Rogers (2008) for a more detailed discussion.
- Profitability studies. If data on share-market value are not available, it may be possible to look at trademarking in the current year and profitability over a subsequent period. This approach attempts to capture the association between trademarking now and future performance. Feeny, Harris and Rogers (2005) provide a discussion of profitability studies.

In the sections that follow, we refer to results from using these techniques. Since space is limited, we often cannot describe the methods used in detail (interested readers should use the aforementioned references for more information).

EMPIRICAL RESULTS ON THE ROLE OF
TRADEMARKS TO UK FIRMS

This section uses the methods previously described to assess the effect of trademarks on various measures of firm performance using the two UK data sets already presented. Some of the techniques are only applicable to large firms, because of a lack of data for smaller firms, which makes a somewhat different approach necessary to analyse the association between trademarks and SME performance.

Large Firms and Share-Market Value

This section reports on the results of using the share-market value of firms to assess the importance of trademark activity. The share-market value should be the expected value of future profits of the firm and has been used extensively in studies on innovation and performance. In our analysis of large UK firms, we are interested in any association between the share-market value of the firm and current trademark activity. As is standard, we also use control variables for whether the firm is R&D-active, patent-active, highly diversified, selling in European or North American markets, or experiencing high sales growth. We also include the debt-to-equity ratio, the book value of intangible assets, and a control for the industry it is located in as further control variables. By using these control variables, we hope to isolate the association with trademark activity.[14]

The first result found by the share-market value analysis is that trademarking firms have a substantial share-market premium. For example, a firm that takes out at least one UKTM in a given year has around a 20 per cent share-market premium. Looking at manufacturing and service firms separately, we find that the premium for manufacturing firms is lower, at around 10 per cent, but is higher for service firms (almost 30 per cent). The share-market premia for firms that take out a CTM are even higher for service firms (around 50 per cent). Finding such large premia for trademarking firms was unexpected. By way of comparison, firms that are R&D active also have a premium of between 15 and 30 percent.

How should we interpret such large share-market premia for firms that trademark? It is important not to claim that the simple act of applying for a trademark will somehow transform a firm into a highly profitable business. Instead, trademarking is correlated with a range of other activities and firm-level characteristics, and it is the entire bundle of activities that gives rise to the premium. For example, trademarking may be associated with the launch of a new product, a new marketing campaign, and higher advertising expenditure.[15] Another possibility is that trademarking may be associated with better managers (i.e. managers who think more strategically and are more likely to use IP).

A further aspect of the analysis was to investigate trademark intensity, which is defined as the number of trademarks per million assets. The previously discussed results suggest that applying for at least one trademark is associated with high share-market values, but we can also investigate whether having more trademarks brings further benefits. Since firms differ in their size, and we would expect larger firms to do more trademarking, investigating whether 'more is better' entails the use of trademark intensity (with intensity defined as 'trademarks/assets'). Does higher trademark intensity raise share-market value? The basic answer is 'no'. However, if one investigates a little further, there appears to be a more complex story. In 1996, higher trademark intensity (both UKTMs and CTMs) did appear to be associated with higher share-market value, but by 2000 this association seemed to have disappeared. Relating this back to our discussion in section 2, the rapid rise in trademarking in the late 1990s appears to be associated with the falling marginal value of each new trademark.

Productivity and Trademarking in Large UK Firms

Greenhalgh and Rogers (2007) also provide an analysis of the links between trademark activity and productivity in large UK firms. The basic method is to link a firm's current net output, or value added, with its trademarking activity in the previous year plus a number of other control variables. This is done using multivariate regression techniques. Once again, the existing literature suggests a large number of control variables, including capital stock, employment, R&D, patents, diversification, European or North American exposure, book value of intangible assets, and industry controls. The analysis controls for the fact that larger firms—in terms of assets and employment—will have higher value added, hence, if any of the control variables show significance, we say they have an association with firm-level productivity.

A first set of results comes from assessing the association between trademark activity and the level of productivity across firms. Once again, we find that trademark activity has a substantial positive correlation with productivity. For example, a manufacturing firm that applies for both a UKTM and a CTM in a given year is associated with a 15 per cent higher productivity, compared to nontrademarking firms. A service sector firm that applies for only a UKTM in such a year has a 17 per cent higher productivity. As before, it is wrong to interpret these as causal effect: the act of trademarking is associated with a range of other firm-level activities. However, it does show that the bundle of activities that include trademarking appears to be very important. Looking at the intensity of trademark activity (we now use the number of trademarks per employee as an intensity measure), we find less evidence of significant associations. In manufacturing, higher UKTM intensity is associated with higher productivity, but CTMs and service sector firms show no significant associations. Hence, when analysing the level of productivity, we find that some level of trademark activity is beneficial, but more trademarking may have little effect.

The analysis can also tackle a further question: is trademark activity associated with higher productivity growth? To be clear, the aforementioned results were based on differences in productivity levels between firms, while this question asks whether trademarking by a firm has an association with productivity growth. In order to answer this question, the analysis needs to use data on firms that have either (a) not had a trademark in each year of the available data or (b) varied their intensity of trademarking over the period. Again, the data used is for 1,600 large firms over the period 1996–2000. There are relatively few firms that fall under category (a), since most large firms that trademarked in 1996 do so in every subsequent year. However, it is possible to analyse firms that varied their trademark intensity. The results from this analysis indicate some positive associations with productivity growth, but, overall, there is not a consistent relationship. Once again, we are back to the main result from all analysis on the large-firm data set: doing some trademarking is associated with better performance, but doing more and more trademarking has limited significance.

SMEs and Trademarking: What do we Know?

Rogers, Helmers and Greenhalgh (2007) and Rogers, Greenhalgh and Helmers (2007) analyse a new database of the IP activity of UK SMEs. Table 3.3, which shows the distribution of trademark registrations by industry size in 2004, indicates that trademarking is relatively less frequent for SMEs than for large firms. Should we expect trademark activity to be associated with increased SME performance? An initial response is 'yes', since the previous arguments regarding search costs and innovation should also apply to SMEs. There is, however, a substantial literature about the differences between SMEs and large firms, especially if the SMEs are innovative and entrepreneurial (see, for example, Sexton and Lanstrom 1999). A core argument in this literature is that the innovative SMEs are much more resource constrained than large firms. As a result, innovative SMEs may have a lower survival rate or, if they do survive, the 'pay back' period may be longer. Another implication from this discussion is that the profitability of IP-active SMEs should be lower in the short run than for IP-inactive SMEs. Equally, there is strong interest in whether the IP system provides sufficient benefits for SMEs to undertake innovation, an activity that is inherently risky (Gowers 2006).

The analysis presented in this subsection is based on tracking the performance of the cohort of 130,082 SMEs in the database in 2001.[16] A first step was to identify how many of these SMEs survived. Table 3.3 shows that a little more than 5 per cent of SMEs in 2001 failed by 2004. Although firms that had a UKTM in 2001 exhibit a slightly lower failure rate, the difference is small. It is, however, noteworthy that SMEs with a CTM in 2001

Table 3.3   Percentage of Trademark Registration by Firm Size in the United Kingdom and the European Union, 2004

Outcome groups in 2004	UK trademark		Community trademark		UKTM & CTM	All firms
	No UKTM in 2001	UKTM in 2001	No CTM in 2001	CTM in 2001		
Large	6.4	8.5	6.4	7.8	11.5	6.4
SME	77.9	79.7	78.0	76.3	77.0	77.9
Micro	10.4	7.4	10.3	9.7	6.9	10.4
Exited	5.3	4.4	5.3	6.2	4.6	5.3

exhibited a slightly higher failure rate than firms without any trademark. In terms of growth, the overwhelming share of SMEs remained SMEs, trademarking and nontrademarking firms alike. However, the share of SMEs that managed to grow out of the SME category into the large-firm category is over two percentage points higher for firms with a UKTM, and over one percentage point higher for firms with a CTM in 2001. The share of SMEs falling into the micro category is three percentage points lower for UK trademarking firms, but only half a percentage point lower for Community trademarking firms. Interestingly, firms that had both UKTMs and CTMs in 2001 were less likely to exit than all but the UK trademarking firms, and are almost twice as likely to fall into the large-firm category by 2004 than the SME category as a whole.

To assess whether trademarking by SMEs had an association with survival, Roger, Greenhalgh and Helmers (2007) made use of a multivariate Probit model. The Probit model allows us to control for a range of other factors on the firm and industry level, such as age, industry, ownership, and industry market structure. The Probit model not only tests the possible effect of a wide range of variables on the probability of failure for all SMEs in the sample, but distinguishes between three subsets of the sample ordering firms into three age categories: firms younger than five years, firms between 5 and 10 years, and firms older than 10 years. The explanatory variables of most interest are the binary variables for UKTMs and CTMs (a binary variable simply indicates whether the SME trade marked or not). The coefficient for UKTMs shows that taking out a UKTM lowers, in a statistically significant sense, the likelihood of failure. The same is true for firms in the age categories 5–10 years and more than 10 years. In contrast, UKTMs seem to have little influence on the survival probability of firms younger than five years. Also, the coefficient of CTMs is negative for the whole sample, but is not statistically significantly different from zero. Only for firms in the age category over 10 years does taking out a CTM lower the likelihood of failure. It is noteworthy that patents from the UK Intellectual Property Office or from the European Patent Office (EPO) do not seem to influence the likelihood of failure in a statistically significant way.

Growth of SMEs and Trademarking

Rogers, Greenhalgh and Helmers (2007) also look at whether SMEs that trademarked experienced higher subsequent growth rates. The data available allow us to analyse the growth in assets and turnover (data coverage for the former is 82 per cent and 28 per cent for the latter). The analysis looks at growth over the period 2001 to 2004 and categorizes performance into 'poor', 'weak', 'solid', or 'high', based on the quartiles of the distribution of growth rates.

Table 3.4 shows SMEs' relative growth performance in terms of firms' total assets. IP-inactive firms form the benchmark category and we can see that each category has roughly 25 per cent in it (as would be expected since we define the categories by quartiles). Looking at the next column, we can see that IP-active firms are less present in the second quartile. These firms are concentrated within the first and fourth quartile, which means that they either perform better or worse than IP-inactive firms. This pattern is present for UK trademarking SMEs. In the first quartile, it is most pronounced for firms taking out CTMs, yet in the fourth, high-growth quartile, it is most pronounced for firms taking out UKTMs.

Table 3.5 looks at the relative growth performance with regard to firms' turnover.[17] The pattern is similar to the pattern detected in table 3.4. However, here IP-active firms are more concentrated in the high growth quartile. This is even more the case for both trademark groups, indicating that firms taking out trademarks may achieve stronger turnover growth than patenting firms.

Table 3.4 SMEs: Growth of Assets (2001 to 2004) and IP Activity (2001)

Growth Quartile	Non-IP Active	IP Active	UKTM Active	CTM Active	UK Patent Active	EPO Active
Poor growth (1st quartile)	24.9	27.9	24.4	33.4	31.3	35.3
Weak growth (2nd quartile)	25.2	16.7	15.9	15.1	20.6	16.6
Solid growth (3rd quartile)	25.0	24.9	26.2	21.6	24.6	21.7
High growth (4th quartile)	24.9	30.6	33.6	29.9	23.6	26.5

Note: Table shows the percentages of SMEs in each of the four growth groups: poor, weak, solid and high. If there were no association between the column header and the growth groups, we would expect 25.0 in all growth groups. Deviations from this suggest growth and IP are not independent. A chi^2 test confirms that each of the IP types has a significantly different distribution to non-IP-active firms. Rounding causes some columns to total more than 100.

Table 3.5   SMEs: Growth of Turnover (2001 to 2004) and IP Activity (2001)

Growth Quartile	Non-IP Active	IP Active	UKTM Active	CTM Active	UK Patent Active	EPO Active
Poor growth (1st quartile)	25.1	23.8	20.8	25.9	24.2	32.9
Weak growth (2nd quartile)	25.1	22.8	21.7	23.3	24.2	24.9
Solid growth (3rd quartile)	25.1	24.1	26.1	18.1	26.8	18.6
High growth (4th quartile)	24.8	29.3	31.4	32.7	24.8	23.9

Note: As per Table 3.4.

Overall, these results suggest the following. Trademarking is associated with higher SME growth rates in assets and turnover over the next three years. By contrast, patenting is weakly, and perhaps negatively, correlated with SME growth rates over the same period. It is important to check these results, controlling for other possible influences affecting asset and turnover growth. For this purpose, Rogers, Greenhalgh and Helmers (2007) use a multivariate regression framework to asses the effect of trademarking on growth. As in the survival analysis, Rogers, Greenhalgh and Helmers (2007) distinguish between three firm-age categories. The results point to a statistically significant and economically important correlation of UKTMs with asset growth and turnover growth. The same holds for CTMs, but this effect shows up in a statistically significant way only for turnover growth using the whole SME sample. As with firm survival, the effect of trademarks on growth in assets and turnover distinguishes itself sharply from that of patents. Neither UK nor EPO patents have any statistically significant impact on firm growth.

Profitability of SMEs and Trademarking

This section analyses the possible association between trademark activity by SMEs in 2001 and profitability in the period 2002 to 2004. Profitability is defined as the ratio of net profit before tax to total assets. Ultimately, the profitability of an SME is of critical importance as persistent low profitability signals that the products, efficiency, and strategy of the SME cannot compete in the market place. However, as discussed, innovative SMEs may be making substantial investments, hence profitability may be low or even negative for a number of years. This said, one might expect, on average, only younger SMEs to be investing at a rate that causes profitability to be very low or even negative.

Again profitability is analysed by splitting firms into four categories based on the quartiles of the distribution. Table 3.6 shows the relative performance of SMEs with regard to profitability. IP-active firms are more concentrated in the first and fourth quartile relative to IP-inactive firms. More precisely, the largest share of IP-active firms falls into the first quartile, providing support for the hypothesis that creating IP may go along with substantial expenditures for SMEs, significantly lowering profitability. This pattern is even more pronounced for CTM and EPO patent-active SMEs (for EPO nearly half of all firms fall into the poor profitability category). The UKTM-active column shows that profitability is 'polarized', but in a less pronounced way than for CTM or EPO-active SMEs.

The following tables provide a breakdown by firm age. This allows further insight into our hypothesis that creating IP results in lower profitability of SMEs in the short run. Table 3.7 looks at the same relative distribution specifically for young firms that have been in the market for less than 5 years. Note that the first column of each table shows how the non-IP-active age cohort performs relative to all SMEs in the sample. Hence, in table 3.7 we can see that younger SMEs do worse than normal (e.g. 35 percent are in poor profitability). This means that the remaining columns in the age cohort tables always need to be compared to the first column. Table 3.7 provides additional strong support that undertaking innovation in the form of trademarks and patents puts young SMEs under considerable pressure in terms of profitability. 50 per cent of SMEs that take out a UKTM fall into the 'poor' profitability category, and almost three-quarters of young SMEs taking out CTMs do so.

The situation for older SMEs is shown in tables 3.8 and 3.9. Table 3.8 shows the results for SMEs aged between 5 and 10. The hollowing out of the middle of the distribution is present, but it is not as pronounced as SMEs under 5 years old. Table 3.9 shows the results for SMEs over 10 years old. As might be expected, the hollowing out of the distribution is less pronounced. Older SMEs are likely to have established products, cash flow, and profits, hence, one would expect these to offset the costs of investing in new innovations. This view is supported by the data. Nevertheless, even in the oldest SMEs, we still see the polarization of profit outcomes (at least as experienced in the 2002 to 2004 period). For example, for the SME EPO patentees in 2001, 34.5 per cent end up in the poor profitability group.

Table 3.6　SME Profitability (2002–2004) and IP Activity (2001)

Profitability Quartile	Non-IP Active	IP Active	UKTM Active	CTM Active	UK Patent Active	EPO Active
Poor (1st quartile)	24.7	33.5	28.7	44.0	30.3	48.2
Weak (2nd quartile)	25.3	17.8	18.4	14.1	18.7	14.8
Solid (3rd quartile)	25.2	21.4	22.6	18.3	23.6	12.2
High (4th quartile)	24.9	27.4	30.4	23.6	27.4	24.8

Note: As per Table 3.4.

Table 3.7   SMEs under 5 Years of Age: Profitability and IP Activity

Profitability Quartile	Non-IP Active	IP Active	UKTM Active	CTM Active	UK Patent Active	EPO Active
Poor (1st quartile)	35.2	58.7	50.0	72.8	54.8	69.2
Weak (2nd quartile)	23.8	12.6	13.0	7.8	23.8	12.8
Solid (3rd quartile)	17.5	12.0	15.9	8.7	11.9	5.1
High (4th quartile)	23.6	16.7	21.2	10.7	9.5	12.8

Note: As per Table 3.4.

Table 3.8   SMEs between 5 and 10 Years of Age: Profitability and IP Activity

Profitability Quartile	Non-IP Active	IP Active	UKTM Active	CTM Active	UK Patent Active	EPO Active
Poor (1st quartile)	27.3	41.7	32.5	51.5	45.4	65.3
Weak (2nd quartile)	22.8	11.4	11.8	9.6	9.3	9.5
Solid (3rd quartile)	21.9	12.9	16.6	9.6	9.3	5.3
High (4th quartile)	28.1	34.1	39.1	29.4	36.1	20.0

Note: As per Table 3.4.

Table 3.9.   SMEs Over 10 Years of Age: Profitability and IP Activity

Profitability Quartile	Non-IP Active	IP Active	UKTM Active	CTM Active	UK Patent Active	EPO Active
Poor (1st quartile)	21.1	23.5	21.7	27.6	22.2	34.5
Weak (2nd quartile)	26.4	21.6	22.2	19.3	20.8	18.1
Solid (3rd quartile)	28.5	27.3	26.5	27.2	29.5	17.5
High (4th quartile)	24.1	27.6	29.6	25.9	27.4	29.9

Note: As per Table 3.4, except that the UK patent-active distribution is not found to be statistically different from the non-IP-active firms by the chi^2 test.

Rogers, Greenhalgh and Helmers (2007) also use a linear regression model to check some of the results presented. A drawback of such regression models is that they cannot capture the 'polarizing' aspect of the data. Nevertheless, the regression results confirm some of the results from the tables. CTMs are associated with lower profitability only for younger SMEs, yet profitability is statistically unaffected for the whole SME sample and the older firm categories. UKTMs are associated with higher profitability for the entire SME sample, but they do not have any association with profitability for the subset of young firms.

INDUSTRY-LEVEL TRADEMARKING: SCHUMPETERIAN EFFECTS

So far, we have assessed the association of trademarking and firm performance from a wide range of different angles. In this section, we broaden the analysis and investigate the influence of other firms' innovation within specific sectors of firm performance. The underlying idea is based on the Schumpeterian paradigm, which regards the innovation process as one of 'creative destruction'. According to this notion, the innovation process is dynamic: firms constantly try to improve on existing innovations; once a firm successfully creates a new innovation, the new innovation supplants the existing ones. Hence, this process creates a winner, the successful innovator, but due to the obsolescence of the previously existing innovation, it also creates a loser. Nevertheless, this process results in a constant improvement in the productivity of the industry. All firms in the industry are spurred on by the dynamic competition and, in addition, there may be substantial spill-overs between competitors. Within such an industry, we should observe various effects. Rapid innovation by other firms within the product group or sector should reduce a firm's ability to profit from its own innovation(s), as obsolescence is likelier to occur. However, the Schumpeterian competition for new innovations between firms is expected to raise the productivity, and possibly the profitability, of all surviving firms in the industry. For example, if the industry is competing in world markets, both productivity and profitability might be expected to rise.[18] These issues suggest that we should also be interested in the trademark intensity of the industry as a whole and, specifically, its association with the short- and long-term performance of an individual firm within that industry.

Large Firms and Industry-level Trademarking

To recap, the large-firm database reported on around 1,600 firms over the period 1996 to 2000. In analysing this database, we used three dependent variables: (a) the market value of the firms, (b) the level of productivity, and (c) growth of productivity. Cases (a) and (c) capture more long-term aspects of performance. Hence, for those cases, we might expect to find evidence for Schumpeterian effects. In contrast, case (b), the level of productivity of a firm, can be thought of as capturing short-run differences in performance between firms. Given this, for (b) we might expect the static competition effect to dominate (i.e. higher trade marking by rivals in your industry has a negative impact on your performance).

In order to measure the innovation of a sector, an industry level variable measuring trademark intensity is constructed as follows. For each firm and year, the trademark activity (defined as the number of trademark publications) is summed for all its rivals in its four-digit standard industry classification (SIC). This sum is then divided by the total assets of the rivals (for larger firms we use total employment as the denominator). This yields a measure of industry trademark intensity (ITMI) which can be summarized as follows:

$$ITMI_{it} = \Sigma_j \, TM_{jt} \, / \, \Sigma_j \, Assets_{jt} \text{ for all } j \neq i \text{ firms within the four-digit SIC at time } t$$

This industry-based variable is added as a further control variable to the various multivariate regression analyses previously discussed. When the industry-based trademark variable is added to the regressions on the level of productivity, we find that all the coefficients are negative. This means that higher industry trademark intensity is associated with lower productivity—as per our expectation.[19]

In contrast to the short-run competitive effects on productivity, the impact of industry trademarking on productivity growth and on share-market value is almost uniformly non-negative. In the productivity growth rate regressions, the competitive pressures from high rates of trademarking in the industry are significantly positive for the full sample and for manufacturing productivity growth. This suggests that Schumpeterian competition among firms makes the industry experience faster growth. The magnitude of the coefficient is such that a single standard deviation in UKTMs and CTMs would accompany growth of around 2 per cent. However, these effects are smaller and much less significant in services. A parallel set of regression results for the share-market regressions produced the following results. For manufacturing firms, the coefficients on the industry-based trademark intensity variable are positive and significant. This indicates that more trademarking by your rivals correlates with your market value. This is consistent with the idea of dynamic (Schumpeterian) competition in the industry raising every firm's profitability. The results for service sector firms show positive, but not significant, coefficients on the industry trademark intensity variable. This indicates that services firms are not gaining any significant premia due to higher levels of industry trademark activity, something that is consistent with the lack of productivity growth impacts seen above.

SMEs and Industry Trademarking

The data on SME trademarking activity between 2000 and 2005 allow us to investigate similar issues for SMEs. The structure of the database allows us to calculate industry trademarking for both large firms and SMEs. Again, following the methods previously introduced, we analyse the presence of Schumpeterian effects for the SME sample by including industry-based trademark intensity variables in the regression specifications discussed earlier. The industry-based intensity variables are defined as the number of trademark publications in the industry divided by industry total assets (in millions; industry is defined at the three-digit SIC level). Since there may be differences between large-firm and SME effects, we distinguish between large-firm and SME industry-level intensity variables.

The first model analysed for SMEs concerned survival. A Probit model estimated the likelihood of failure between 2001 and 2004 using a range of explanatory variables. We now add two industry-based UKTM intensity variables to the model: one for industry-based intensity for large firms, the other industry-based intensity for SMEs. The results show that the impact of industry-based trademark activity on an SME differs between these two variables. If large firms in your industry are trademarking intensively, it tends to raise the chances of survival for SMEs in that industry. In contrast, if you are an SME in an industry where many other SMEs are trademarking, it tends to reduce your chance of survival. This is an entirely new finding, and we do not claim to fully understand the mechanisms at work. It could be that large-firm trademarking is a proxy for a highly innovative industry where there are opportunities for SMEs, something akin to Schumpeterian creative destruction; whereas high rates among rival SMEs indicates that the competition to fill such opportunities is intense.

We also investigate the growth of assets of SMEs. Again, we add the two industry-level trademark intensity variables as additional explanatory variables in this model. Using growth in assets between 2001 and 2004 as the performance measure, the results tend to confirm those from the survival regression. Higher trademark intensity by large firms in an industry tends to increase the growth rate of a SME in that industry. In contrast, higher industry-level trade marking by SMEs tends to lower the growth in assets of SMEs in the same industry. Once again, this is consistent with a Schumpeterian-type interpretation when large-firm trademark activity is indicative of opportunities and, in contrast, SME trademark activity is indicative of intense competition between SMEs. However, repeating the analysis for growth in turnover does not find similar results (in general, coefficients are insignificant).

The two new industry-level variables were also added to the profitability specification. The results from this analysis differed from those of the survival and growth analysis previously mentioned. Now, higher large-firm trademark intensity in an industry had no significant effect on

SME profitability in that industry. If high large-firm trademark intensity does provide a proxy for an innovative industry, this implies that SMEs in that industry do not benefit in terms of profits (at least within the subsequent three-year period). In contrast, higher industry-level SME trademark activity tends to increase the profitability of an SME in the industry. This result appears inconsistent with those already discussed: if there is intense competition for opportunities between SMEs, it should reduce, not increase, profitability.

What have we learnt from analysing industry-level trademark intensity variables and SME performance? The most important thing to stress is that there are no simple mechanisms at work, since the results do contain inconsistencies. However, we have found that it is also important to distinguish between industry-level activity by large firms, as opposed to industry-level activity by SMEs. In the case of survival and growth in assets, large-firm activity appeared to boost SME performance, whereas activity by rival SMEs tended to weaken performance.

CONCLUSIONS

This chapter has reviewed recent UK evidence of how trademarking influences firm performance. The existing empirical literature on the value of trademarks is miniscule compared to that of patents. Our results indicate that there is no justification for such an imbalance. When we analyse UK databases of large firms and SMEs, we consistently find significant associations between trademark activity and performance. In some cases, these are quantitatively larger than the associations between patenting and performance. One reason for this is that service sector firms have a much lower propensity to patent, but this strengthens the case for using trademark data, since advanced economies are dominated by the service sector.

A short summary of our results is as follows. For the UK's largest firms, trademarking is a common activity—around 48 per cent of manufacturing firms and 28 per cent of service firms take out one or more UKTMs in a given year. Comparing firms that do and do not trademark, we find substantial differences in share-market value and productivity (a premium of 20 per cent is not uncommon). We also find that higher trademarking by rivals in a firm's industry is associated with high growth and high share-market value, but with reduced productivity advantage over rivals. These findings are consistent with a Schumpeterian view of competition, suggesting that trademarks are proxies for innovation activity. In a Schumpeterian world, firms compete through innovation, something that erodes short-run productivity differences between firms but that boosts growth rates and long-run performance of industry (and hence raises share-market values).

For SMEs, we find a more complex role for trademark activity. Relatively few SMEs are trademarking. On average, only 1.32 per cent of SMEs take out a UKTM and 0.66 per cent a CTM. Nonetheless, taking out a UKTM (in 2001) is associated with a higher likelihood of survival (2002–2004), although this is not true for the youngest firms. Taking out a CTM, by contrast, is not generally associated with increased likelihood of survival. One interpretation of these results is that a trademark signals that the SME is innovative, and innovation activity is more risky, hence increasing the chance of exit. This type of interpretation also fits with the results on SME growth and profitability. The analysis shows that the cohort of SMEs that trademark (in 2001) is associated with a 'polarized' distribution in growth and profitability performance (2002–2004). This means that the group of SMEs that trademark tend to have more 'poor' and 'high' performance SMEs than would be expected. Again, this is consistent with innovative activity being risky, hence there being winners and losers from such activities.

The major result here is that trademark activity appears to be a useful proxy for innovative activities of both large and small firms. A common reaction to using trademarks as such a proxy is to say that some trademarks may simply reflect minor changes to the appearance or style of existing products, or just a management decision to trademark an existing product. No doubt, some trademarks do represent small changes, but our results show that being a trademark-active firm is associated with substantial differences in performance. It is clear that trademarking is a proxy for a bundle of innovative activities—such as product design, production, distribution, marketing, and advertising. Further analysis, and the availability of more data, may be able to separate out the value of different aspects, including isolating the pure 'intellectual property right' value of a trademark. However, it is important to remember that innovation is a complementary bundle of activities.

How do our results contribute to understanding innovation and economic growth? A major contribution is that we now have a metric for gauging innovation in the service sector, something that patent and R&D data were poor at capturing. Trademark data also allow an economy-wide assessment of trends in innovation. Trademark data also provide a way of investigating the Schumpeterian world of creative destruction—or competition through innovation across time. For larger UK firms, we find evidence of such creative destruction: highly innovative industries (using trademarking as a proxy) tend to have higher growth and future profits. Our initial results for SMEs indicate a more complex world of innovation and performance. An SME that trademarks appears more likely to find itself in either a 'high' or 'poor' performance group. This polarization may reflect the risk associated with innovation. For SMEs, Schumpeterian competition does appear to separate winners and losers, something that we expect to benefit economic growth in the economy.

NOTES

1. We shall use the term 'trademark' to cover both trade and service marks.
2. The legal framework for UKTMs and CTMs is largely the same, since the UK's Trade Mark Act [1994] was based on the European Trade Marks Directive, hence the choice between the two comes down to balancing the expected costs and benefits. If a UK firm never expects to sell in the EU, then a UKTM is cheaper and will offer all the protection needed. If there is any expectation of sales in the EU then, as long as the firm can afford the greater costs, it should use Community trademarks.
3. Some trademark applications are not registered due to invalid claims or oppositions. The UK Intellectual Property Office states that around 85 per cent of trademark applications are registered within eight months (http://www.ipo.gov.uk/ accessed 4 December 2007). For Community trademarks, out of the 57,373 applications in 2000 there were 11,495 oppositions. Assuming half of oppositions resulted in registrations, the approximate success rate is around 90 per cent. The delay in getting a Community trademark appears somewhat longer that a UK patent at around 15 months (based on 2004 data at http://oami.europa.eu/ _ accessed 4 December 2007).
4. Multiple classes per single application are allowed, although each additional category requires an additional fee of around £50 (http://www.ipo.gov.uk/tmapply.pdf _ accessed 4 December 2007).
5. US Patent and Trademark Office (2006; 2007): 'Performance and Accountability Report'.
6. German Patent and Trade Mark Office (1999; 2006): 'Annual Report'.
7. Japan Patent Office (2001; 2007): 'Annual Report'.
8. These figures come from the UK IP website (http://www.ipo.gov.uk/ _ accessed 4 December 2007).
9. Landes and Posner (1987) provide excellent overviews of the economics of trademarks.
10. Classic articles include Schmalensee (1978) and Shaked and Sutton (1982), but reviews are contained in modern textbooks (Tirole 1988; Cabral 2000).
11. The EU defines an SME as a firm with total assets greater than €2 million and less than or equal to €43 million. Alternatively, an SME may be defined in terms of employment or turnover. Firms with employment less than 250 employees or turnover greater than €2 million and less than €50 million also fall into the SME category. Our definition of SME uses a combination of these criteria and, in addition, makes adjustments for the ownership structure of the firms contained in the data base (for more information, see Rogers, Helmers and Greenhalgh 2007).
12. In both cases, the construction of the database involves matching trademark applicant names to firm names. For firms that have subsidiaries, we match trademarks to both parent and subsidiary names, and hence provide an accurate measure of their (consolidated) trademark activity. Further details of the matching process are contained in Greenhalgh and Rogers (2006; 2007) and Rogers, Helmers and Greenhalgh (2007).
13. The 'hotels/catering' sector has a high mean value due to the presence of a firm called Chorion PLC. Information on this company in 2005 shows it to be a company that manages and owns brands (http://www.chorion.co.uk/ _ accessed 4 December 2007). The influence of this firm on the analysis in this chapter has been checked and, despite its high values, it does not have a notable effect on results.

14. We use a multivariate regression analysis with share-market value as the dependent variable. Greenhalgh and Rogers (2007) contains full details of the analysis summarized in this section.
15. If we had data on all these activities it might be possible to isolate each of these effects. However, it is highly likely that they act together to raise share-market value, hence trying to attribute separate effects to each is missing the point.
16. Full details of the analysis can be found in Rogers, Greenhalgh and Helmers (2007).
17. As noted, only 28 percent of SMEs in the sample report turnover data. These will tend to be the larger SMEs, since larger firms have to report more financial data. Hence, any table showing growth rate of turnover is based on a subsample of larger SMEs in both 2001 and 2004.
18. McGahan and Silverman (2006) contrast 'market stealing' where a rival's patent gives it an advantaged position to the detriment of the focal firm, with 'spill-over' effects, where a breakthrough by a rival firm triggers greater technological opportunity and provides information on which the focal firm can build. In their study of US firms using patent data, positive spill-over effects dominate negative market-stealing effects in the intellectual property rights (IPR) competition between rivals in the same industry. Bloom, Schankerman and van Reenen (2007) provide similar empirical evidence.
19. To give an order of magnitude to these coefficients: the results predict that, in services, the effect of an increase of one standard deviation in trademarks by other firms in the four-digit industry would be to reduce an incumbent's productivity by 2 per cent.

BIBLIOGRAPHY

Bloom, N., M. Schankerman and J. Van Reenen (2007) 'Identifying technology spillovers and product market rivalry', NBER Working Paper 13060.

Cabral, L. (2000) *Introduction to Industrial Organization*, Cambridge, MA: MIT Press.

Feeny, S., M. Harris and M. Rogers (2005) 'A dynamic panel analysis of the profitability of Australian tax entities', *Empirical Economics*, 30(1): 209–234.

Greenhalgh, C. and M. Rogers (2006) 'The value of innovation: The interaction of competition, R&D and IP', *Research Policy*, 35(4): 562–580.

――― (2007) 'Trade marks and performance in UK firms: Evidence of Schumpeterian competition through innovation', Department of Economics, University of Oxford. Available online: <http://www.economics.ox.ac.uk/Research/wp/pdf/paper300.pdf>.

Griliches, Z. and J. Mairesse (1995) 'Production functions: The search for identification', NBER Working Paper 5067.

Gowers, A. (2006) 'The Gowers review of intellectual property'. Report for the UK Treasury. Available online: <http://www.hm-treasury.gov.uk/independent_reviews/>.

Hall, B. (2000) 'Innovation and market value' in R. Barrell, G. Mason and M. O'Mahoney (eds.) *Productivity, Innovation and Economic Performance*, Cambridge, UK: Cambridge University Press: 177–198.

Hart, P. and N. Oulton (1996) 'Growth and size of firms', *Economic Journal*, 106: 1242–1252.

――― (1999) 'Gibrat, Galton and job generation', *International Journal of the Economics of Business*, 6(2): 149–164.

Helmers C. and M. Rogers (2008) 'Innovation and the survival of firms across UK regions', mimeo, Department of Economics, University of Oxford.

Landes, W. M. and R. A. Posner (1987) 'Trademark law: An economic perspective', *Journal of Law and Economics*, 30(2): 265–309.

Macpherson, A. and R. Holt (2007) 'Knowledge, learning and small firm growth: A systematic review of the evidence', *Research Policy*, 36(2): 172–192.

McGahan, A. and B. Silverman (2006) 'Profiting from technological innovation by others: The effect of competitor patenting on firm value', *Research Policy*, 35: 1222–1242.

Mendonça, S., T. Pereira and M. Godinho (2004) 'Trademarks as an indicator of innovation and industrial change', *Research Policy*, 33: 1385–1404.

Penrose, E. (1959) *The Theory of the Growth of the Firm*, Oxford: Basil Blackwell.

Perry, M. K. and R. H. Groff (1986) 'Trademark licensing in a monopolistically competitive industry', *Rand Journal of Economics*, 17(2): 189–200.

Rogers, M., C. Greenhalgh and C. Helmers (2007) 'An analysis of the association between the use of intellectual property by UK SMEs and subsequent performance', Report for UK Intellectual Property Office, October 2007.

Rogers, M., C. Helmers and C. Greenhalgh (2007) 'An analysis of the characteristics of small and medium enterprises that use intellectual property', Report for UK Intellectual Property Office, October 2007.

Schmalensee, R. (1978) 'Entry deterrence in the ready-to-eat breakfast cereal industry', *Bell Journal of Economics*, 9: 305–327.

Sexton, D. and H. Lanstrom (1999) *Blackwell Handbook of Entrepreneurship*, Oxford: Blackwell.

Shaked, A. and J. Sutton (1982) 'Relaxing price competition through product differentiation', *Review of Economic Studies*, 49: 3–13.

Tirole, J. (1988) *The Theory of Industrial Organization*, Cambridge, MA: MIT Press.

Varian, H., J. Farrell and C. Shapiro (2004) *The Economics of Information Technology*, Cambridge, UK: Cambridge University Press.

4 Cobranding Product and Nation
Danish Modern Furniture and Denmark in the United States, 1940–1970

Per H. Hansen

'Denmark for Design' read the headline in the *New York Herald Tribune* on 27 May 1959 (Berry 1959). The 1961 edition of Temple Fielding's *Selective Shopping Guide to Europe* claimed that many Americans considered Danish shopping the finest on the continent: 'Most of the merchandise is outstandingly tasteful and handsomely designed, in the special national way'. The *Guide* concluded, 'If it's Danish, it's almost certain to wear well and to give pleasure' (Fielding 1961: 22, 29). Anecdotal evidence of this sort indicates that, by the 1960s, Denmark had established a strong national image in the United States with respect to design. In fact, the two concepts 'Denmark' and 'design' had merged into one strong metaphor: Denmark for Design. This is, thus, an example of the anthropologist McCracken's (1988) transfer model where meaning is transferred from the culturally constituted world to the product. The result, according to McCracken, is that the consumers identify 'sameness' between product and world. When such a transfer is successful, the 'good now "stands for" cultural meaning of which it was previously innocent' (McCracken 1988: 79).

In this case, Denmark had come to stand for a type of design, as certain meanings assigned to Denmark had been transferred to the concept/brand of Danish Design or Danish Modern. More than McCracken's one-way transfer, however, a reciprocal relationship was established between goods and the culturally constituted world so that the image of the Danish nation, in the United States, was also partly shaped by consumers' perception of Danish Design (see also Anholt 2007: 9). This association between Denmark and Danish Modern furniture can be considered a special sort of 'cobranding' of a nation and certain products from that nation.

In this chapter, I offer a first attempt at an analysis and discussion of how country image and product brand are constructed and how they interact as a cobrand. In contrast to most studies of brands, whether product or place brands, my point of departure is that branding is not about identifying a product's or place's essence or DNA, but about constructing powerful narratives that create certain meanings, which address consumers' self-fashioning and lifestyle needs in their specific cultural contexts. The point is, then, that meaning is not immanent in a product, a corporation, or a nation. Meaning is constructed by narratives that create order and coherence in an otherwise chaotic and fragmented world. I want to go beyond the idea that 'a brand signals to consumers that the product satisfies basic requirements for consistency and quality . . . and embodies a combination of characteristics that differentiate it from other brands' (Lopes and Casson 2008: 655) and try to understand how these signals and characteristics are constructed, how they work, and how consumers use them.

I use the case of Denmark's country image and Danish Modern furniture (Danish Design or Danish Modern), and their interaction and reception in the United States in the 1950s and '60s. I argue that a nation brand and a specific image of Denmark were constructed in the United States in this period by a number of different authors. For a limited time period, the images of the nation and of Danish Design came to enjoy a special harmony and metaphoric identification, as already suggested, and I further argue that this reciprocal relationship was important for Danish Design as a brand, influencing US consumers' taste and, hence, purchasing decisions when furnishing their homes.[1]

I apply a material culture framework for analysing and understanding the relationship between nation brand, nation image, and product brand. I draw, in particular, on McCracken's (1988; 1989; 2005; 2006) and marketing professor Douglas Holt's (2004) contributions to material culture and cultural branding respectively.

In the next section, I briefly discuss traditional branding approaches and their shortcomings with regard to understanding how brands work. I then discuss the concepts of a 'nation brand', a 'nation image', and a 'product brand', and their relationship with the cultural context of the consumer. I next present the theoretical framework of the chapter, which is followed by the empirical part of the chapter, with a focus first on the development of Danish Modern as a brand and, second, on Denmark's image in the United States. Finally, I offer a few remarks to suggest that more work is needed both on the theory and on the practice of branding.

BRANDING THEORY AND THE CONSUMER

The American Marketing Association defines a brand as a 'name, term, sign, symbol or design, or a combination of them intended to identify the goods or services of one seller or group of sellers and to differentiate them from those of competition' (Kotler and Gertner 2002: 249). Kotler and Gertner expand this definition to argue that 'brands differentiate products and represent a promise of value. Brands incite beliefs, evoke emotions and prompt behaviors' (Kotler and Gertner 2002: 249) This expansion, however, does not suffice to describe what a powerful brand does or how consumers use brands.[2]

Especially when it comes to identity products—products that reflect certain meanings from the culturally constituted world, and communicate a narrative or myth that addresses specific needs and dreams of the consumer (McCracken 1988; 2005; Holt 2004)—brands are more than logos, design, attributes, and trademarks. Therefore, branding theory must look to material culture studies in order to understand how brands actually work. This can help us distinguish between the brand as constructed by a company or a nation on the one hand, and the brand image used by consumers to construct their lifestyle and identity on the other. Consumers' identity projects and their cultural context must be included in the analysis of brands in order to understand why consumers use brands and how they work. Consumers use material objects and the stories and cultural meanings that come with them as brands to construct themselves as individuals according to a number of cultural categories and principles (McCracken 1988), but this process of construction is absent in the dominant focus of branding theory on economics and psychology, which therefore misses an important part of why brands work and how they add value.

Furthermore, branding seems to have become ever more important not only to companies, but also to nations, as well as to regions and cities. Globalization, increasing productive forces, technological innovations, intense international competition, and growing convergence of markets have obliged nations and companies to seek distinction and authenticity by means of branding. With regard to nations, this is a matter of place branding, which is pursued in order to compete for exports, human capital, foreign direct investments (FDI), and tourism. In many respects, the recent focus on the experience economy (Pine and Gilmore 1998) further increases the need for the construction of strong national brands that differentiate one nation and its products from those of other countries. Thus, in recent theories of corporate branding, the nation is almost considered as a corporation (Olins 1999; Anholt 2002; Csaba 2005; Schultz 2005).

Although Olins argues that there are similarities between nation and corporate branding, there are also important differences between nations and corporations, not least with respect to the degree to which the two entities can control their brand at home and abroad. Even though it is hard enough for companies to control their brand, and even more so their image, most literature on corporate branding assumes that this is possible (see, for instance Aaker and Joachimsthaler 2000; Olins 2003; Schultz 2005).[3] For a country to control its image abroad is next to impossible. A nation, after all, is a much more complex entity than a corporation, and comprises many more diverse interests, each of which seeks to promote its own narrative (Papadopoulos and Heslop 2002; Anholt 2007, especially pp. 7–8, 75ff). Anholt argues that 'although nations and regions and cities do *have* brand images, they can't usually *be* branded' (Anholt 2007: 5). Consequently, there are many more narratives and counternarratives in circulation about a country at any given time (Czarniawska 2004; Hansen 2007). Thus, although there is more than enough evidence to suggest that while corporate brands such as Starbucks and Nike also encounter problems with respect to controlling their brands and images, the problem is greater for nations.[4]

Although state-of-the-art knowledge of corporate branding argues that the corporation must communicate one consistent brand message at all levels (Schultz 2005), a nation brand may need to communicate different images, depending on which groups it wants to represent and which to target. The nation brand is important for a country's ability to attract foreign capital, human resources, and tourists, and to increase its exports of goods and services, but these different targets further complicate the task of designing one unified strategy for the construction of a nation brand. The attraction of FDI, labour and tourists, and increasing exports can hardly be done on the basis of one unified nation branding strategy (Anholt 2002: 230; 2007: 90). Each area must be branded in a distinct way and create distinct images of the country, without invoking too obvious or explicit conflicts between the different areas (Kotler and Gertner 2002: 254; Papadopoulos and Heslop 2002: 308). The degree to which this process can actually be managed is not obvious, however. As a matter of fact, it is doubtful whether a nation brand—and even less so a nation image—can be managed in any precise way. The dream of marketing research and practitioners that the process of marketing a country must involve 'government, citizens and businesses, all with a shared vision' (Kotler and Gertner 2002: 254) is hardly realistic.

The challenge is to construct brand narratives of a country that address specific target groups (tourists, consumers, investors, employees, and so forth) in selected areas of special competitive advantage of the given country. Whenever there is a conflict between the relevant brand narratives, a choice will probably have to be made in order not to confuse or dilute the brand.[5] For instance, when it comes to exports, the national brand is supposed to influence foreign consumers' preferences and, therefore, demand for all or specific goods or services from this country. This means that if, for instance, Denmark has a positive reputation in other countries, consumers and businesses of these countries are supposed to have a preference for Danish goods. In other words, the reliance by a company or an industry on a nation brand can be considered a variety of cobranding or celebrity endorsement, with the country in question being the celebrity (Csaba 2005).

Conversely, if there are negative connotations connected with the country, this may have an adverse effect on consumer preferences. The crisis in 2006, and again in 2008, over the Danish cartoonists' depiction of the Prophet Muhammad is a case in point. Practically overnight, the Danish dairy company Arla saw its business in Muslim countries in the Middle East reduced almost to nothing. This crisis vividly illustrates how brand management depends not only on the product or corporate brand, but also on the nation image of the brand's home country and on the cultural context of foreign consumers. These contexts are not controllable by the company or the home country: Both company and nation have to adapt their brand narratives to the cultural context of the consumers, investors or tourists they want to attract.[6]

To complicate the situation even further, a nation brand cannot be taken to add value—i.e. a price premium—to all goods and services from the country. According to Jaffe and Nebenzahl (2006: 108), country image effect is product specific. In other words, a positive country image influences consumers' purchase of particular products, not all products in general from the relevant country. Finally, country image and the value it adds to specific products must also be assumed to be specific to certain consumers and groups of consumers according to their self-fashioning and lifestyle needs and perceived or wished for identity. Since most lifestyle and identity brands, such as Danish Modern, appeal to the consumer groups who look for only certain of the meanings carried by this particular brand, other consumer groups may not share the same image of the country in question.

The implication of this discussion is that, even though a great deal of research has been done on nation branding and nation image, it is still not clear how they are used by consumers, how they relate, and how they should be defined in order to deal with these questions. What is clear is that corporate branding theory alone cannot provide a satisfactory model for nation branding. In the following section, I try to outline a basic understanding of nation brand and nation image through an analysis of the successful cobranding of Denmark and Danish Design in the United States during the 1950s and '60s.

Nation Brand, Nation Image and Product Brand

Nations, Olins (2002) has argued, have branded themselves for more than two centuries, with the purpose of constructing a shared national identity among the nation's citizens. I expand on this line of thinking by using research on the construction of nations. The educational system, along with print-language media such as newspapers, novels, and textbooks, were all instrumental in nation building exercises, and the result was the construction of the nation as an imagined community (Anderson 1991). This was backed by the invention of traditions that traced the nation's history by projecting a unified identity backwards in time (Hobsbawm and Ranger 1983). A nation, in short, is an imagined community where the inhabitants feel a sense of belonging together without actually knowing each other, and this sense is reinforced by its traditions and the general use of symbols (*lieux de memoire*) and historical narratives. The citizens of a nation develop certain cultural categories and principles or values that are, at least to a certain degree, shared. Language, the vernacular, and shared historical narratives are instrumental in this national building process. Thus, Olins (2002) argues: 'as nations emerge they create self-sustaining myths to build coherent identities' (245). For Olins, 'many brands help to create a sense of identity, of belonging, just like the nation' (248).

According to this argument, nations and nation branding involve communicating the identity of the nation and its citizens internally. However, this definition misses the external communication of the nation brand, and will have to be expanded in order to fit the present purpose. Thus, in this chapter, nation (or place) branding is a concerted and (mostly) conscious effort by authorities and private and public organizations to assign certain general meanings that are not product specific to a place such as a city, a region, or a country. This effort is directed mostly to international audiences with the purpose of attracting FDI, human resources, and tourism and of increasing exports. This definition suggests that a nation brand is a construction communicated both within and outside the nation in order to represent a certain image of the nation. Thus, nations and nation brands do not have an essence, but rather aim to construct narratives that communicate the meanings that the nation (or place) wishes to represent.

The result, if achieved, will be a place brand that communicates certain basic characteristics and important cultural categories and principles of the place in question. In order to be reliable and credible, the place brand cannot contradict the perceived and experienced identity and image by various domestic and foreign groups. The general, nonproduct-specific part of the brand delineates the nation brand from well-known product-specific place brands such as Bordeaux and wine, Porto and Port Wine, which are all product- or product-line-specific. Although these are also examples of cobranding, the important difference lies in the more limited meanings assigned to these places and their products.[7]

How the brand is perceived at the receiving end of the communication is another, but no less important, story, for this is not entirely controllable by the 'owners' of the nation brand. In the process of place branding, the nation brand is turned into a nation image, which will also be influenced by the cultural context of the recipients, and the way they use the brand to create their own meanings, lifestyle, and self. Moreover, although the 'owners' of the brand narrative strive to control the communication and perception of the nation brand, they cannot do this to any full extent. Controlling one's own narrative is always problematic, because alternative, and sometimes even contradictory, narratives will circulate.

For the purpose of this chapter, then, a nation image consists of the meanings assigned to a country by consumers embedded in a specific cultural context. The nation image held by consumers will be influenced by, but will not necessarily reflect, the nation brand as intended by the authors of that brand narrative and does not, therefore, necessarily correspond to basic characteristics of the nation. However, for the nation image to have any authority, it must reflect the dominant narratives of the country in question and, at the same time, interact with the cultural context of the consumers in the receiving country. This means that for narratives to be effective among these consumers, it must address their cultural needs. This argument challenges standard assumptions, which hold that country images influence the attitude of consumers towards a country and its products (see Kotler and Gertner 2002; Papadopoulos and Heslop 2002; Jaffe and Nebenzahl 2006). Such arguments take no account of the cultural contexts in which the country image is perceived. In fact, nation branding efforts coalesce with other ideas and narratives in circulation about a given country to form consumers' image of that country. This image will vary with these consumers' specific cultural context, and the way and purposes for which they use the image and the narratives that lie behind.

Where do narratives about other nations come from? Nations have always interacted through war, trade, tourism, diplomacy, and so on. Moreover, for many countries, citizens and organizations have established a more or less well-informed image of other nations based on the available information, some of which have been controlled by the nation and related organizations, while some have other sources such as travel, newspapers, radio and television programs, and hearsay. Moreover, national efforts at what could at least be likened to nation branding have been widespread since the mid-nineteenth century, at the latest, as evidenced for instance by the world exhibitions such as the ones in Paris in 1937 and New York in 1939.[8] In many cases, national (or place) narratives have been used by producers of a number of product brands in order to influence the taste and preferences of the consumer. As a special sort of cobranding, country image and product brand provide a central link to consumers, who consume the product not only because of its functional attributes but also to construct lifestyle and self. An important part of this construction is the use consumers make of the cultural meanings assigned to the product. If the meanings of the product and the meanings of the country in question relate in a special way that addresses certain consumer groups' cultural projects, then a successful cobranding process of metaphorical identification is going on. Coca-Cola is just one example of how the American Dream and the soft drink went into such a metaphorical identification. Luxury cars such as Jaguar and Rolls Royce, on the other hand, draw on certain meanings attached to Britain.[9]

In sum, a complicated circulation of meanings is at play when nation image and corporate or product brand, in combination, are planned to appeal to specific consumer groups embedded in specific cultural contexts. Depending on the country and the product, companies can use the nation brand and the image of their home country to strengthen their corporate and product brand, and the consumers' perception of the brand will feed back and influence their perception of the country, and thus the country image. A further complicating factor is that it is not a straightforward job to name the country of origin for a product. As Rivoli demonstrates in *The Travels of a T-Shirt in the Global Economy*, many products travel between countries before being sent on the market (Rivoli 2005). More concretely, in the case of Danish Modern furniture, although it was designed and produced in

Denmark until the 1970s, today this is no longer necessarily true, because of plagiarism and outsourcing, which may blur any country image effect. Thus, a product may be designed in one country, manufactured in one or several other countries, assembled in yet another country, and the country of origin may not be included in any of them. The country of origin is the country that consumers associate with the product—as in Danish Design or the Swedish furniture giant, IKEA. Today, at least, country of origin does not necessarily indicate where the product was designed, produced, or assembled. It is exactly for this reason that it is highly important for companies to consider how a given country image relates to their products.

These findings and observations raise a number of more specific questions, such as how meanings are assigned to a nation brand and transferred to specific products, and how these meanings influence the product and/or the corporate brand. We might also ask how and why these meanings change over time, and what role the consumers' cultural contexts (nationality, demographics, psychographics, lifestyle or identity) play in influencing their perception of the product brand and its country image. Related to these questions, and most important, is the problem of how consumers use brands and country images.

In the next section, I discuss these questions by applying theories on meaning transfer and cultural branding developed by McCracken and Holt respectively to the case of Danish Design in the United States from *c.*1948 to *c.*1980.

Meaning Transfer and Cultural Branding

According to Jaffe and Nebenzahl (2006) country image is related to the performance and quality of a given product—i.e. if a country has a good reputation for producing quality electronics or cars, the country image will be positive and vice versa. This is too narrow an understanding of how country image and nation brand are constituted, and what they mean and do. The most important elements in a product, and especially in an identity product, are not its physical properties but the meanings the product carries. Any country will carry multiple meanings that do not stem from product quality and reputation, but that are culturally constructed and reconstructed over time. The important question, then, is how countries and products come to carry certain meanings and how and for what purposes consumers use them. According to McCracken (1988) meanings are unstable and flowing in the social world. A number of interests (designers, producers, advertisers, consumers) aim to influence and direct these meanings that are 'drawn from a culturally constituted world and transferred to the consumer good . . . [and] then drawn from the object and transferred to the indivdual consumer' (McCracken 1988: 71–2).

In McCracken's model, meaning resides in the culturally constituted world as the cultural categories that cultures construct to make sense of their world, and as the cultural principles according to which meaning is assigned to these categories. Among typical cultural categories are time, space, class, status, age, race, ethnicity, and gender, and the principles are the basic values that determine what these categories signal in a given culture or subculture. Both meanings as cultural categories and as cultural principles are transferred from the culturally constituted world to goods by communities or groups, such as the advertising industry and the fashion system—or what Holt terms the culture industry (Holt 2004).

In the case of the advertising industry, the meaning transfer process is carried out by the advertising agency and its clients. The fashion system has several sources of meaning, agents of transfer, and media of communication. In the case of Danish Design, the fashion system consisted of a network of producers, designers, organizations, and critics who promoted Danish Modern (Hansen 2006b). Although the actions of a fashion system are harder to coordinate, the effect of the meaning transfer process carried out by a fashion system is probably stronger than if carried out by a single company and its advertising agency. In any case, meanings are transferred from the culturally constituted world to the good in question, and, according to McCracken, the process can be managed.

This process happens, for instance, in advertisements, and when it has taken place, the next step is for the consumer to transfer these meanings from the product to him- or herself. This last transfer happens by means of possession rituals, in which the consumer takes the product in his or her possession, for instance by talking about it, using it, showing it to friends, and so forth. The meanings thus transferred express cultural categories and principles and the consumer uses them in his or her individual cultural project to express him- or herself with regard to gender, class, social status, and lifestyle.

McCracken (2005) has applied the cultural meaning transfer model to celebrity endorsement, and this may be particularly interesting when discussing nation image and products. In celebrity endorsement of products, cultural meanings residing in the celebrity are transferred to the product, and the consumer then uses rituals to transfer these meanings to him- or herself. The interesting question is whether the celebrity might be a country? If the answer is affirmative, the cultural categories will be different and at another level, because categories invoked by celebrities are related to the level of the individual, and categories invoked by a country are related to other cultural categories such as governments, politics, space, geography, nature, and culture, to name a few.

Another problem that is not well covered by McCracken's discussion is how, more precisely, nations, companies, and consumers produce, communicate, use, and circulate these meanings. The cultural meaning transfer model has a strong explanatory power when it comes to understanding the production and use of meaning. It does need, however, to be extended with a theory about how these meanings are communicated more widely and about the importance of the cultural context in which these meanings are interpreted. The position taken in this chapter is that narratives—or myths as they are called by Olins (1999; 2002) and Holt (2004)—play a crucial role in the dissemination of cultural meanings that consumers use to construct lifestyle and self.

Holt's (2004) theory of cultural branding is built on the assumption that context matters a great deal for consumers' interpretation and use of brands. Moreover, although the contextualization introduces a dynamic element of time into the framework, strong narratives or myths are important as well. According to Holt, successful brands communicate narratives that effectively address a consumer's hopes and anxieties that are provoked by changes in the historical context or, as Holt (2004) calls it, the national ideology. By constructing narratives that bridge the conflict between consumers' identity projects and the national ideology these brands support, the consumers' endeavour to make sense of their own lives and to construct their own identities and lifestyles in a meaningful way (Holt 2004).

The important part is the role of narratives. Narratives are (hi)stories that explain a phenomenon and its development by assigning meaning, order and direction to that phenomenon. Efficient brands are built on narratives that address consumers' need for construction of identity, lifestyle, and self. Although narratives in their substance contain a beginning, a middle, and an end; a plot; a hero; and villains, over time they need not be circulated in their full form, but can be condensed in the shape of certain key concepts that frame (Lakoff 2004) the consumers' understanding of the brand. Thus, Danish Modern could be viewed as a frame that activated certain key concepts that referred to the narrative from which they are derived. Danish Modern, as a brand, referred to the idea of hand-crafted wooden furniture, simplicity, and democracy. Furthermore the concept of Denmark activated frames that referred to a number of key concepts, several of which fitted well with the narrative of Danish Modern (discussed later in the chapter). The result was cobranding of Denmark and Danish Design, but which consumers actually preferred Danish Modern depended entirely on the cultural and social context that influenced their preferences.

Narratives may, and will, conflict, and this is probably one of the main reasons why identities, brands, and images will always contain a certain degree of differentiation or even fragmentation, and why no brand will ever appeal to all consumers. Consumers' social and cultural contexts differ, and the difference influences their taste, their self-fashioning needs, and their preferences. Countries, companies, and consumers cannot control their own narratives, because other authors tell stories, too. For a period, however, certain groups may be able to come up with strong and convincing narratives that capture the imagination of specific groups of consumers and help them make sense and direction of their world. This is what happened during the Golden Age of Danish Design (1940–1970), and in this process Danish Modern drew heavily on a country image of Denmark that was constructed in the same period.

DANISH MODERN AS A BRAND

Elsewhere, I have argued that the concepts Danish Design and Danish Modern became firmly established as a brand in the United States from the late 1940s (Hansen 2006a; Hansen 2006b) and that this brand experienced a decline from the mid-1960s when the context changed. In the 1970s, Danish Modern increasingly lost market share, and in 1980 the *New York Times* reporter, Ada Louise Huxtable, answered her own rhetorical question, 'Whatever happened to Danish Modern?' with a firm, '[It] went out of style' (Huxtable 1980: C6).

Modern furniture was introduced in Denmark around 1930 when young architects with a modernist orientation joined forces with a group of cabinet-makers and started exhibiting modern furniture at the Copenhagen Cabinet-Makers' Guild Exhibitions. The cooperation was a marriage of convenience in the sense that industrial furniture producers did not foresee any demand for modern furniture, yet the cabinet-makers were under increasing pressure from industrial and imported furniture competition.

As early as the 1930s, architects and cabinet-makers had started to circulate a narrative about the unique qualities of Danish Modern furniture and how it all began. The story emphasized the combination of modernist functional furniture, based on scientific methods with high-quality, traditional handcrafted furniture made out of wood. The story also promoted a number of other key concepts related to Danish Modern furniture, which was portrayed as honest, democratic, simple, and opposed to all sorts of fashion, distinction, and representation. Here was McCracken's meaning-transfer model in action, and over time it established a firm and shared understanding of the meanings of Danish Modern. For that very reason, it appealed to some consumers who associated Danish Modern with good taste, yet others distanced themselves from this style. For instance, in interviews with a number of working-class Americans, McCracken (1989) found that many intensely disliked 'Scandinavian' style.

The breakthrough for Danish Modern furniture in Denmark happened in the late 1940s when an increasing number of middle-class consumers began showing an interest and gradually prompted producers and furniture dealers to revise their early opposition to the new style. The success of Danish furniture did not come easily, however, and required a massive marketing effort before certain consumer groups accepted it. This marketing effort went on at several levels such as exhibitions, books, newspapers and magazines, and film and radio interviews. Moreover, it was executed and supported by a fashion system and network, and orchestrated by some critically important organizations with close relations to the architects and the cabinet-makers (Hansen 2006a; 2006b).

The increasing success of the furniture and the architects, such as Hans Wegner and Finn Juhl, who came to be considered as celebrities in their own right, was followed by changes in the relative distribution of power in the supply chain. The cabinet-makers who cooperated with well-known architects started branding the furniture with text such as 'Cabinet-maker Niels Vodder, Copenhagen, Denmark. Design: Finn Juhl'. In branding the furniture like this, they activated frames in the consumers' minds referring to the broader narrative promoted by the network, and at the same time they laid the foundation for a future conflict between industrial producers of modern furniture and furniture dealers. Until the late 1940s, most furniture dealers purchased the furniture from producers and branded it with their own name. However, producers increasingly became aware of the value of a brand, and around 1950, much to the frustration of the dealers, the power balance tipped in favour of the producers who started branding the furniture with their own names, as well as with the name of the designer. This was an example of vertical competition in the supply chain (Duguid, this volume), and the result was increased brand awareness among Danish consumers (Hansen 2006a: 336–44).

Danish Design had been introduced to the US market before the Second World War. At that time, it was mostly industrial arts and crafts such as silver, textiles, and pottery, however. At the World Exhibition in New York in 1939, the Danish pavilion also exhibited furniture, but among the Scandinavian countries, US consumers were most aware of Swedish Modern. At the 1939 World Exhibition, the story was circulated of Danish furniture as scientific in design, high in quality and handcrafted, but it was only after the war that this early circulation of the narrative of Danish Design reached a popular audience.

In 1960, the Danish Society of Arts and Crafts and Industrial Design organized *The Arts of Denmark*, an exhibition in the United States with substantial support from the Danish State. In the book-length catalogue, it was stated that:

> The basic work for the design of light, modern types of furniture that fit naturally into a modern, democratic milieu was carried out in the thirties by architects in cooperation with cabinet-makers. A great influence on the development in this period is due to the architect Kaare Klint. (Hiorth 1960: 119–20)

This short text sums up the basic elements of the story of Danish Modern. Since the late 1940s, these various elements coalesced in the narrative that laid the foundation of the Danish Modern as a brand in the United States. Although the idea of Danish Modern as a brand may not have been intentional initially, there is no doubt that the Danish network that authored the story set its eyes on the United States as a potential export market.

In March 1945, the Association of Danish Crafts initiated a discussion of how to enter foreign markets, and especially the US market, which was perceived to offer huge rewards if it could be entered successfully. In the following years, several other organizations, the Danish state, and influential individuals participated in a concerted, networked effort, which succeeded during the 1950s in positioning Danish Modern as an important brand for imported modern furniture. The results did not fail to materialize, and Danish furniture exports to the United States took off in the early 1950s, assisted by the Danish devaluation of 1949.

The success of Danish Modern among certain consumer groups in the United States was based on the narrative behind the brand. The story fitted well with US consumers with a high level of education and a progressive lifestyle. The narrative enabled consumers to bridge one of the main conflicts in the United States, namely how to be an individual in a mass-production and mass-consumption, conformist society, where Fordism was the direct contrast to the content of the Danish Modern brand.

In October 1952, *House Beautiful* proclaimed that 'quietly and privately, people in every class all over the country are hammering out a philosophy of individualism', and it went on asking the central question of 'How to be an individual in a society dependent on mass production?' (Barry 1952: 176). One of *House Beautiful*'s own answers was to decorate with Danish furniture, and in the same year *Retailing Daily* reported on Georg Jensen Inc. in New York City, one of the first stores to sell Danish Modern furniture, commenting that 'individuality is what they sell' (Katzen 1952: 44).

Another well-informed observer of the modern furniture market in the United States noted that Danish Modern was well positioned to alleviate the 'atmosphere of insecurity in which we live—economic, intellectual, physical, emotional—which has encouraged . . . escapism'. The furniture could do this because it

> reflects the maturity of the social climate surrounding its birth and development. It is predicated on the assumption that men and women today are grown up or ought to be grown up enough to face the facts, even the hard ones, of their world. It attests to the belief that this does not preclude finding dignity, beauty and graciousness in our own time. (van Houten 1954)

Van Houten, continued that there was a

> growing number of young men and women who feel drawn to the work of particular designers. They ask for them by name, taking a purely aesthetic pleasure in a silhouette, a construction detail, a recognizable form. These are the middle-class young, the kids who recognize a Gauguin or Matisse when they see one but who can never hope to own an original. They can, however, own . . . chairs and tables originating in the workshops of craftsmen artists. (van Houten 1954)

Besides the wish for individuality, van Houten (1954) touches upon another important aspect of brands and their function in constructing consumers' lifestyle and identity. Brands need to demonstrate distinction and individuality, but also to belong to one or more socio-cultural group. As indicated by van Houten, the young consumers who purchased modern furniture designed by well-known architects were liberal, progressive, well educated, and living in the urban areas on the West coast, the East coast, and around Chicago (Hansen 2006a; 2006b).

Evidence from interviews with a few consumers of Danish Modern confirms this picture. A family in which the husband was an army officer and a professional purchased Danish Modern in 1959. The wife says that 'We were very cool. Two or three other families purchased Danish furniture as well. We were all very cool'. A male customer adds that 'about 46 years ago my new bride and I purchased furniture for our first apartment. Danish Modern was the "in" thing for my fellow Landscape Architects and it was what we bought'. Some US officers stationed in Europe were also interested in Danish Modern furniture. A doctor, stationed in London, reports that 'Danish Modern was being talked about by many of the officers and occasionally an Air Force plane would fly to Denmark to pick up a load of furniture for the PX and individual officers' (Hansen 2006a: 433–6).

Danish Modern's attractiveness to these consumers was based on a narrative that helped to bridge an identity conflict, as characterized by Holt (2004), between consumers' wish for individuality and distinction in a society based on large-scale industrial production. The narrative of unique, hand-crafted furniture appealed to consumers with a need to distance themselves from the Fordism and conformity of contemporary American consumer society. This conclusion corresponds well with the hypothesis that successful brands are based on myths that address the hopes and anxieties of consumers (Holt 2004), and it also underlines the insight of material culture studies that objects such as furniture carry meanings that are important in influencing consumers' taste and preferences and—therefore—their purchasing decisions.

The meanings carried by Danish Modern were partly a result of a narrative initiated and circulated by the network of architects' and cabinet-makers' organizations in cooperation with the state and the media, as well as other private and public organizations. However, the meanings of Danish furniture were merged with the broader meanings of Denmark in the United States—in other words, with the nation image of Denmark. This claim is vindicated by the Federal Trade Commission's advisory opinion in 1968 that terms like 'Danish' and 'Danish Modern' must only be used to describe furniture that was produced in Denmark, but the term 'Danish designed' could be used for furniture designed in Denmark only (Federal Trade Commission 1968: 234). The *Journal of Marketing* added that the Commission had recognized that consumers might have a preference for goods identified with a foreign culture (Werner 1969). Thus, the next step will be to trace the development of the nation brand and image of Denmark in the same period.

BRANDING DENMARK

In October 1949, Axel Dessau came to New York as the newly appointed manager of the new Danish Tourist Office. During the next 30 years, Dessau orchestrated the branding of Denmark as a destination for American tourists (Dessau 1990). It is not altogether surprising that Denmark wanted to intensify the communication with prospective American tourists, since the United States was, in many ways, looked upon as the Promised Land in the years after the Second World War. Danish engineers, architects, and managers all looked to the United States in order to learn about production methods, rationalization, marketing, architecture, export opportunities, and so on. And since the United States was the only country to have actually come out of the war with purchasing power not only equal to, but in better shape than before, it was also a logical step to try to encourage Americans to travel to Denmark. Some persuasion was needed, and Axel Dessau was appointed by the Danish Tourist Association as the person in charge of this persuasion.

The efforts of Dessau consisted primarily in establishing contacts with several thousand travel agencies, magazines, newspapers, freelance writers, and radio- and TV-stations all over the United States, and to provide them with brochures and other material about Denmark. According to Dessau, more than 30 million Americans watched Danish tourist films during his 30 years as head of the Danish Tourist Office, and the number of American tourists increased from 25,000 in 1950 to 400,000 in 1973. Danish export-oriented consumer goods firms and industries and the events they organized aimed to construct, circulate, and maintain a specific image of Denmark as a tourist destination (Dessau 1990: 23). The general image portrayed drew on a number of stereotypes and export-items, such as Vikings, fairy tales, food (butter and bacon), beer (Carlsberg, Tuborg), industrial arts (silver, furniture), and fashion (fur). The first slogan designed to capture prospective tourists' interest was 'Denmark—Famous For Food, Fun & Fairy Tales' (Dessau 1990). At the same time, other events, such as the exhibitions *Design in Scandinavia* (1954–57) and the *Arts of Denmark* (1960–61), were staged by other Danish (and Scandinavian) actors, and a number of American writers, newspapers, and magazines with a specific or general interest in Denmark also contributed to constructing an image of the country (Dessau 1990; Hansen 2006a; 2006b).

Denmark is a lovely land is the title of a book published by a writer and professor of creative writing, Hudson Strode, in 1951. Strode wrote enthusiastically about the Danish welfare state and the friendliness and openness of the Danes. He credited much of this to the agricultural cooperative movement and the folk high schools, which had contributed to the happiness of the people. 'Throughout the world "Made in Denmark" is recognized as a symbol of value and durability' Strode claimed (Strode 1951: 206).

In November 1952, Samuel Goldwyn released *Hans Christian Andersen,* a fairy tale picture about the famous Danish author. The film was well received and it left an image of the capital of Denmark that is still with us: *Wonderful Copenhagen* (Crowther 1952). Danny Kaye, who played Hans Christian Andersen, sang this song to fame to the extent that, even today, many Americans pronounce Copenhagen like in the German Kopenhagen. The Danish Tourist Association immediately made the song title into a slogan, and in 1953, a famous Danish tourist poster was designed by Viggo Vagnby. Its title was, of course, 'Wonderful Copenhagen', and it depicted a police officer holding back the traffic in order to allow a mother duck and her ducklings to cross the street.

Both the poster and the movie pictured Denmark and Copenhagen as an idyllic, picturesque society unharmed by industrialization and the spirit of capitalism. The Danes were represented as a relaxed people who could afford to stop the traffic while the mother duck and her ducklings crossed the road. Before the film was made, the Danish Foreign Office strongly opposed the particular image of Hans Christian Andersen being made, claiming that 'the Goldwyn version would insult the memory of the beloved fairy tale writer'. However, when Danny Kaye visited Denmark in July he was received as a statesman, because 'he is going to bring Hans Christian Andersen's and Denmark's name to millions of filmgoers around the world' (Anon 1952a; 1952b).

The social institutions and organizations that formed the foundation of the welfare state were also frequently commented upon, for instance in the *New York Times.* In 1952, the newspaper carried a story about Denmark and the 'Meet the Danes' program initiated by Dessau and the National Travel Association. Copenhagen's modern social institutions, it read, 'have set the pace for similar developments all over the world', and kindergartens and nursery homes arranged a 'World of Tomorrow' tour where tourists could see, with their own eyes, how the Danish welfare state arranged the lives of its citizens (Schwimmer 1952; Anon 1956).

It was quite a typical feature of many newspaper articles about Denmark that they represented Denmark as something 'other', but at same time representing certain elements of 'sameness', compared to the United States. Denmark and the Danes were different, it was understood, but not so different that any American would fail to recognize the basic cultural categories and principles. That many Danes spoke English at a decent level was mentioned regularly, along with the usual suspects such as design objects, Tivoli, and Hans Christian Andersen.

The Danes were presented as 'gay and hardworking', and the Copenhagener 'will keep you amused. He is of ready wit, and is sharp in business' (Arnold 1954). The country was 'so lovely and picturesque', and the Danes were said to be giving American tourists a particularly fine welcome. The result was that an increasing number of American tourists visited the country, and one of them reported from his visit that 'sophisticated Danes can teach us how to mix work and pleasure'. At the same time, there were strong similarities between the Danes and the Americans, the writer thought. Danes had a 'strong American-style sense of humor. These people enjoy life, like to laugh at themselves, and at and with their guests'. In the mind of this visitor, the people of Denmark had a certain way of getting things done without the stress and rush that characterized contemporary American work culture. 'These are a sophisticated people with a life that is so close to the American ways' (Andersen 1955; P.J.C.F. 1956). On and on it went. 'The Relaxed Danes' said another headline, and the author noted that more and more Americans went to Denmark to acquaint themselves with this country that was, at the same time, well-known and yet unknown (Lassen 1957).

Many of these articles almost resembled advertisements, and some of them were written by reporters with Danish names. In October 1960, however, the *New York Times* carried a lengthier article by Henry Commager, an academic well-known for his popular histories, but who also knew Denmark well, having written a dissertation on Danish politics. The occasion was a visit by the Danish King Frederik IX and Queen Ingrid to the United States in connection with the opening of the *Arts of Denmark* exhibition. Commager stressed that Denmark was a democracy like the United States but a much more egalitarian one whose leaders 'have all but wiped out poverty, as they have wiped out slums, unemployment, and preventable diseases' (Commager 1960).

Commager was clearly impressed and sympathetic towards Denmark and its social institutions. The Danish temper was liberal, progressive and experimental, but instead of 'liberal', he preferred to call it 'advanced'. 'The most striking . . . manifestation of Danish democracy and progressivism is in the operation of the welfare state. . . . The most comprehensive and successful and certainly one of the best advertised.' Denmark was different, but it has still 'vindicated the logic that Toqueville so confidently applied to America more than a century ago'. And then, of course, there were the Danish dressmakers, the beer, the porcelain, the silversmiths and the furniture (Commager 1960, passim).

Danish Modern furniture was frequently mentioned and promoted as part of the Danish national image. During the hugely successful *Design in Scandinavia* exhibition that toured the United States and Canada from 1954 to 1957, about 650,000 people in 22 US cities could see Danish Modern for themselves, and in *House Beautiful* they could read about an

> unbroken tradition of homecraft, which not even victorious industrialism has been able to extinguish. The hand loom, for instance, is still fairly frequently found in the country, and organized commercial homecraft is . . . based on traditional artisan skills. (Hald 1954)

The connection between country image and Danish furniture was completed in the argument that

> The artist-craftsman plays a prominent role in Scandinavia. . . . Denmark offers the finest example of how artisan culture may become part of modern living in general. . . . [E]ach year the newest handmade furniture is displayed at an exhibition. (Hald 1954: 153)

Thus, the image of Denmark and the story about Danish Modern fed on each other. The tourist-oriented promotion of Denmark as a welcoming destination for US tourists fitted very well with the narrative of Danish Modern as democratic, hand crafted, natural, and high quality. It was, indeed, a small fairy tale on its own. At the same time, during *Design in Scandinavia*, a number of Danish and Scandinavian interests also promoted information about the Scandinavian countries in the cities visited by the exhibition. In Houston, for example,

> All high schools . . . are devoting February to studies of the Scandinavian countries. Literature, films and lectures on each of the four countries have been supplied to 40 high schools arranging contests for their students on the best essay on Scandinavia. . . . Leading department stores and many travel offices, banks, libraries, air lines, and stores in Houston are arranging window displays of Scandinavian products to include posters, literature, flags etc.[10]

All this publicity seems to have worked well, as evidenced by the increase in export of Danish furniture from Denmark to the United States (see figure 4.1). Denmark was not the United States; it did not represent the same hectic pace of life; sense of conformity; and anonymous, mass-produced products that most American consumers were used to. A US woman even claimed that Scandinavians were more materialist than the Americans because there was such a focus on the things that they became attached to them, but the American 'buy and waste' mentality was unacceptable to the Scandinavians (Hald 1954).

However, as already hinted, there was also a perception that the United States and Denmark had many things in common. Denmark, with its democratic and open-minded people, was very different from Germany, for example, as was argued in 1953 by Elizabeth Gordon, the prominent editor of *House Beautiful*. In an influential article with very clear Cold War overtones, Gordon attacked the international style of the Bauhaus School architects such as Walter Gropius and Mies van der Rohe. They were dictators of taste, Gordon claimed, and if Americans accepted this dictatorship, there was only a short way to accepting other dictatorships (Gordon 1953). The next year, Gordon strongly endorsed Danish and Scandinavian furniture, claiming that it was democratic.

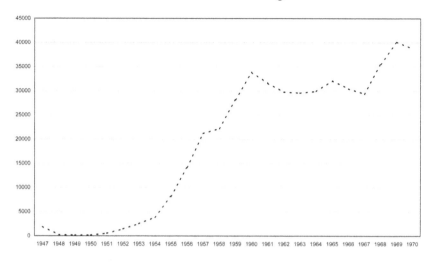

Figure 4.1 Danish furniture exports to the United States, 1947–1970.

The concept of democracy was emphasized several times in articles in the *New York Times*. Danish furniture was consistently represented as democratic, natural, and functional by the network of producers, architects, and the cultural industry that promoted it (Hansen 2006a). Assuming for the moment that Denmark and Scandinavia can be treated as synonyms—a not altogether unreasonable assumption in this connection—the values assigned to furniture were the same as in the more general articles on Denmark. Also, the cosy and picturesque image of Scandinavia was repeated. These values were not, however, values shared by all Americans. Categories and principles such as liberal, cosmopolitan, progressive, democratic, and advanced appealed to certain groups of Americans who wanted to demonstrate a lifestyle associated with these values.

One clear cut example of this link between liberal and progressive US values and Danish furniture appeared when John F. Kennedy was pictured in 1960 in a chair designed by Hans Wegner during the presidential debate with Nixon. The picture of Kennedy in Wegner's chair is very well known indeed, yet, to my knowledge, no picture of Nixon in the same chair has ever been used in the marketing of Danish Modern. This is hardly accidental, since Kennedy carried all the meanings that corresponded with the image of not only Denmark but also Danish Modern.[11]

The editor of *House Beautiful* commented on the popularity of Scandinavian furniture in the United States, arguing that this was due to the similarities between the two nations:

> Why are their home furnishings so well designed and so full of meaning for us? Because they are so well designed and so meaningful for the Scandinavians themselves. Aimed at Scandinavian home life, their designs have a natural beauty and usefulness . . . , for we are both deeply democratic people. Home is their center—and people are the center of their homes. Their design is human and warm. Therefore it is natural, national and universal. (Gordon 1954: 94)

Natural, human, democratic, and warm were not exactly values that went well with the big US corporations focusing on standardization, mass-production, and economies of scale and scope. At the same time, the need to be an individual in a mass consumer society made certain consumer groups demand furniture and other goods that carried meanings, which enabled them to bridge the identity conflicts that they encountered in their everyday lives.

It was the metaphorical identification process pointed out by McCracken (1988; 2005), where Denmark's country image and the meanings of Danish Modern lend each other value and merged into one, that appealed to US consumers who felt a need to construct an alternative lifestyle and an alternative personal and group identity. Arguably, the reason that a particular narrative of Denmark could circulate relatively freely was that only few people had actual knowledge of Denmark, and this meant that it did not encounter alternative or even conflicting narratives. Thus, the authors of the official narrative were able to circulate the story without encountering many obstacles.

'The Danish Way is the Only Way' (Anon 1966) announced an advertisement in a Canadian interior decorating magazine. Although this was clearly an overstatement, the discussion so far indicates that Danish Modern came to occupy a special place among imported furniture to North America during a certain time period. As already mentioned, the fairy tale didn't last forever, and in 1980 the *New York Times* flatly pointed out that Danish Modern had gone out of fashion. The most likely explanations for this is that the meanings assigned to both Denmark and Danish Modern referred to a Denmark that no longer existed.

The cabinet-makers and the designers went on using the same design expressions and same materials that once worked so well, but from the mid-1960s they experienced increasing problems due to the introduction of new materials, new production technology, and new and more fragmented consumer lifestyles and preferences. At the same time, Denmark became an industrial country during the 1950s and '60s, and the nation brand and image portrayed came into conflict with social reality in Denmark. The meanings of Denmark and Danish Design that had been so attractive to consumers took on new connotations and consumers looked elsewhere for the meanings and narratives that could help them make sense of an ever more chaotic world (Hansen 2006a; 2006b).

At the same time that Denmark was branded as an idyllic, traditional, even agricultural utopia, the Danish Government, in 1956, published a pamphlet, *Investment of Foreign Capital in Denmark*, for US companies (Royal Danish Ministry of Foreign Affairs 1956). Aimed at an entirely different audience from that addressed by the Danish Modern discourse, the pamphlet portrayed Denmark as a country of low company taxation with easy access to the wider European market, a well-trained workforce, few restrictions on foreign trade, efficient infrastructure, and so on.

This image conflicted with that portrayed by the tourist associations, and for good reasons. However, one interesting question for further research will be to understand better how such conflicting narratives influence the effort to brand nations effectively (see also Anholt 2002: 231).

CONCLUSION

This chapter has argued that traditional branding theories cannot present an adequate understanding of how the branding of products and nations work, and how sometimes product, brand, and country image enter into effective ways of cobranding each other. Based on a cultural understanding of branding promoted by such scholars as McCracken and Holt, and on the case of Danish Design and Denmark, I have argued that branding and the way it works can be better understood when the cultural context and consumers' use of brands for the construction of lifestyle and self is brought into the framework. Furthermore, I have suggested that narratives play a significant role in the construction of efficient brands that consumers can use to create order, meaning and direction in their lives.

The case study is on Danish Modern and Denmark's country image in the United States from 1940 to 1970. It has been demonstrated how an elaborate network of designers, producers, organizations, and the press produced a powerful narrative of Danish Modern as handcrafted, scientific, and functional furniture that appealed to certain US consumers who wanted to construct themselves as individualists in a conformist US society based on mass production. The Danish Modern narrative worked well with the view of Denmark as a country that, unlike the United States, had a strong social welfare system and an unstressful lifestyle. Even though Denmark, itself, was becoming increasingly industrialized, the image of both Danish Modern and of Denmark was that of a romantic and idyllic society that well-educated US consumers could use to construct an identity and lifestyle that put some distance between themselves and the conformist US society. During the 1950s and '60s, Danish Modern and Denmark was a powerful example of efficient cobranding. In Anholt's words, 'for a brand's home country to add this helpful dose of free additional equity, the product should "chime" with its country of origin in the consumer's mind, and some logic must link the two' (Anholt 2007: 95). In the 1970s, however, this chime, no longer worked. Denmark increasingly industrial-ized while the narrative of Danish Design remained unchanged, even in the face of a dramatically changing cultural context in the United States as well as in Denmark.

In telling this story of Danish Desigh, this chapter has touched briefly upon some of the most important issues in approaching a better under-standing of what brands do and how they work. Much more research needs to be done in order to continue the scholarly conversation on this topic. The main argument of this article has been to suggest the need for a more nuanced culturally and historically based debate on brands, their consum-ers, and their cultural context. Without such research, branding will never be fully understood.

NOTES

1. In this article, Danish Modern and Danish Design are used synonymously, as are Denmark's image, country image and national image.
2. Apart from a brief mention, Kotler and Armstrong (2006: 249) don't treat the role of culture in branding strategy in their influential textbook *Principles of Marketing*. See Kotler and Armstrong 2006: 249–57. See also McCracken 2006.
3. The distinction between corporate brand, identity, and image is quite prob-lematic. A widespread definition contends that corporate identity expresses the organization's internal identity, corporate brand is the external com-munication of this identity, and corporate image is the external perception among consumers and other stakeholders of the corporate brand. It seems, however, that this distinction is only sustainable as long as identity, brand, and image (what Anholt 2007 calls brand purpose, brand identity and brand image) are essentialized, and thus kept distinct from each other. If identity, brand, and image are considered social constructions, it becomes very diffi-cult to distinguish identity, brand, and image, because they will tend to blur, or even merge. For example, how can a company or a nation project a brand identity that differs from the brand image that consumers and others hold of the brand? To make things even more complicated, and as emphasized throughout this text, the reception of a brand—that is the brand image—depends on the cultural context in which it is interpreted. As for the internal side of the organization or the nation, does it make sense to speak of one singular identity? Any observer of nations and companies would probably grant that it does not, because there will always be, at the same time, inte-gration, differentiation, and fragmentation within organizations and nations (see Martin 2002; Schultz 2005; Hansen 2007; and Anholt 2007: pp. 4–6).
4. It may be argued that trademarks and logos enable companies to control who use their mark, which is not the case for nations. However, this posi-tion misses the point, which is not so much about control of trademarks and logos, but of the narratives that assign meanings to them, and these are not easily controlled. So, for example, when the Federal Trade Commission ruled in 1968 on the use of Danish, Danish Modern, and Danish Design, its opin-ion did not help the Danish Modern brand, because, as I argue, the problem was more related to a changing context and to the narratives related to Dan-ish Modern.

5. Of course, the question of who should make this choice and how to enforce and coordinate it takes us right back to the problem of controlling narratives.
6. In this connection, it is interesting that, in the wake of the first cartoon crisis in 2006, the Danish Government allocated DKK 412 millions to brand Denmark. This effort, of course, is based on an idea that it is, indeed, possible to brand a nation in a way that improves the general image of that nation across space. As this chapter argues, this is hardly possible.
7. It seems that place branding in general has undergone a transformation over time. Initially, place-of-origin brands such as Champagne, Cognac, Port, etc. essentialized the nature of places, arguing that champagne, cognac, and port proper could only be produced in these places, due to specific physical characteristics of the place. Later, with the shift to more recent place branding, it is not nature, but culture, that is essentialized. The idea that Danish Modern and Denmark have certain characteristics that are part of a unique Danish culture and, therefore, cannot be replicated outside of Denmark is but one example. (I am grateful to the editors of this volume for making this point.)
8. Ingeborg Glambek has written an interesting book on how Nordic architecture and design was perceived in other countries by means of a number of exhibitions such as Design in Scandinavia, etc. (Glambek 1997).
9. Steen Eiler Rasmussen argued that there was a unique British way of designing everyday applied art, and that this way reflected a unique culture related to the English upper class, noble simplicity, durability, and functionality (Rasmussen 1965: 5).
10. The quotation is from a press release dated 6 February 1956 and issued by the press office of Design in Scandinavia: to US correspondents of the Scandinavian Press (Hansen 2006a: 397–8).
11. I am grateful to my colleague at Copenhagen Business School, Mads Mordhorst, who directed my attention to this point.

BIBLIOGRAPHY

Anon. (1952a) 'Danes okay Kaye, who feared kayo', *New York Times*, 22 July.
Anon. (1952b) 'Danes weigh protest on Andersen picture', *New York Times*, March 15.
Anon. (1956) 'Sightseeing Copenhagen and Sealand', (brochure), S. Johnsen & Co.
Anon. (1966) 'The Danish way . . . is the only way', Advertisement in *Canadian Interiors*, November issue.
Aaker, D. A. and E. Joachimsthaler (2000) *Brand Leadership*, London: Free Press.
Anderson, B. (1991), *Imagined Communities: Reflections on the Origin and Spread of Nationalism*, New York: Verso.
Andersen, G. (1955) 'Denmark's sights', *New York Times*, 13 March.
Anholt, S. (2002) 'Foreword', *Journal of Brand Management*, vol. 9, No. 4–5: 229–39.
Anholt, S. (2007) *Competitive Identity: The New Brand Management for Nations, Cities and Regions*, New York: Palgrave MacMillan.
Arnold, F. (1954) 'Smiling Danes', *New York Times*, 14 March.
Barry, J. A. (1952) 'Free taste: The American style of the future,' *House Beautiful*, October issue: 176–80, 228–32.
Berry, N. (1959) 'Denmark for design', *New York Herald Tribune*, Europe Edition, 27 May.
Commager, H. S. (1960) 'Big lesson from a small nation', *New York Times Magazine*, 2 October: 16–17 and 82.

100   *Per H. Hansen*

Crowther, R. (1952) 'The screen in review: "Hans Christian Andersen" in technicolor arrives at the Paris and Criterion', *New York Times*, 26 November.
Csaba, F. F. (2005) 'The limits of corporate branding: The application of branding to non-profit organizations and places', in Schultz, M., Y. M. Antorini and F. F. Csaba (eds.), *Corporate Branding: Purpose/People/Process*, Copenhagen: CBS Press: 127–49.
Czarniawska, B. (2004) *Narratives in Social Science Research*, Thousand Oaks, CA: Sage Publications.
Dessau, A. (1990) *30 Sjove år for Dansk Turisme i*, New York and Århus: De samvirkende danske turistforeninger.
Duguid, P. (2008) 'Brands in chains', this volume.
Federal Trade Commission (1968) 'Advisory opinion digest no. 301', *Federal Trade Commission. Advisory Opinion Digest 1–313, 1 June 1962 to 31 December 1968*: 234.
Fielding, T. (1961) *The Temple Fielding's Selective Shopping Guide to Europe*, New York: Fielding Publications.
Glambek, I. (1997) *Det Nordiske I Arkitektur og Design* Sett Utenfra, Oslo: Arkitektens Forlag.
Gordon, E. (1953) 'The threat to the next America', *House Beautiful*, April, 126–30, 250–1.
Gordon, E. (1954) 'Why the new Scandinavian show is important to America', *House of Beautiful*, February issue: 94–6.
Hald, A. (1954) 'A fresh breeze from the Northeast', *House of Beautiful*, February, 97, 152–4.
Hansen, P. H. (2006a) *Da Danske Møbler blev Moderne: Historien om Dansk Møbeldesigns Storhedstid*, Copenhagen: University Press of Southern Denmark/Aschehoug.
Hansen, P. H. (2006b) 'Networks, narratives, and new markets: The rise and decline of Danish modern furniture design, 1930–1970', *Business History Review*, 80: 449–83.
Hansen, P. H. (2007), 'Organizational culture and organizational change: A narrative analysis of the transformation of savings banks in Denmark, 1965–1990', *Enterprise & Society*, 8: 920–53.
Hiorth, E. (1960) 'Trends in contemporary Danish design', in Lassen, E. (ed.), *The Arts of Denmark, Viking to Modern*, Copenhagen: Berlingske Bogtrykkeri: 119–32.
Hobsbawm, E. and T. Ranger (1983) *The Invention of Tradition*, Cambridge, UK: Cambridge University Press.
Holt, D. B. (2004) *How Brands Become Icons: The Principles of Cultural Branding*, Cambridge, MA: Harvard Business School Press.
Huxtable, A. L. (1980) 'The melancholy fate of Danish modern style', *New York Times*, 21 August.
Jaffe, E. D. and I. D. Nebenzahl (2006) *National Image and Competitive Advantage: The Theory and Practice of Place Branding*, Copenhagen: CBS Press.
Katzen, J. (1952) 'Prestige—The intangible asset', *Retailing Daily*, 28 April: 44.
Kotler, P. and G. Armstrong (2006) *Principles of marketing*, 11th edition, Upper Saddle River, NJ: Pearson Education.
Kotler, P. and D. Gertner (2002) 'Country as brand, product, and beyond: A place marketing and brand marketing perspective', *Journal of Brand Management*, 9 (4–5): 249–61.
Lakoff, G. (2004), *Don't Think of an Elephant: Know Your Values and Frame the Debate*, White River Junction, VT: Chelsea Green.
Lassen, P. (1957) 'The relaxed Danes', *New York Times*, 3 March.

Lopes, T. da Silva and M. Casson (2008) 'Entrepreneurship and the development of global brands', *Business History Review*, 81: 651–680.

Martin, J. (2002) *Organizational Culture: Mapping the Terrain*, Thousand Oaks, CA: Sage Publications.

McCracken, G. (1988) 'Meaning manufacture and movement in the world of goods', in McCracken, G., *Culture and Consumption*, Bloomington: Indiana University Press: 71–89.

McCracken, G. (1989) '"Homeyness": A cultural account of one constellation of consumer goods and meanings', in Hirschman, E. (ed.), *Interpretive Consumer research*, Provo, UT: Association for Consumer Research: 168–83.

McCracken, G. (2005) 'Who is the celebrity endorser?: Cultural foundations of the endorsement process', in McCracken, G., *Culture and Consumption II*, Bloomington: Indiana University Press: 97–115.

McCracken, G. (2006) *Flock and Flow: Predicting and Managing Change in a Dynamic Marketplace*, Bloomington: Indiana University Press.

Olins, W. (1999) *Trading Identities: Why Countries and Companies are Taking on Each Others' Roles*, London: Foreign Policy Centre.

Olins, W. (2002) 'Branding the nation—The historical context', *Brand Management*, 9 (4–5): 241–8.

Olins, W. (2003) *Wally Olins on Brand*, London: Thames & Hudson.

Papadopoulos, N. & L. Heslop (2002) 'Country equity and country branding: problems and prospects', *Journal of Brand Management*, 9 (4–5): 294–314.

Pine II, B. J. and J. Gilmore (1998) 'Welcome to the experience economy', *Harvard Business Review*, 76 (4): 97–105.

P.J.C.F. (1956) 'Happy memories of Denmark', *New York Times*, 29 July.

Rasmussen, S. E. (1965) *Britisk Brugskunst*, Copenhagen: Det danske Kunstindustrimuseum.

Rivoli, P. (2005) *The Travels of a T-shirt in the Global Economy: An Economist Examines the Markets, Power and Politics of World Trade*, New York: John Wiley and Sons.

Royal Danish Ministry of Foreign Affairs (1956) *Investment of Foreign Capital in Denmark*, Copenhagen: Berlingske Bogtrykkeri.

Schultz, M. (2005) 'A cross-disciplinary perspective on corporate branding', in Schultz, M., Y. M. Antorini and F. F. Csaba (eds.), *Corporate Branding: Purpose/People/Process*, Copenhagen: CBS Press: 23–55.

Schwimmer, R. (1952) 'Denmark organizes 'life-seeing' tours', *New York Times*, 30 March.

Strode, H. (1951) *Denmark is a Lovely Land*, New York: Harcourt Brace.

van Houten, L. (1954) 'Furniture', *Arts and Architecture*, August issue: 25–9.

Werner, R. O. et al (1969), 'Legal developments in marketing', *Journal of Marketing*, 33 (2): 70–81.

Part II

Trademarks and the Law

5 Trademarks and Infringement in Britain, c.1875–c.1900[1]

David M. Higgins

This chapter discusses the general problem of infringement in Britain between the Trade Marks Registration Act [1875][2] and 1900. The Act was the culmination of concerted and sometimes intense pressure on government to alter the law on misrepresentation in all of its forms.[3] Following the Act, infringement is deemed to occur when any person who is not the proprietor of a registered trademark uses a mark identical to, or having a strong resemblance to, the registered mark. Consequently, consumers are deceived or confused into believing that the imitating mark is the registered mark and the trade that would ordinarily accrue to the registered owner is diverted to the imitator.

Trademark infringement continues to attract publicity, especially when household names are affected. Recent examples of cases involving familiar names include Philips *v.* Remington (2006); Chocosuisse (and others) *v.* Cadbury Ltd (1998); Easyjet *v.* Dainty (2001), and Inn Crystal *v.* Waterford Wedgewood PLC (2005).[4] Each of these cases brought up the issue of confusion in the minds of consumers about the true provenance of the goods, as well as the damage to goodwill.

The legal remedies that govern infringement in cases such as these have been evolving for over 100 years. However, between 1875 and 1900, the period covered by this chapter, the law governing infringement was still in its infancy and a number of issues remained to be resolved. The precise ways in which evolving case law determined the rights of trademark owners were numerous, and in many cases had still to be determined. As I demonstrate later in this chapter, providing the parameters within which these rights—and others—were determined had a direct bearing on the competitive strategies that could be adopted by firms.

This chapter is organized as follows. In section one, I examine the importance of trademarks to business strategy. In section two, I provide a brief review of the state of the law as it existed prior to 1875, and the fundamental changes that followed as a result of the Trade Marks Act [1875]. Section three discusses some of the prominent cases involving infringement. In section four, I argue that, despite the advantages conferred by the various trademarks acts in the nineteenth century, recourse to actions for passing-off were still prominent. In other words, consumer perception of products was only partly determined by trademark. Other indicia, for example labels and wrappers, were also valuable in differentiating the products of one manufacturer from those of others. In the concluding section, I review the developments in trademark legislation and litigation between 1875 and 1900, and argue that the growing emphasis on brands, rather than trade-marks, in the twenty-first century appears to be undermining the impor-tance of the latter as an indication of trade origin.

THE BUSINESS–ECONOMIC ADVANTAGES OF TRADEMARKS

To address the issue of why businesses expend considerable energy pro-tecting their trademarks, we need to answer the question: What is it that makes trademarks so valuable? Because infringement adversely affects producers and consumers, the benefits that trademarks confer to each need to be assessed.

As far as producers are concerned, the literature indicates a number of advantages generated by trademarks. It is recognized that they are a crucial means for the conveyance and building of reputation, especially when extended distribution networks undermine the traditional familiarity between buyer and seller (Schecter 1927: 824; Wilkins 1992: 68; Ramello 2006: 550). The reputation effects conveyed by trademarks can assist entry into new markets where high search costs would otherwise represent a sig-nificant barrier to entry (Griffiths 2008). Trademarks provide an endog-enous mechanism for producers to maintain and uphold quality (Klein and Leffler 1981: 617, 622–24, 629–31; Landes and Posner 1987: 270; Ramello 2006: 552; Shapiro 1983: 660–61). To the extent that trademarks provide an indication of quality, they help to reduce price and cross-price elasticity effects, thereby allowing their owners to achieve monopoly profits (Ramello 2006: 557). Recent empirical work has indicated that the size of premia earned by particular brand names can be considerable (Png and Reitman 1995: 216; Wiggins and Raboy 1996: 378–79). Moreover, to the extent that they induce inertia in consumer preferences, trademarks facilitate the main-tenance of monopoly power (Png and Reitman 1995: 216; Ramello 2006: 558; Davis and Maniatis, this volume).

From the consumers' perspective, it has long been recognized that the deception of the public by misrepresentation is wrong and actionable. In 1878, for example, the noted barrister Lewis Sebastian wrote in his *Law of Trade Marks*:

> The function of the trade mark is to give the purchaser a satisfactory assurance of the make and quality of the article he is buying. . . . It is

on the faith of the mark being genuine, and representing a quality equal
to that which he has previously found a similar mark to indicate, that
the purchaser makes his purchase (Sebastian 1878: 2).[5]

In economic terms, the precise benefits that trademarks offer consumers
include the following: they overcome the problem of asymmetric information which is particularly important when expensive items are being
purchased (Akerlof 1970; Ramello 2006: 551). Apart from their intrinsic
attractiveness, it has been argued that consumers attach particular weight
to salient trademarks (Griffiths 2008). At a more general level, it has been
argued that trademarks reduce search costs and improve overall market
efficiency, both of which help consumers match their particular preferences
with specific products (Landes and Posner 1987: 269).

At first sight, it appears that trademarks simultaneously benefit producers and consumers. Actions for trademark infringement and passing-off are
distinctly separate legal principles and are based, respectively, on the prem-
ise that the protection of the property of the plaintiff and the prevention of
fraud upon the public are important. Consequently, when a business sells
products of its own manufacture as being those of another, it simultaneously violates both of these principles.

However, the law in the nineteenth century did not always recognize
congruence in the interests of producers and consumers. Some legal scholars have argued that the positive benefit of trademarks to producers has
been understated: too much emphasis has been placed on the injury done to
consumers by misrepresentation; and the early development of trademark
law—particularly its emphasis that the function of trademark was to indicate origin—was not viewed as in producers' best interests (Schecter 1927:
822; McKenna 2007: 1857). Moreover, some of the most recent research
has shown that a number of fundamental issues governing trademark law
remained to be determined. For example, what constituted a trademark?
Was infringement simply a matter of deceiving consumers—or did owners
have rights of property in their mark? (Bently 2008a). In order to understand how changes in the law affected business strategy during our period,
it is necessary to have some understanding of the law as it existed before
the Trade Marks Act [1875].

LAW AND REGISTRATION OF MARKS

The fundamental principle governing the law on misrepresentation is that
the deception of the public by the offer for sale of products as possessing
some connection with a particular trader that they do not, in fact, possess is wrong, and the trader has a legal remedy against any person who is
responsible for the deception. Legislation governing misrepresentation falls
into two main categories. The first concerns actions for passing-off, and

the second concerns actions for infringement. In the first case, it is alleged that the defendant is using means that are calculated to pass-off products as those of the plaintiff and the means *may or may not* involve the imitation of a trademark (for example, imitation of the packaging, colouring, or any other aspect of 'get-up'). In the second case, the complaint by the plaintiff is that the defendant has infringed his/her trademark either by copying it exactly, or by closely imitating it, and the plaintiff relies on the exclusive rights to that mark that have been conferred by registration.

Before the Trade Marks Act [1875], *only* passing-off actions could be instigated against misrepresentation, because rights to exclusive legal property in trademarks had not been established (McKenna 2007: 1853–55; Bently 2008b). In 1842, Lord Langdale stated:

> A man is not to sell his own goods under the pretence that they are the goods of another man; he cannot be permitted to practise such a deception, nor to use the means which contribute to that end. He cannot, therefore, be allowed to use names, marks, letters, or other *indicia* by which he may induce purchasers to believe that the goods which he is selling are the manufacture of another person.[6]

Unfortunately, the outcome of passing-off cases was, in practice, highly uncertain. The basic legal principle at stake was straightforward: Was the defendant passing-off his goods as those of the plaintiff? Answering this question proved more difficult and involved consideration of all the circumstances affecting the plaintiff and the defendant and their respective trades. But the view taken of the facts of the case was a matter entirely personal to the presiding judge. Moreover, witness statements before the trial often differed significantly from those made in the witness box. And for a judgement, an assessment had to be made whether competition that was unjustifiable was also illegal (Cutler 1904: 3–5). Furthermore, before the landmark case of Millington *v.* Fox (1838),[7] the plaintiff also had to establish that there was an *intent* to deceive.

From the early nineteenth century, the risk of 'passing-off' increased both in domestic and export markets. Growing unease about the current state of the law culminated in the appointment in 1862 of a Select Committee.[8] Evidence given before this committee demonstrated that the law was unsatisfactory in a number of respects. The legal issues surrounding the definition and functions of merchandise marks and trademarks were numerous, thorny, and controversial (Bently 2008a). The principal concerns of businesses were that the law was expensive, that the outcome of actions was uncertain, and that the absence of domestic registration of trademarks exacerbated difficulties when seeking redress abroad (Higgins and Tweedale 1995: 8–17).

As a result of the Select Committee's deliberations, the Merchandise Marks Act [1862] was introduced.[9] This Act imposed a variety of penalties in cases where misrepresentation of products involving trademarks and other indicia occurred. These penalties were severe and included forfeiture of articles, payment equivalent to their value, together with a fine ranging from 10 shillings to five pounds. Persons convicted of offences under this Act were liable to imprisonment for up to two years, possibly with hard labour.[10]

However, because the Merchandise Marks Act [1862] did not provide for the registration of trademarks, the legal footing upon which actions could be taken for infringement was not advanced.[11] Consequently, it has been argued that the Merchandise Marks Act [1862] merely reinforced the view that protection of trademarks was necessary to prevent consumer deception, not because trademarks were valuable *per se* (Bently 2008b).

The Trade Marks Act [1875] not only provided for the registration of marks, but also established the parameters within which registration could be refused. By this act, registration conferred upon the proprietor 'prima facie evidence of his right to the exclusive use of such trade mark'.[12] Of particular importance also, the registrar was not permitted to register in the same class of goods 'a trademark identical with' or 'so nearly resembling a trademark already on the register with respect to such goods or classes of goods as to be calculated to deceive'.[13]

Enshrining property rights in trademarks, the Trade Marks Act [1875] represented a considerable advance in the law. For the first time in Britain, the courts no longer required plaintiffs to establish their rights to a particular mark or to prove that a particular mark was understood in the trade to designate their products. The Act was extremely popular and businesses responded with alacrity to the new rights conferred by it: between 1876 and 1881, for example, 32,367 trademarks were registered;[14] by the end of 1900, over 100,000 marks had been registered.[15] However, as with all significant legislation, the interpretation of the courts was critical to the determination of the actual rights of trademark owners and prospective owners.

EVOLUTION OF TRADEMARK LAW

This section discusses aspects of the evolution of trademark law following the Trade Marks Act [1875]. Prior to this Act, there were no official means by which businesses could ascertain whether the marks they used were identical with, or similar to, those of others. Following the Act, applications for registration were published in the *Trade Marks Journal*, which provided the means by which businesses and the registrar could assess whether marks put forward for registration were likely to clash with marks already registered. But what degree of resemblance was necessary to prevent registration or instigate actions for infringement? The 1875 Act provided that the fundamental principle governing this matter was whether use or registration of a trademark was 'calculated to deceive'.[16] Because infringement could be effected in an almost infinite number of ways, it is necessary to limit the discussion to those that acquired prominence after 1875. Two broad categories of action are considered. First is the use of identical or similar marks by different manufacturers. This category includes honest concurrent use; use of the same marks by manufacturers in different geographical markets; and use of the same marks in different product classes. The second set of actions to be considered are those involving marks common to the trade, particularly 'fancy' marks.

By the Trade Marks Act of 1875, registration was *prima facie* evidence of exclusive rights to a particular trademark. One of the key problems this raised was whether different manufacturers were entitled to register the same mark in the *same class* of goods.[17] Resolution of this issue was important, because the ensuing public confusion would have undermined the ability of the trademark to denote trade origin; further, this confusion had the potential to undermine the goodwill that a particular manufacturer had established in that mark.

Unfortunately, the 1875 act failed to make clear provision on this matter, stating only that the registrar was to prevent identical or similar marks unless he had 'special leave of the court'.[18] Similar provision was made in the Trade Marks Act [1883] and by the Trade Marks Act [1905].[19] Unsurprisingly, perhaps, determining the conditions that would allow multiple registration was a complex issue. In some of the earliest cases, the issue of 'calculated to deceive', or confuse, was sufficient for the court to grant an action for infringement. For example, in Wilkinson *v.* Griffith Bros. and Co. (1891), it was decided that the defendant was using a mark consisting of a red balloon and two red medals, which infringed the plaintiff's mark of two red medals.[20] Another case involved the dissolution of Ehrmanns' business partnership (1897), which raised the question of whether the individual partners could independently use the trademarks originally used by the firm. In this case, it was decided by the registrar that registration should not be permitted because harm was likely to arise from confusion or the probability of deception.[21]

However, in Aerated Bread Company *v.* Albert Baker (1898), both companies successfully secured registration of the mark 'A.B.C.' for cigarettes. Dual registration was permitted because it was thought that confusion of the public was unlikely and because the Aerated Bread Company disclaimed exclusive rights to the mark 'A.B.C.' in its application.[22] Later cases suggest that the courts took a more liberal interpretation of the trademarks acts, recognizing that the threat of confusion among the public was but one consideration in determining whether multiple firms could use the same trademark. Thus, for example, in 1915, Mr. Justice Sargant stated:

> It seems to me that the intention was to allow the Court to weigh against a slight possibility of deception, or a slight possibility of confusion, in

the minds of the public, the commercial claims which a proprietor of a common law trade mark might have acquired through a considerable amount of concurrent use.[23]

The use of the same or similar trademarks by manufacturers in different markets, or as applied to different products, raised further problems. The basic complaint here was that a mark that had acquired repute in one market was being used by another manufacturer in another market or with respect to a different class of products. This practice could involve the deliberate copying or significant imitation of a particular mark and could have severe adverse consequences for the value of the original mark. For example, the greater the dilution of a mark, the greater is the loss in its communicative value (Landes and Posner 1987: 306). Although the use of the same mark by different manufacturers on different products does not mean they are in actual competition, it does undermine the ability of a particular mark to compete with other marks in the *same* class of products for which it was originally registered. Thus, it has been argued that, 'the preservation of the uniqueness of a trademark should constitute the only rational basis for its protection' (Schecter 1927: 831).

Where the same or similar mark was used by different manufacturers in different *geographical* markets, the legal issues could be highly complex. For example, in Paine and Co. *v.* Daniell and Sons' Breweries. Limited (1893), the plaintiffs sought exclusive rights to the mark 'John Bull', which they had registered in connection with beer. The defendants claimed that they had used the mark 'John Bull' without knowledge of the plaintiff's use of the same mark. It was established that both companies used the same mark in different markets: Paine and Co, who were based in St Neots, had a large export trade and a limited domestic trade centred on Middlesex; Daniell and Sons, based in Colchester, sold their beer largely within the eastern counties. One of the fundamental issues that had to be addressed in this case was whether use of the 'John Bull' brand by the defendant was 'calculated to deceive'. Initially, the presiding judge, Mr. Justice Kekewich, was prepared to rule in favour of the plaintiff, but on receiving communication from Lofthouse and Bell (Sheffield brewers) that they, too, used the 'John Bull' mark, it was ruled that Paine and Co. did not have exclusive rights to 'John Bull', and it was ordered that this mark should be expunged from the register.[24]

Even in situations where infringement was not 'calculated to deceive,' there was no guarantee that an application to register a mark similar to a registered mark would succeed. A classic example of such a case occurred in 1896, when John Dewhurst and Sons (manufacturers of cotton thread) sought to register a device symbolizing 'The Golden Fan Brand'. The registrar refused registration of this mark on the grounds that it conflicted with an earlier mark. The significance of this case is that Dewhurst's had obtained the consent of the owners of the registered mark. It was argued that this consent indicated that the proposed mark was not 'calculated to deceive'; if it was, the owners of the registered mark would not have given their consent. Dewhurst's application failed because consent provided no justification for registration; even when consent had been obtained, it might not be known outside the register, with the result that Dewhurst's proposed mark could mislead the public.[25]

The second class of actions to be discussed is the registration of marks that were common to the trade. In a number of industries, it was the practice for many firms to use similar indicia, for example, diamonds and triangles in alcoholic beverages, especially beer and porter. This immediately influenced the interpretation of the law on the following questions: should one firm be allowed exclusive rights to a common mark? To what extent would combinations of common marks, or common words, suffice to distinguish a mark from a single mark in common use? More fundamentally, what restrictions should be placed upon word marks? Another issue closely related to these questions concerned the use of geographical appellations: suppose a geographical region had acquired repute for a product based on the output of incumbent firms. Was a new entrant entitled to use the same geographical appellation as the incumbents?[26]

Some of these questions were addressed by the Trade Marks Act [1883], which repealed the Trade Marks Act [1875] but reenacted many of its key provisions. For our purposes, the key changes introduced by the Trade Marks Act [1883] were as follows. First, it was provided that existing marks could be altered to include marks, devices, or other indicia that were common to the trade.[27] Second, registration of any distinctive word or combination of words was permitted, even when such indicia were common to the trade, provided such marks were not used prior to the Trade Marks Act [1875].[28] Finally, definition of a trademark was extended to include any 'fancy word or words not in common use'.[29]

However, it soon became apparent that these provisions were insufficient and that the Trade Marks Act [1883] needed to be amended. The Herschell Committee (1888), appointed to review the law on trademarks, reported as follows. First, the combination of common marks was not, in itself, sufficient to be regarded as a new mark. What was crucial in this instance was whether the combination of common marks conveyed a new idea. Thus, for example,

> Assuming a cat and a fiddle to be each an old mark, we do not think the mere representation of a cat and a fiddle together would be new mark, but the representation of a cat playing upon a fiddle, the idea conveyed by which would be neither the cat nor the fiddle, but a cat playing upon a fiddle, would be a good combination, and might properly be registered.[30]

Determining which word marks could be registered posed the greatest difficulties for the Committee. Although the Trade Marks Act [1883] provided for the registration of 'fancy words', this term was never defined.

Consequently, considerable differences of opinion arose as to its meaning. One witness giving evidence before the Committee stated, 'The difficulty we have to face now is what is a good fancy word? . . . So far as I am aware, every word mark that has been tested in the Appeal Court has failed'.[31] In its final report, the Herschell Committee stated: 'The expression "fancy word" is certainly not a happy one, and has naturally given rise to considerable differences of opinion as to its meaning'.[32]

The Trade Marks Act [1888] amended the Trade Marks Act [1883]. The term 'fancy word' was replaced with the terms 'invented or invented words' and 'A word or words having no reference to the character or quality of the goods, and not being a geographical name'.[33] But this change in the law had only limited initial impact: 'fancy words' registered under the 1883 Act, were still valid after 1888. There was, then, scope for further differences of opinion.

Some of the early cases on this point indicate that the court adopted a very strict interpretation of the statutes, for example, 'Gem' as applied to guns (1887), 'Jubilee' for note paper (1887), 'Melrose' for hair restorer (1887), and 'Electric' for velveteens (1887).[34] In each of these cases, it was decided that the word mark being used was descriptive of the article to which it was applied. To succeed as a 'fancy word', the key criteria were that the word 'must be obviously meaningless as applied to the article in question'[35]; in fact, 'the more ridiculous it is, the better it is'.[36]

A classic case that exemplified this definition was that of 'Bovril'. This mark was registered as a fancy word on 2 November 1886, in Class 42 (substances used as food or as ingredients in food). Bovril Ltd. argued that 'Bovril' was widely understood among the public to denote their fluid beef and that 'it would be a fraud upon the public, as well as an invasion of the Company's rights, if anyone used the term "Bovril" to describe or denote any extract of beef or other food produced not of the Company's manufacture'.[37] In 1896, Rosetree and Co., also manufacturers of fluids and meat extracts, wished to use 'Bovril'. Rosetree contended that, as 'Bovril' was founded on 'Bov', implying beef (bovine), the mark had reference to the character of the product; consequently, Rosetree sought to expunge the mark from the register. The presiding judge, Mr. Justice Kekewich, stated that there was no doubt that 'Bovril' was not in common use when it was adopted; moreover, as 'Bovril' was applied to a wide range of other articles produced by Bovril Ltd.—such as 'Bovril Celery Salt' into the manufacture of which the extract of beef did not enter—it was clear that the mark 'Bovril' was not necessarily descriptive. Rosetree appealed but lost.[38]

TRADEMARKS, LAW, AND BUSINESS

The previous section discussed two prominent categories of litigation that followed the Trade Marks Act [1875]. By stipulating that registration was *prima facie* evidence of exclusive rights to a particular mark, this Act provided the foundation on which all British trademark legislation was based. However, it should not be assumed that the Trade Marks Act [1875] and subsequent legislation were a panacea for all businesses that had an interest in trademarks. First, considerable scepticism was expressed about the benefits of the Trade Marks Act [1875] as it applied to the Lancashire cotton textile industry. Second, even when businesses owned registered trademarks, their products were still vulnerable from misrepresentation by rivals using a similar 'get-up'.

The Lancashire cotton textile industry owned the greatest number of registered trademarks in the years immediately following the Trade Marks Act [1875]. Between 1876 and 1881, for example, the marks registered in the 'cotton classes' were 20 per cent of all registered trademarks; during the same period, registrations in these classes were 10 times the average for all classes, and registrations in cotton piece goods alone exceeded the next highest class—fermented liquors and spirits—by a factor of 1.7.[39] In this industry, there were numerous users of identical or strongly similar trademarks. Evidence given before the Herschell Committee (1888) indicated the peculiar problems confronting this industry. Cotton textile merchants were constantly urging that a similar mark should be registered for a particular market. For example, one merchant would register a diamond for the Indian market, another for the West African market, and so on. This practice existed because many trademarks registered in this industry belonged to merchants, not manufacturers. It was estimated that 75 per cent of textile shipments was made by merchants, not manufacturers.[40] Dealing with multiple buyers in different markets, merchants were obliged to use a greater variety of trademarks than manufacturers because 'there may be buyers in the same market who would not like the same goods to be brought in competition with the same stamp'.[41]

The solution proposed for this dilemma was the 'Three Marks Rule', by which three or fewer owners were allowed to register the same, or very similar, marks. Although this solution appeared to work well, it was only a temporary expedient.[42] As far as the Lancashire cotton textile trade was concerned, the basic problem remained that the marks Manchester merchants wished to register were not considered sufficiently distinctive. Consequently, the view was expressed that legal protection of trademarks was on a stronger footing prior to the Trade Marks Act [1875]. Thus, for example, Charles Bailey (an employee of Ralli Brothers, who were the biggest owner of trademarks in the Lancashire cotton textile trade, and a member of the Manchester chamber of commerce), stated:

> In fact, my own view is that we do not want the 1883 Act at all in Manchester. Personally, I would prefer to have the whole of the marks of my firm in the position in which they stood prior to the passing of the Act of the 15th August 1875, because we hold that we have better rights at

common law for the protection of our marks than we have had either by the Act of 1875 or the Act of 1883.[43]

The second argument to be presented is that firms used a variety of means, other than trademarks, to distinguish their products from those of other firms. Irrespective of whether a firm owned a particular trademark, its products were vulnerable to misrepresentation if a rival used a similar 'get-up'. However, unlike trademark infringement, actions for passing-off remained complex affairs after the Trade Marks Act [1875]. Viewed from this perspective, protection afforded by this and subsequent acts was only efficacious so far as infringement, *per se*, was concerned: in cases where nonregistered indicia were used to 'pass-off', traditional remedies had to be relied upon, with all their inherent difficulties. After 1875, a number of cases occurred where owners of registered trademarks sought relief from misrepresentation. Two of these cases indicate that the plaintiffs viewed misrepresentation as seriously as trademark infringement. Moreover, these cases also indicate that reliance had to be placed on 'passing-off' actions.

In Lever *v.* Goodwin, which lasted between November 1886 and May 1887, the plaintiff owned the registered mark 'Sunlight Self-Washer Soap', and sold this soap in 12-ounce tablets wrapped in distinctive, legend-bearing, imitation parchment paper. The defendants also began to sell soap using a different mark, 'Goodwin's Self-Washing Soap', also in 12-ounce tablets, using similar wrappers to those of the plaintiff. Establishing that Goodwin had been using a form of 'get-up' calculated to deceive the public proved complex. It was freely admitted that no one had a monopoly over 12-ounce tablets or the use of parchment paper or the printing on it. Although an injunction was obtained that prevented Goodwin using wrappers similar to those of Lever, the plaintiff nonetheless argued that the mark 'The Self-Washer Soap' would be struck-off the register. Goodwin appealed, reiterating their claim that no one had a monopoly on the size or shape of soap tablets wrappers, and Lever relied on the traditional argument against misrepresentation that,

> You, the Defendants, are selling your soap in a wrapper and dress which represents it to be our soap, and, therefore, on the old common law doctrine enforced in Court of Equity by injunction we seek to restrain you from passing off your goods as our goods.[44]

The appeal was unsuccessful because the judges, Lords Justices Cotton, Lindley, and Bowen, were satisfied that Goodwin had intentionally misrepresented his products as those of Lever.

An even more striking example is provided by the 'Yorkshire Relish Case', which was fought between February 1893 and July 1897. In this case, the plaintiff, William Powell, trading as Goodall, Backhouse and Co., had registered 'Yorkshire Relish' as a trademark in 1884. In 1893, Powell brought an action against the Birmingham Vinegar Co. to restrain them from using upon their 'London Relish' a label resembling, in terms of colour, that used by Powell for his 'Yorkshire Relish'. Powell did not claim for infringement of his registered trademark. In the first action, it was decided that Powell had not used 'Yorkshire Relish' as a trademark; moreover, this mark had never been used alone but always in conjunction with the registered label, stopper label, and paper wrapper in which the bottles were sold. It was ordered by Mr. Justice Chitty that the mark 'Yorkshire Relish' be expunged from the register.[45] However, despite successive appeals by the defendants to the Court of Appeal and the House of Lords, Powell, in 1897, did establish that by using 'Yorkshire Relish' the Birmingham Vinegar Co. was attempting to pass-off their products as those of Powell.[46]

CONCLUSION

This chapter has discussed aspects of the evolution of British trademark law between 1875 and 1900. Looking back through the lens of the twenty-first century, it is clear that it evolved in directions very different from those conceived in the late nineteenth century, and it is on the basis of this evolution that two conclusions are made.

As the introduction made clear, there can be little doubt that trademark infringement and passing-off are practices that continue to be taken very seriously by business and the courts. Why, then, more than 130 years after the passing of the Trade Marks Act [1875], are businesses still instigating actions for infringement? The answer appears to lie in the longevity of trademarks (Lury 2004: 101). Unlike patents and copyrights, trademarks do not have a fixed term; indeed, many of the leading trademarks in existence today were registered in the 1880s and 90s.[47] This indicates that, over the life of a mark, different generations of consumers will rely on the same marks to inform their purchases. Over time, therefore, registered owners of reputable marks must ensure that rivals do not succeed in registering marks that will deceive or confuse the public. This is particularly important because an injunction that is obtained against infringement at one point in time does not apply to rival marks that may be introduced in the future. Effectively, therefore, trademarks will always become victims of their own success.

In the nineteenth century, at least in a British context, the registration of brands as trademarks had to await the Trade Marks Act [1883]. Prior to this Act, the registration of brands was not permitted, although it was recognized that they performed functions similar to trademarks.[48] Thereafter, the indicia that firms used to differentiate their products has widened considerably, and much more emphasis is now placed on brands rather than trademarks (Lury 2004: 18). One consequence of this trend is that producers and consumers now place much more emphasis on the cultural appeal of the brand, for example the extent to which it is associated with youth, vitality, sophistication, intellect, and maturity. Conversely, it has been argued that the role of the trademark as a mark of origin and as a means of protecting consumers from confusion has become increasingly outmoded. Thus, for example, consumer legislation has superseded trademark law as a guarantor of quality, and the multinational activities of global firms mean that indications of origin are becoming increasingly less important for consumers (Lury 2004: 109).

NOTES

1. A version of this chapter was presented to the Globalization and Trade Marks workshop held at Queen Mary University, London, on 11 May 2007. I am grateful to the participants for their useful comments. Particular thanks are due to the editors, Teresa da Silva Lopes and Paul Duguid, and to Dev Gangjee.
2. 38 & 39 Vict., Ch.91. Hereafter Trade Marks Act [1875]. The other principle statutes enacted within the period covered by this chapter were the *Patents, Designs and Trade Marks Act* (1883), 46 & 47 Vict., Ch.57 (hereafter, Trade Marks Act [1883]), and the *Patents, Designs and Trade Marks Act* (1888), 51 & 52 Vict., Ch.50 (hereafter, Trade Marks Act [1888]).
3. Following the conventions established in the legal literature, infringement applies to registered trademarks, and passing-off is used to refer to misrepresentation, which need not involve such marks.
4. Philips Electronics NV *v*. Remington Consumer Products (2006) *European Trade Mark Reports* (hereafter, ETMR) 42. This case, which was fought between 1998–2006, concerned whether Remington were to be allowed to use a picture of a three-headed electronic shaver similar to the ones used by Philips and known as 'Philishave'. Chocosuisse, Kraft Jacobs Suchard (Schweiz) AG and Chocoladefabriken Lindt & Sprungli (Schweiz) AB *v*. Cadbury Ltd. (1998) ETMR 205. Cadbury's had launched a chocolate bar under the name 'Swiss chalet', and the confectionary was enclosed in a wrapper which bore a picture of the Matterhorn mountain and a picture of a Swiss chalet. Easyjet *v*. Dainty Easyjet *v*. Dainty (t/a EasyRealestate), (2001) *Fleet Street Intellectual Property Reports* 6. In this case, the well-known budget airline argued that the use of the domain name 'easy Realestate' represented an intention by the defendant to 'pass-off' their Website as belonging to the claimant. Inn Crystal Vertriebs GmbH's application: opposition of Waterford Wedgwood plc. (2005) ETMR 102. The applicant sought to register the word mark 'LISA MORI' for glassware in class 21. Waterford-Wedgwood objected that there was a risk of confusion with its earlier marks consisting of a pattern known as 'Lismore' and the word 'LISMORE'.
5. This quotation raises an important distinction between the economic advantages claimed for trademarks and the protection afforded them. In the first case, as discussed in the first section of this chapter, it is well established that owners of reputable trademarks have a strong incentive to maintain quality. However, as far as the law was concerned, it was not necessary for the plaintiff to establish that the defendant was using his/her mark on inferior or superior products.

6. (1842) 49 *English Reports* (hereafter, *ER*) 749.
7. (1838) 40 *ER* 956. Removing the need to prove intent to fraud was an important first step in facilitating the legal actions that could be taken by owners of trademarks. Nonetheless, as I show in section three, significant areas of the law on trademarks remained to be resolved after the Trade Marks Act [1875]. For example, what degree of resemblance between marks would cause confusion among consumers.
8. *Report from the Select Committee on Trade Marks Bill and Merchandise Marks Bill*, 1862, (212) . Hereafter, Select Committee, 1862.
9. 25 & 26 Vict., Ch.88. Hereafter, Merchandise Marks Act [1862].
10. Merchandise Marks Act [1862], s.4; s.7–8; s.14. Following this Act, misrepresentation was made a penal offence. Consequently, and unlike Millington *v.* Fox (1838), a higher evidence threshold was required. It has been indicated to me that this threshold was so severe that it was relaxed in subsequent legislation. I am grateful to Dev Ganjee for bringing this to my attention.
11. Even though the Merchandise Mark Act [1862], s.2, stipulated that, where intent to defraud was established, fraudulent use of a trademark was a misdemeanour, recent scholarship (Bently 2008b) has shown that witnesses before the Committee of 1862 feared that registration of trademarks would facilitate fraud because the transfer of marks between traders would mislead the public about the true provenance of the goods.
12. Trade Marks Act [1875], s.3.
13. Ibid., s.6 . Following this act, 50 trademark classes were established.
14. *Second Report of the Comptroller General of Patents, Designs and Trade Marks*, C. 1428,1885: Appendix I, p.12. The Trade Marks Act [1875] did not become operational until 1 January 1876.
15. Calculated from *Report of the Comptroller General of Patents, Designs and Trade Marks*, 1884–1915.
16. Trade Marks Registration Act [1875], s.6. A committee appointed by the Board of Trade in 1888, recognized that determining the degree of resemblance between marks was vexatious. The solution proposed by this committee was as follows. First, the image conveyed by the mark as a whole was paramount. Second, 'when the question arises whether a mark applied for bears such a resemblance to one on the Register as to be calculated to deceive it should be determined by considering what is the leading characteristic of each'. (Herschell Commitee 1888).
17. The issue of identical marks being used in different trademark classes and/or different geographical markets is discussed later in this section.
18. Trade Marks Act [1875], s.6.
19. Trade Marks Act [1905], 5 Edw.7, Ch.15.
20. Wilkinson *v.* Griffith Bros. and Co. *Reports of the Patent Commissioners* (hereafter, *RPC*) (1891), VIII, 41, 370. Both the plaintiff and the defendant were manufacturers of French polish.
21. In the Matter of Ehrmann's Trade Marks, *RPC*, (1897), XIV, 23. The Ehrmann brothers were wine and spirit merchants based in London.
22. In the Matter of an Application for a Trade Mark by Albert Baker & Co. (1898) Ltd, and In the Matter of an Application for a Trade Mark by the Aerated Bread Company Ltd. *RPC* (1898), XXV, 16.
23. In the Matter of an Application by Joseph Emil Maeder to Register a Trade Mark, *RPC*, (1915), XXXIII, 4, 82. Maeder was a manufacturer of condensed milk. See also, Aerated Bread Company *v.* Albert Baker, *RPC*, (1898), XXV, 513, and Paine and Co. *v.* Daniel and Sons, *RPC* (1893), X, 71, where common law rights are emphasized.

24. Paine and Co. *v.* Daniell and Sons' Breweries, Limited, RPC (1893), X, 8. In this case. it was ruled that 'John Bull' was, in fact, common to the trade. This particular matter is discussed later in this section.
25. In the Matter of Dewhurst's Application for a Trade Mark, *RPC*, (1896), XIII, 288. A further problem in this case was that no provision existed by which registration could be limited to particular geographical markets. A further set of actions during this period was the use of the same mark by different manufacturers in different product classes. However, the issues generated by this practice, for example dilution and defensive registration, became more prominent after 1914. But see, for example, The Eastman Photographic Materials Company Ltd., and Another *v.* The John Griffith's Cycle Corporation, Ltd., and the Kodak Cycle Company, Ltd., and In the Matter of the Trade Mark No. 207,006 (Kodak) RPC (1898) XV, 5, 105.
26. The issue of geographical marks is discussed further in Higgins (2008).
27. Trade Marks Act [1883], s.74, (1), (a). Common to the trade was defined as any indicia used by more than three persons on the same or a similar description of goods before the Trade Marks Act, [1875], was introduced. Ibid., s.74, (3).
28. Trade Marks Act [1883], s.74, (1), (b). However, in any case where a mark common to the trade was registered, the applicant had to disclaim exclusive use of such marks.
29. Trade Marks Act [1883], s.64, (1), (c).
30. Herschell Committee (1888), p. ix. This Committee also recommended that where several common marks were grouped together in a new design, such a combination may be entitled to registration, but it was advisable that all of the common elements in such a mark should be disclaimed. Ibid., p.xi.
31. Herschell Committee (1888), Q. 1113.
32. Ibid., p.xi.
33. Trade Marks Act [1888], s.64, (1), (d), (e). It was clearly desirable that 'no one ought to be granted the exclusive use of a word descriptive of the quality or character of any goods. Such words of description are the property of all mankind'; further, 'geographical words which can be regarded as descriptive of the place of manufacture or sale of the goods are open to obvious objections. One manufacturer or merchant cannot properly be allowed to prevent all his competitors from attaching to their goods the name of the place of their manufacture or sale.' Herschell Committee (1888), p. xi.
34. The last two cases, involving the applications by Van Duzer, and Leaf, Son & Co., respectively, were especially protracted. In both cases, initial application was refused by the Comptroller-General; both parties appealed to the Board of Trade, which referred the matter to the courts. Vice Chancellor Bacon, before whom both cases were heard, agreed that 'Melrose' and 'Electric' were fancy words. The Comptroller-General was finally successful in the Court of Appeal before Lords Justices Cotton, Lindley, and Lopes. Van Duzer's Trade Mark and Leaf's Trade Mark, *RPC* (1887), IV.
35. Ibid., 39.
36. (1862) 9 *Jurist Reports*, (New Series) 322.
37. In the Matter of Trade Mark No. 58,405 (Bovril), *RPC* (1896) 13, 384. This case also provides an excellent example of trademarks improving the efficiency of information: the product was originally sold as 'Fluid Beef Brand Bovril' but over time the public simply asked for 'Bovril'.
38. Ibid.
39. Cotton classes were defined as class 23 (cotton yarn and thread), class 24 (cotton piece goods), and class 25 (cotton goods such as small wares). Total

numbers are calculated from *Second Report of the Comptroller General of Patents, Designs, and Trade Marks*, C. 1428, 1885, Appendix I, p.12.
40. Herschell Committee (1888), Q. 285. Giving evidence before a later Select Committee, John Holden estimated that only 5 per cent of the cloth was marked with the manufacturer's mark or name. Report from the Select Committee on Merchandise Marks Act [1887], [1890], Q. 4278 .
41. Herschell Committee (1888), Q. 286; Q.291; Q.299.
42. A Committee of Experts was appointed in Manchester to oversee registration of marks in the cotton classes. Of the 40,000 decisions taken by this Committee, only 170 were appealed and the decision reversed. Ibid., Q.180. For a further discussion of the trademark problems facing Lancashire, see, for example, Higgins and Tweedale (1996).
43. Herschell Committee (1888), Q. 760.
44. Lever *v*. Goodwin, *RPC*, (1887) IV, 505.
45. In the Matter of Powell's Trade Mark, *RPC*, (1893) X, 63.
46. Powell *v*. The Birmingham Vinegar Company Ltd., *RPC*, (1897) XIV, 720.
47. For example, 'Huntley & Palmers', *Trade Marks Journal* (hereafter, *TMJ*) 457, p. 1405, 29 December 1886; 'Bisto', *TMJ* 924, p.1030, 11 December 1895.
48. Herschell Committee (1888), p.xi.

BIBLIOGRAPHY

Akerlof, G. (1970) 'The market for "lemons": Quality uncertainty and the market mechanism', *Quarterly Journal of Economics*, 84: 488–500.
Bently, L. (2008a) 'The making of modern trade marks law: The construction of the legal concept of trade mark (1860–1914)', in L. Bently, J. Davis and J. Ginsburg (eds), *Trade Marks and Brands: An Interdisciplinary Critique*, Cambridge, UK: Cambridge University Press.
Bently, L. (2008b) 'From communication to a thing: Historical aspects of the conceptualisation of trade marks as property', in G. Dinwoodie and M. Janis (eds.), *Trade Mark Law and Theory: A Handbook Of Contemporary Research* (forthcoming), Cheltenham: Edward Elgar.
Cutler, J. (1904) *On Passing Off*, London: Gay and Bird.
Griffiths, A. (2008) 'A law and economics perspective on trade marks', in L. Bently, J. Davis and J. Ginsburg (eds.), *Trade Marks and Brands: An Interdisciplinary Critique*, Cambridge, UK: Cambridge University Press.
Herschell Committee (1888): 'Report of the Committee appointed by the Board of Trade to inquire into the duties, organization, and the arrangements of the Patent Office under the Patents, Designs, and Trade Marks Act, 1883, so far as relates to trade marks and designs; together with minutes of evidence, appendices, etc', British Parliamentary Papers (1888), LXXXI, C. 5350.
Higgins, D. and G. Tweedale (1995) 'Asset or liability? Trade marks in the Sheffield cutlery and tool trades', *Business History*, 37: 1–27.
Higgins, D. and G. Tweedale (1996) 'The trade marks question and the Lancashire cotton textile industry, 1870–1914', *Textile History*, 27: 207–28.
Higgins, D. (2008) 'The making of modern trade mark law: The UK, 1860–1914. A business history perspective', in L. Bently, J. Davis and J. Ginsburg (eds.), *Trade Marks and Brands: An Interdisciplinary Critique*, Cambridge, UK: Cambridge University Press.
Klein, B. and K. B. Leffler, (1981) 'The role of market forces in assuring contractual performance', *Journal of Political Economy*, 89: 615–41.

Lury, C. (2004) *Brands: The Logos of the Global Economy*, London: Routledge.

Landes, W. M, and R. A. Posner (1987) 'Trademark law: An economic perspective', *Journal of Law and Economics*, 30: 265–309.

McKenna, M. P. (2007) 'The normative foundations of trademark law', *Notre Dame Law Review*, 82: 1839–1916.

Png, I. P. L and D. Reitman (1995) 'Why are some products branded and others not?', *Journal of Law and Economics*, 38: 207–224.

Ramello, G. B. (2006) 'What's in a sign? Trademark law and economic theory', *Journal of Economic Surveys*, 20: 547–65.

Schecter, F. (1927) 'The rational basis of trade-mark protection', *Harvard Law Review*, 40: 813–33.

Sebastian, L. B. (1878) *The Law of Trade Marks and Their Registration, and Matters Connected Therewith* , London: Stevens and Sons.

Shapiro, C. (1983) 'Premiums for high quality products as returns to reputations', *Quarterly Journal of Economics*, 98: 659–79.

Wiggins, S. N. and D. G. Raboy. (1996) 'Price premia to name brands: An empirical analysis', *Journal of Industrial Economics*, 44: 377–88.

Wilkins, M. (1992) 'The neglected intangible asset: The influence of the trade mark on the rise of the modern corporation', *Business History*, 34: 66–95.

6 Trademarks, Brands, and Competition

Jennifer Davis and Spyros Maniatis

Trademark rights are exclusive rights. They allow their owners to exclude others from certain uses of the signs that constitute the subject matter of protection. The justification behind this lies in the distinguishing function of trademarks. They allow consumers to distinguish between products and express their preferences. As a result, they allow traders to compete. Once a trademark becomes established through use and advertising, however, it can be transformed into a powerful barrier against smaller players or new entrants. These two issues demonstrate the complexity of the relationship between the inherently procompetitive nature of trademarks on the one hand, and the inherently monopolistic effect of the exclusionary scope of trademark rights on the other.

According to the European Court of Justice (ECJ), the essential function of a registered trademark is:

> to guarantee the identity of origin of the marked goods or services to the consumer or end user by enabling him, without any possibility of confusion, to distinguish the goods or services from others which have another origin. For the trade mark to fulfil its essential role in the system of undistorted competition which the Treaty seeks to establish and maintain, it must offer a guarantee that all the goods or services bearing it have been manufactured or supplied under the control of a single undertaking which is responsible for their quality.[1]

If one looks simply at the essential functions of a registered trademark, as identified by the ECJ, it would appear that trademark registration should be neither anticompetitive nor an obstacle to innovation. On the contrary, the contribution of a trademark as a badge of origin is generally considered to be entirely benign. For example, it has been pointed out that trademark registration will reduce consumer search costs. Provided the trademark is not duplicated, it will allow a consumer familiar with the mark to identify, with precision, the goods or services he or she may wish to purchase.[2]

Furthermore, this benefit will only be obtained if the proprietor of a trademark ensures that his or her goods maintain, 'a consistent quality over time and across consumers'.[3] Thus, a second benefit of trademark registration is that it provides an incentive for its proprietor to invest in his or her goods or services in order not to disappoint consumers' expectations.[4]

Nonetheless, it is argued here that when the protection of a registered trademark strays beyond its ability to act as a badge of origin and embraces what might be described as 'brand values', then such protection might function as an impediment to innovation in two, albeit related, ways. First, traders might find it difficult to introduce new products into a market where established brands and trademarks already operate. Second, traders might take the view that the acquisition of well-established trademarks or brands would be more profitable than seeking to provide the same, or related, goods or services under a different trademark or brand. This chapter examines both of the ways in which trademarks and brands might discourage innovation. But first, it is necessary to examine the relationship between a trademark and a brand.

The first section of this chapter distinguishes between a trademark and a brand, and seeks to examine the ways in which trademarks *qua* brands might discourage innovation. It then goes on to explore the seeming antithesis between trademarks' procompetitive nature on the one hand, and the exclusionary scope and monopolistic effect of trademark rights on the other. It does so by focussing on two areas of trademark law that exemplify this contrast: comparative advertising and functionality. In doing so, the chapter refers to trademark law both in the European Union, where it is governed by the Trade Mark Directive, and in the United States.

TRADEMARKS AND BRANDS

In order to understand how a trademark may act as a barrier to market entry, it is first necessary to examine the relationship between a trademark and brand. Despite the value placed upon successful brands, there is no generally accepted definition of a brand, as such. However, the literature relating to brands (rather than trademarks) does identify a number of attributes that are likely to be ascribed to a brand. For example, according to the International Trademark Association (INTA):

> A brand is a trade mark (or combination of trade marks) that, through promotion and use, has acquired a significance over and above its functional use by a company to distinguish its goods or services from those of other traders.[5]

This is a very narrow definition of a brand, and not one that would be recognizable to those involved in brand development. At the other extreme,

L. D. Chernatony and F. D. Riley identify nine aspects of a brand. Thus a brand is:

1. a legal instrument,
2. a differentiating device,
3. a company,
4. an identity system,
5. an image in consumers' minds,
6. a personality,
7. a relationship,
8. adding value, and
9. an evolving entity.[6]

In fact, although markedly different, both these approaches view registered trademark(s) as an essential attribute of a brand. However, the latter approach also suggests, as do most definitions of a brand, that a brand's value extends beyond the value of the product with which it is associated. As one marketing expert put it, brands 'offer value to the customer which goes beyond the product alone and becomes synonymous with the brand'.[7] Second, most definitions of a brand emphasize its quality of 'transferability'. In other words,

> A brand has the unique ability to transfer consumer loyalty between products, services and categories over time and to separate it from tangible production. The ability to franchise and license brands has enabled recognition of this intangible property as the most powerful and productive asset owned by modern business. [8]

The question then arises as to what extent trademark registration will protect a mark's added value, beyond its origin function, and also its transferability. According to another observer:

> A brand asset's unique identity is secured through legal definition which firstly, protects the seller from competitors who may attempt to provide similar goods and/or services and secondly, enables it to exist as an entity in its own right and therefore be capable of being transferred independently of the goods or services to which it was originally linked. [9]

The ECJ considered the same question from the perspective of trade origin in a recent case concerning the interpretation of the European trademark law provisions covering deceptive marks. In *Elizabeth Florence Emanuel*,[10] a dress designer who had registered her name as a trademark and used it in order to attract funding into her business found that, following a number of transfers, the trademark belonged to a new entity, unconnected with the designer.

Again, the function of the trademark became the starting point for the Court: for the trademark to be able to fulfil its essential role in a system of undistorted competition, it must offer a guarantee that all the goods or services bearing it have been manufactured or supplied under the control of a single undertaking, which is responsible for their quality. Having identified consumer protection as the public interest behind the provision on deceptive marks, the Court considered whether the risk that consumers might think that Elizabeth Emanuel, who originally personified the goods bearing the ELIZABETH EMANUEL mark, was still involved with the production of the garments might give rise to deceit. It found that the trademark would still function as a guarantee of quality despite the transfer; 'even if the average consumer might be influenced in his act of purchasing a garment bearing the trade mark ELIZABETH EMANUEL by imagining that the appellant in the main proceedings was involved in the design of that garment, the characteristics and the qualities of that garment remain guaranteed by the undertaking which owns the trade mark'.[11]

THE SCOPE OF TRADEMARK RIGHTS

Trademark registration in the European Union is governed by the Trade Mark Directive (89/104/EEC).[12] As we have seen, the essential purpose of trademark registration is to protect the origin function of the mark. Thus, a sign will conflict with a registered mark if it is identical to the registered mark and is used on identical goods or services, or if it is similar to the registered mark and is used on similar goods or services, and the average consumer would be confused as to origin.[13] However the Directive goes further and will protect a mark with a reputation if an identical or similar sign is used on similar goods or dissimilar goods and, without due cause, would take unfair advantage of, or be detrimental to, the distinctive character or repute of the earlier mark.[14] In the latter case, it is not necessary for the average consumer to be confused as to the origin of the goods sold under the later sign; instead he or she need only associate the sign with the earlier registered mark in such a way that its distinctiveness will be blurred or diluted or, alternatively, that its reputation will be tarnished. Although there is considerable debate at present as to what sort of association (or link) might be deemed to dilute or damage the reputation of a registered trademark with a reputation,[15] for the purposes of this chapter the crucial question is whether the legal protection of brand values through trademark registration will inhibit innovation.[16]

We have already noted that there is little disagreement over whether the role of a trademark as a badge of origin is conducive to market efficiency and should have no adverse effect on innovation. There is, however, far less consensus as to whether the legal protection of the trademark as a brand would be equally benign. The most influential argument for protecting brand values by trademark registration was offered in the seminal essay by Frank I. Schecter in 1927.[17] According to Schecter, the value of 'modern' trademarks is their advertising function, or as he put it, 'their selling power'. Furthermore, such selling power need not necessarily stem from the quality of the goods to which a trademark is affixed. It could also arise from the attractiveness of the trademark itself. Therefore, Schecter argues, trademark law should be premised on the need to protect not just the origin function of a registered trademark, but also its advertising function.[18]

Although Schecter was not concerned with market entry, critics of his approach to trademarks have highlighted that protecting the brand function of a trademark might inhibit both innovation and market entry. Thus, Ralph S. Brown, in another influential essay first published in 1948, argued that advertising has two main functions, to inform and to persuade. Against a competitive market background, at its best, advertising will inform the consumer about the nature of the relevant goods. At its worst, persuasive advertising, notably through the nurturing of brands, will allow the brand holder to charge premium prices and to gain a certain amount of immunity from competition.[19] Furthermore, informative advertising might be said to encourage innovation, since it alerts consumers to new products and improvements on existing products. Conversely, persuasive advertising might be said to discourage innovation, since capital expenditure that might be spent on product improvement is, instead, diverted to nurturing the brand as a means of maintaining or increasing market share.[20] Finally, Brown argues that a competitive price system will not automatically 'purge' inefficient producers, as pricing may be the result of the success or failure of branding, rather than a reflection of efficient production.[21]

Both Schecter and Brown have their latter day disciples. Thus, Landes and Posner argue that the protection given to the advertising function of a trademark does not result in a loss of market efficiency or innovation through the use of resources in wasted competition. Instead, they suggest, consumers will be willing to pay a price premium for branded goods, even if there is a generic equivalent on the market, because of the reassurance it gives of predictable quality.[22] Conversely, Jessica Litman has endorsed the view of branding taken by Brown.[23] She accepts that, since Brown's day, the protection of trademarks as a valuable persuasive advertising tool—what she terms the trademark's atmospherics—has been generally accepted by both the legislature and the courts. But she also adopts Brown's argument that the emphasis placed on brand advertising diverts expenditure from product innovation. According to Litman,

> American industry seems to proceed on the assumption that we can make the consumer richer simply by revising a product's packaging, without having to make any changes to the product itself.

She adds that persuasive advertising allows companies to address niche markets without 'needing to redesign anything but the ad campaigns' for the products in question.[24]

To what extent are either Landes and Posner or Litman correct in their approaches, when applied to the real world of commerce? If we take the argument that an established brand may deter market entry and innovation, then recent studies suggest Litman may be right. One study based upon interviews with consumers found that, when given the choice of an established branded product and a product of higher quality that had just entered the market, they were more likely to choose the former. Consumers, according to this study, prefer to avoid the risk taking involved in buying technically superior products sold under a nonestablished brand and will remain faithful to the established brand with which they are familiar, even if the goods to which they are attached are of a lesser quality.[25] Such a finding may offer ammunition to both those who see the brand as a barrier to innovation and to those who view it as giving the consumer reassurance when faced with a diversity of products, some of which, like generic medicines, may actually be unbranded.[26]

Another study that dealt with industrial, rather than consumer, products made a similar finding. Research into the manufacture and purchase of precision bearings discovered that price and the actual quality of the product were not a sufficient explanation for consumer choice. Even in such a specialized industry, the decision to buy was rooted in intangible qualities that purchasers associated with the brand.[27]

The issue of whether innovation may be stifled because traders take the view that the acquisition of well-established trademarks or brands would be more profitable than seeking to provide the same or related goods or services under a different trademark or brand is far less ambiguous. Ever since Rank Hovis McDougall, in 1988, became the first listed company to show the value of its nonacquired brands on its balance sheet while defending itself from a 'take over bid', it has been widely recognized that the value of a good brand (or trademark) may far exceed the tangible assets to which it attaches.[28] An almost contemporaneous study of the white goods market in Italy explains why market actors may find that acquisition of an established brand is more profitable than seeking to introduce a new product.[29] According to Praba, a 'strong brand segmentation' of white goods manufacturers in Europe 'has greatly reduced the internal growth of firms'.[30] Instead, he suggests that large players in the marketplace did not achieve their preeminence because of 'their superior efficiency in production' or their 'superior product quality'. On the contrary, Praba's study suggests that 'the best way to secure markets has proved to be to acquire existing market shares by taking over brands with a good reputation among consumers'.[31] As a result, he argues for the 'inertial role of brand quality reputation'.

Glenn Thomas, on the other hand, argues that in order to assess the competitive strength of major brand owners, we must take into account (i) the magnitude of price differences between major and minor brands; (ii) the extent to which these differences may be attributable to quality or cost differences, rather than the exercise of market power by suppliers of major brands; (iii) the cost of launching a new brand relative to market value; (iv) the extent to which small and new firms face a cost disadvantage because they have to spend a higher proportion of their sales revenue on advertising to promote their products effectively; and (v) the extent to which new or minor brands—including own-label products—have gained market share from major established brands in the relevant product market.[32]

There is indeed an alternative argument that the acquisition of brands may facilitate innovation, through the tactic of brand (or line) extension. Thus, a brand owner may seek to facilitate the entry of a new product onto the market by associating it with already established products sold under the same brand. The market entry of a new product may thus take a considerable time to reach fruition, and therefore will reflect the brand owner's long-term interest in its brand.[33] Nonetheless, it is also the case that the strategy of obtaining market dominance in the face of brand-segmented markets through brand acquisition has continued apace since Praba completed his study.[34] A more recent example that attracted a great deal of attention involved the US motor company Ford's acquisition of the Swedish car company Volvo in 1999.[35] At the time, it was widely noted that this acquisition would give Ford entrée into the European luxury car market, without the trouble of having to develop its own brand, which was widely associated with less expensive cars. Ford, itself, planned to achieve economies of sale by common parts purchases for both Ford and Volvo cars and common platforms. In addition, according to the CEO of Ford, the company would hope to extend Volvo's range to include mini-vans and sports utility vehicles, since it viewed the Volvo brand as having 'quite a lot of flexibility and versatility' or, in other words, transferability.[36] According to one observer, Ford, which has also subsumed other 'brands' such as Jaguar, Aston Martin, and Land Rover, has reduced its physical asset base in favour of investment in intangible assets.[37]

It can be argued that the acquisition of brands as a substitute for market entry through innovation and product development has reached its apotheosis with the growth of private equity buyouts. A substantial number of such buyouts have involved the acquisition of well-known brands, such as Dunkin' Donuts, Hugo Boss, Tommy Hilfiger, Valentino, Chrysler, Boots, and the Automobile Association (AA), to name but a few. It is generally accepted that the private equity firms that undertake such buyouts are seeking short-term profits, and arguably these are achieved not by undertaking R&D or by introducing innovative products, but rather by disposing of capital assets, slimming the workforce,[38] or taking well-known brands into the growing global market.[39] In 2007, a number of observers predicted that Ford would sell Volvo to the highest bidder. It was, one observer said, a reasonable acquisition for a private equity buyout, because Volvo's 'recently updated range of models [are] attractive because little investment will be required for renewal'.[40]

OVERCOMING THE BARRIERS: COMPARATIVE ADVERTISING

Classic advertising refers only to one brand. However advertising can also be indirectly comparative, with indirect references to competing products without mentioning specific brands; or directly comparative, where brands of competing products are specifically mentioned or can be clearly recognized. Noncompeting 'referential' advertising refers to more than one branded product that is not directly competing; for example, brands for different products—beer and ice cream—used in the 'plot' of the advertisement.

Established brand owners argue that it is wrong to allow latecomers to the market to engage in comparative advertising in order to associate their products with well-known branded products. It is argued that this allows the latecomers a 'free ride', since they may benefit by such association. As a result, some argue that comparative advertising cannot be fair unless the comparison is conducted by independent bodies.[41] On the other hand, new players may argue that comparative advertising is one of the most effective ways for bringing down the barriers to market entry raised by established brands. After all, trademark registration should favour competitive markets. In fact, courts both in the United Kingdom and the United States increasingly appear to favour comparative advertising. There are uses of registered trademarks that fall outside the scope of protection; in comparative advertising, the general principle is that as long as the use of the competitor's mark is 'honest', then there is nothing wrong with telling the public of the relative merits of competing goods and services and using registered trademarks to identify them.[42]

Indicatively, a US Court of Appeal had found back in 1966 that there is no cause of action where there is no misrepresentation or confusion. Thus, the statement on a dress label 'Original by Christian Dior—Alexander's Exclusive—Paris—Adaptation' could be detrimental to Dior, but was, nevertheless, true. Trademark law 'does not prohibit a commercial rival's truthfully denominating his goods as a copy of a design in a public domain, though he uses the name of the designer to do so. Indeed it is difficult to see any other means that might be employed to inform the consuming public of the true origin of the design'.[43] This principle remains valid today, despite the adoption of an antidilution basis of protection for registered trademarks.

Turning back to Europe, the Court of Justice has examined the balance between trademark protection and comparative advertising in a number of cases, in all of them opting for a liberal approach towards comparative advertising. Adopting a common position on comparative advertising was a difficult exercise; there was divergence at the national level with Germany and the United Kingdom positioning themselves at the two extremes, against and for comparative advertising respectively.

Turning back to Europe, the ECJ has examined the balance between trademark protection and comparative advertising in a number of cases. Adopting a common position on comparative advertising across the EU has been a difficult exercise for the ECJ; for example, there was considerable divergence at the national level between Germany and the UK, with the former inhospitable to comparative advertising and the latter seeing it as largely benevolent. In the event, the ECJ has used the Directive on Comparative Advertising and its trademark jurisprudence as tools both for limiting the scope of trademark rights and as an argument for nurturing comparative advertising.[44]

Recently, the Court of Justice has been asked to clarify further the balancing between trademark protection and comparative advertising; the Advocate General, having underlined the problems the Court has been facing in delineating the proper scope of trademark protection, has urged the Court to decide that the comparative advertising directive trumps the provisions of the Trade Marks Directive.[45]

TRADEMARKS, PATENTS, AND INNOVATION

The protected life of a registered trademark is open ended, provided the mark remains a badge of origin. The same is not true of other intellectual property rights, including, most relevantly for the purpose of this chapter, patents. The maximum length of protection afforded to a patent in the United Kingdom is 20 years. In addition, none of the existing intellectual property rights offers protection for a mere idea.[46] This section of the chapter discusses the ways in which trademark proprietors have attempted to use the monopoly provided by registration to circumvent both the limited lifespan given to a patent and the limited subject matter that other intellectual property rights embody.

Broadly, there are two justifications for allowing an invention the protection that is afforded by patent registration. The first is that a patent registration provides an incentive to create, since it endows the patent holder with a time-limited monopoly during which the costs of research and development leading to the invention may be recouped. The second justification is that the patent application, which provides details of the invention, allows others to use such information for equally innovative inventions, so long as they do not trespass on the ground covered by the patent itself.

However, once the patent expires, it is open to competitors of the patent owner to enter the market by working the invention. At this point, the cost of the article embodying the patent may well decrease, since those who are exploiting the expired patent do not have to carry the original costs of research and development.[47] It is this latter feature of the patent system that demonstrates the attraction for a proprietor of an expired patent to seek to protect its invention by other means, including the potentially unlimited protection afforded by trademark registration.

It is precisely for this reason that Philips Electronics obtained trademark registration for a depiction of a three-headed shaver when applied to electronic shavers in the United Kingdom In this case, Philips had marketed the three-headed rotary shaver, with its head arranged in an equilateral triangle, since 1966. Originally protected by patent registration, the patent had expired and, in 1985, Philips registered its two dimensional depiction of a three-headed shaver as a trademark. Until Remington Consumer Products began marketing its own rotary shaver, with a similar head design but with the mark 'Remington' prominently displayed, rotary shavers were unique to Philips. In the event, Philips sued Remington for trademark infringement and Remington countered by arguing that Philips' trademark was invalid. In the High Court, it was agreed that Philips' registration would be treated as a three-dimensional mark.[48] A key issue in this case was how to interpret the wording of Article 3(1)(e) of the European TM Directive, which applies specifically to shape marks. According to this article, a sign will not be registered as a trademark when it consists exclusively of a shape that results from the nature of the goods themselves, a shape that is necessary to obtain a technical result, or a shape that gives substantial value to the goods for which registration is sought. In the Philips case, Remington argued that the Philips mark, treated as a three-dimensional shape, fell at all three hurdles, although in this and subsequent judgments, the real controversy related to whether the shape was *necessary* to obtain a technical result.[49] In his judgment, in the high court, Jacob held, against the Philips' argument, that this prohibition was effective even if there were other shapes that could obtain the same result. The Court of Appeal (CA) took a similar view, noting that the purpose of the prohibition of trademark registration for functional shapes arose from a concern 'that to enable monopolies granted in respect of patents, registered designs and the like to be extended by trade mark registration, would be contrary to the public interest unless justifiable on grounds of the public good'.[50] The CA then went on to suggest that the proper question to ask in relation to this prohibition was, 'Does the shape solely achieve a technical result whether or not other shapes might obtain the same result?' In the event, the CA held that Philips's mark did indeed fall at this hurdle. Somewhat earlier, a Swedish case between the same two protagonists on similar facts was decided in Philips's favour. The Swedish court held that Philips's trademark was not necessary to obtain a technical result, because the same result could be obtained without any considerable change in cost or efficiency by the use of a number of different shaving heads.[51]

Because of the uncertainty regarding the relationship between trademark registration and functional shapes reflected in the differing outcomes in the UK and Swedish courts, the CA decided to ask the ECJ for a definitive interpretation of the relevant provision of the directive. In the event, the ECJ preferred the UK interpretation of necessity.[52] According to the ECJ, where the essential functional characteristics of a shape of a product are attributable solely to the technical result, Art. 3(1)(e) second indent precludes the registration of a sign consisting of that shape, even if the technical result can be achieved by other shapes.[53] It noted that this approach to Art. 3(1)(e) reflects the legitimate aim of not allowing individuals to use registration of a mark in order to acquire or perpetuate exclusive rights relating to technical solutions.[54]

This was not the end of the matter, however. In 2005, Philips again sued Remington, on the basis that it had infringed an existing trademark registration for a three-headed shaver, although, in this case, its trademark included, unlike its earlier mark, a raised face plate of a cloverleaf design, which it claimed was (although performing a technical function) an embellishment and unnecessary for the shaver to function. Once again, both the High Court[55] and the Court of Appeal ruled against Philips. The latter held, *inter alia*, that the question to be asked was whether the cloverleaf design had separate 'eye impact'. If it did not, it could not overcome the effective functionality of the shape protected by the Philips trademark as a whole. Once again, the CA noted that the purpose of refusing to register a functional design as a trademark ensured that the competition between the would-be proprietor and competitors who wished to sell goods of the same shape was not distorted.

Under US trade mark law, it is accepted that trade dress, a term describing the external appearance of a product, can be protected as trademark, provided it is recognized by consumers as a sign that identifies and distinguishes source.[56] However, a general public interest doctrine has been applied by the courts in order to ensure that functional elements of trade dress are excluded from trademark protection. This can cover any aspect of trade dress, including colour.[57] 'The exclusion of functional designs from the subject matter of trademark law is intended to ensure effective competition, not just by the defendant, but also by other existing and potential competitors'.[58]

The aim is to keep innovative products outside the exclusionary scope of trademark rights. The essence of functionality has been captured in Inwood Laboratories Inc. *v.* Ives Laboratories, finding that a product feature is functional if it is essential to the use or purpose of the article or if it affects the cost or quality of the article.[59] This fits very well with Majaro's definition of innovation; he defines creativity as the 'thinking process that helps us to generate ideas' and innovation as the 'practical application of such ideas towards meeting the organization's objectives in a more effective way'; this, in turn, will result in a product that is 'new, better, faster, cheaper, and more aesthetic'.[60]

In TrafFix, the US Supreme Court considered the overlap between patent and trademark protection and held that the existence of an expired patent should imply that the design covered by the patent was functional.

Having noted that '[C]opying is not always discouraged or disfavored by the laws which preserve our competitive economy', Justice Kennedy stressed:

> A utility patent is strong evidence that the features therein claimed are functional. If trade dress protection is sought for those features the strong evidence of functionality based on the previous patent adds great weight to the statutory presumption that features are deemed functional until proved otherwise by the party seeking trade dress protection. Where the expired patent claimed the features in question, one who seeks to establish trade dress protection must carry the heavy burden of showing that the feature is not functional, for instance by showing that it is merely an ornamental, incidental, or arbitrary aspect of the device.[61]

TRADEMARKS AND THE PROTECTION OF INNOVATIVE CONCEPTS

The approach taken by the ECJ and the US Courts has shown a determination not to allow registered trademarks to monopolize the use of functional shapes once they can no longer claim patent protection. The ECJ has taken a similar restrictive approach to an attempt to register the idea or 'concept' of an innovative product; in this case, the transparent bin or collection chamber for a vacuum cleaner that had been introduced by Dyson Ltd. in 1993.[62] In particular, as noted by the ECJ, Dyson did not seek to obtain registration of a trademark in one or more particular shapes of a transparent bin, but rather to obtain registration of trademark in the bin itself, such that the trademark application covered all conceivable shapes of a transparent collecting bin.[63] According to the ECJ, under Art. 2 of the TM Directive, the subject matter of an application for registration must satisfy three conditions. It must be a sign; it must be capable of graphic representation; it must be distinctive.[64]

The ECJ held that the Dyson application did not meet the first criterion. It was not a sign, but a concept. In particular, 'the shape, the dimensions, the presentation and composition of that subject-matter [of the trademark application] depended on the vacuum cleaner models developed by Dyson and on technological innovations. Likewise, transparency allows for the use of various colours'.[65] As a result, the concept of a transparent collection chamber is a 'mere property' of the product concerned and is not a 'sign' as defined in the Directive. The ECJ suggested that to find otherwise would be to hand Dyson an unfair advantage against its competitors, since it would prevent them from marketing vacuums with a transparent collecting bin and hence would distort competition with the European Union.

CONCLUSION

This chapter has examined a variety of ways in which the law relating to trademark protection can both enhance and deter innovation. A trademark as a badge of origin may enhance competition by allowing consumers to make choices between similar goods and by motivating proprietors to maintain the standard of their products. From this perspective, it has also been noted that the law on comparative advertising may facilitate market entry, since it allows newcomers to a market to identify their goods through the association that consumers might make with an already established trademark. However, if one turns to the market effect of trade marks *qua* brands, a well-known brand may act as a disincentive to market entry through its advertising function or by allowing trademark proprietors entry to a new market not through innovation, but rather through the acquisition of an already established brand. Finally, trademark proprietors may seek to use their marks to protect the functionality of their goods once other intellectual property rights such as patents have expired.

The courts in both the United Kingdom and the United States seem to have sought to steer a middle course between the protection afforded to the origin function of a trademark, which may be seen as clearly in the interest of consumers, and the protection afforded to the brand attributes of a trademark, which are seen to be for the benefit of the trademark proprietor.[66] Similarly, in cases involving signs that have a functional role, both the European Union and the United States have sought to protect both innovation and competition by refusing to register such signs as trademarks. It may even be suggested that, given the enormous value of many well-known brands and the easily recognizable functional attributes of some, the courts, both in Europe and the United States, should be commended for continuing to steer such a middle course. It does, however, remain to be seen whether the courts will be able to maintain this balanced approach in the future. The value of many companies is increasingly determined by the value of their brands, rather than by product quality, the material means of production, and the skill of the work force that manufactures them. Thus, the courts will continue to face the question of whether it is their role to protect the increasing value of trademarks as brands, or whether they should ensure that competition, rather than market dominance, dictates how trademark law will be applied.

LIST OF CASES

Application of David Crystal, Inc., 296 F.2d 771, 132 U.S.P.Q. 1 (1961)
Arsenal Football Club *v.* Reed [2003] 1 C.M.L.R. 12
Barclays Bank *v.* RBS Advanta [1996] R.P.C. 307
BMW AG *v.* Deenik [1999] E.C.R, I-905

Brunswick Corp. *v.* British Seagull, 35 F.3d 1527, 1532, 32 U.S.P.Q.2d 1120 (Fed. Cir. 1994)

Coca Cola Trade Marks [1985] F.S.R. 315, [1986] R.P.C. 421 (HL)

Dyson Ltd. *v.* Registrar of Trade Marks [2007] 2. C.M.L.R. 14.

Elizabeth Florence Emanuel *v.* Continental Shelf [2006] E.C.R. I-7605

Fraser *v.* Thames *v.* Thames Television Ltd. [1983] 2 All ER 101

Hoffman-La Roche *v.* Centrafarm [1978] E.C.R. 1139

Ida Line Aktiebolag *v.* Philips Electronics NV (Case No. T7–1316–94) [1997] E.T.M.R. 377.

Intel Corp. Inc. *v.* CPM United Kingdom Ltd. [2006] E.W.H.C. 1878 (Ch), [2007] E.W.C.A. Civ. 431

Koninklijke Philips Electronics NV *v.* Remington [2002] 2 C.M.L.R. 52

Koninklijke Philips Electronics NV *v.* Remington Consumer Products Ltd. [2005] F.S.R. 17 (High Court)

Koninklijke Philips Electronics NV *v.* Remington Products Australia Pty (1999) 44 I.P.R. 551 (Fed Ct. Aus); Richardson (2000)

L'Oreal *v.* Bellure [2006] E.W.H.C. 2355 (Ch), [2007] E.W.C.A. Civ 968

Michael Hölterhoff *v.* Ulrich Freiesleben [2002] E.C.R. I-4187

O2 Holdings Ltd v Hutchison 3G UK Ltd [2008] E.C.R. 0

Philips Electronics BV *v.* Remington Consumer Products [1999] R.P.C. 283.

Philips Electronics NV *v.* Remington Consumer Products [1999] R.P.C. 890

Philips Electronics NV *v.* Remington Consumer Products Ltd. [2006] E.W.C.A. 16

Re Dassler, 134 U.S.P.Q. 265 (TTAB 1962)

Rewe-Zentral *v.* OHIM (LITE) [2002] E.C.R. II-705

Societe Comptoir de l' Industrie Cotonniere Etablissements Boussac *v.* Alexander's Department Stores 299 F2d 33, 132 USPQ 475 (1962).

Toshiba Europe GmbH *v.* Katun Germany GmbH [2001] E.C.R. I-7945

Toy Corp. *v.* Plawner Toy Mfg. Corp., 685 F.2d 78, 216 U.S.P.Q. 102, (3d Cir. 1982)

TrafFix Devices, Inc. *v.* Marketing Displays, Inc., 69 USLW 4172, 532 US 23, 58 USP.Q.2d 1001 (2001)

Two Pesos Inc. *v.* Taco Cabana 120 L. Ed. 2d 615, 112 S. Ct. 2753, 23 U.S.P.Q.2d 1081 (1992)

NOTES

1. Arsenal Football Club *v.* Reed, Case C-206/01 1 CMLR 382, para. 48. See also, *inter alia*, Case 102/77 Hoffman-La Roche [1978] E.C.R. 1139, para. 7.

2. In T-79/00 Rewe-Zentral *v.* OHIM (LITE) [2002] ECR II-70 the Court of First Instance linked distinctiveness—the essential requirement for trade mark protection—with the function of a trademark as product identifiers. Signs devoid of any distinctive character are signs that are regarded as incapable of performing the essential function of a trademark, namely that of identifying the origin of the goods or services, thus enabling the consumer who acquired them to repeat the experience, if it proves to be positive, or to avoid it, if it proves to be negative, on the occasion of a subsequent acquisition.
3. Landes and Posner (1987: 269); Dogan and Lemley (2004: 786).
4. Ibid., 270.
5. International Trade Mark Association, *Brand Valuation*. Available HTTP: <http://*www.inta.or/info/basics.valuation.html*>.
6. de Chernatony and Riley (1997: 45). The authors suggest that attributes 1–4 are the creation of the brand owner (what they term an 'input perspective on brands', and attributes 5–8 represents the blends that the brand holder's input with the consumers' output. Attribute 9 acknowledges that brands evolve from an input to an output perspective.
7. Attributes 5–8 in the previously mentioned definition, Smith (2003: 106). See also Davis (2006: 97–123).
8. Haigh (1998: 1).
9. Attributes 6–8 of the aforementioned definition, Tollington (2001). See also Haigh (1998: 1) and Aaker and Joachimsthaler (2000: 48).
10. Elizabeth Florence Emanuel *v.* Continental Shelf [2006] E.C.R. I-7605.
11. Ibid, para. 48.
12. First Council Directive of 21 December 1988 to approximate the laws of the Member States relating to trademarks (89/104/EEC). The final interpretation of the Directive falls to the European Court of Justice.
13. Art. 4(1)(a)-(b); Art. 5(1)(a)-(b).
14. Art. 4(4); Art. 5(1)(2),
15. The nature of the 'link' that would operate to dilute or tarnish a registered trademark has been questioned in some recent Court of Appeal decisions, for example, L'Oreal *v.* Bellure [2007] and Intel Corp. Inc. CPM United Kingdom Ltd. [2006]. The Court of Appeal has now addressed this issue to the ECJ. See also, C. Howell, 'Case comment: Intel: A mark of distinction?', EIPR ,2007, 29(11), 441–445; I. Simon, 'Dilution in the United States and the European Union, and beyond: Part I: International obligations and basic definitions' J.I.P.L.P. (2006a), 1(6), 406–412 and 'Part II: Testing for blurring', J.I.P.L.J. (2006b), 1(10), 64–659.
16. Note that trademarks can also be protected, irrespective of registration, through unfair competition systems when they become tools for deceiving consumers or denigrating competitors.
17. Schecter (1927): 813–833.
18. Ibid.: 831. Interestingly, at the time Schecter made this argument, there was an increasing separation between the manufacture of goods and the retail outlets through which they passed. Schecter noted that the growth in the value of trademarks coincided with the decline of the 'antiquated theory of neighborhood trade' (824); Davis (2006): 110.
19. Brown (1948).
20. Ibid.: 1631.
21. Ibid.: 1632. See also Nelson (1974), who underlines at 749 that consumers will be rarely deceived as long as they follow the rule 'believe an advertisement for experience qualities when it tells about the functions of a brand;

do not believe the advertisement when it tells how well a brand performs that function'. Landes and Posner (1987): 291.

22. Landes and Posner (1987): 274–275.
23. Litman (1999): 1717–1735.
24. Ibid.: 1726–1727. However, an alternative view was offered by one brand manager, who suggested that, 'technological innovation makes possible customizing of products to ever-smaller target groups', without specifying what that innovation is. M. Goodyear (1996).
25. Muthukrishnan and Wathieu (2007): 1.
26. An example raised by Landes and Posner (1987): 291.
27. Mudambi, Doyle and Wong (1997): 433–446.
28. RHM valued its nonacquired brands at £678 million and its tangible assets at less than £400 million. Haigh (1998): 1, 49. See also. Mcauley (2003) and Davis (2006): 102.
29. Paba (1991): 15, 21–43. White goods include washing machines, refrigerators and so on.
30. Ibid.: 21.
31. Ibid.: 22. In an earlier study (Paba 1986), Paba shows how the white goods industry in Italy grew in part from its willingness to supply unbranded products to established companies with a strong brand.
32. Thomas (1989): 188–189.
33. It is even the case that such brand extension may involve not just a related product but even an entirely new product which embodies a patented invention. Interview with Jack Keenan, Grand Cru Consulting Ltd., 14 March 2008.
34. Blackett (1998): 88.
35. Ford bought only its car marking operation. The Swedish company continues to manufacture trucks and buses.
36. Buerkle (1999).
37. Lindemann (2003): 29. Lindemann also notes that Samsung, 'a leading electronics group, invests heavily in its intangibles, spending about 7.5% of annual revenues on R&D and another 5% on communications'. Another high profile merger was that of Guinness and GrandMet (whose brand assets included Gilbey's Gin and Croft sherry) in 1997. Later, Diageo went on to acquire with Pernod Ricard, the Seagram drinks company, to create the world's largest wine and spirit grouping.
38. Teather and Treanor (2007).
39. Gaibraith (2007).
40. Hampus Engellau, cited in William and Castelli (2007). In the event, Ford decided not to sell.
41. For a review of the legal issues see Jacoby (1994); Llewelyn (1999); Barendt and Firth (eds.) (1999); and Carty (2002).
42. J. Laddie in Barclays Bank *v.* RBS Advanta [1996] RPC 307.
43. Societe Comptoir de l' Industrie Cotonniere Etablissements Boussac *v.* Alexander's Department Stores 299 F2d 33, 132 USPQ 475 (1962).
44. See Michael Hölterhoff *v.* Ulrich Freiesleben [2002] E.T.M.R. 7 and BMW [1999] ECR I-905 as examples of the Court's trademarks jurisprudence and Toshiba Europe *v.* Katun Germany GmbH [2001] ECR I-7945 as an example of its position on comparative advertising.
45. In Case C-533/06, O2 Holdings Ltd *v.* Hutchison 3G UK Ltd.
46. The one exception is the protection given to an idea in the law relating to confidential information. But, even here, ideas will only be protected if they are clearly identifiable, original, of potential commercial attractiveness, and capable of reaching fruition. Fraser *v.* Thames *v.* Thames Television Ltd. [1983] 2 All ER 101.

47. For a discussion of justifications for the patent system, see Cornish and Llewelyn (2007): 132–142.
48. Until the implementation of the 1994 Trade Marks Act in the United Kingdom, it was not possible to register a shape as a trademark, even if it was acting as a badge of origin. The courts took the view that to allow shapes to be registered would create an unhealthy monopoly, since it would prevent other traders from using these shapes for functional reasons. Coca Cola Trade Marks [1985] F.S.R. 315 at 324 as per Sir Denys Buckley in the Court of Appeal. Coca Cola Trade Marks [1986] R.P.C. 421 House of Lords.
49. Philips Electronics BV *v.* Remington Consumer Products [1999] R.P.C. 283.
50. Philips Electronics NV *v.* Remington Consumer Products [1999] R.P.C. 890 at 816.
51. See Ida Line Aktiebolag *v.* Philips Electronics NV (Case-T71316/94) [1997] ETMR 377.
52. Koninklijke Philips Electronics NV *v.* Remington Consumer Products Ltd (Case C-2999/9) (2002) E.T.M.R. 995.
53. Koninkijke *v.* Remington at para. 82.
54. Koninkijke *v.* Remington at para. 83. The battle between Philips and Remington has been repeated across the globe. Thus in Australia the courts held that the three-headed shaver could not be registered as a trademark because it was unclear whether it functioned as a trademark or was a functional device to facilitate shaving. Koninklijke Philips Electronics NV *v.* Remington Products Australia Pty [1999] 816 (Fed Ct. Aus); Richardson (2000): 314–319. See also Firth, Gredley and Maniatis (2001) and Suthersanen (2003).
55. Koninklijke Philips Electronics NV *v.* Remington Consumer Products Ltd. [2005] F.S.R. 17 (High Court); Philips Electronics NV *v.* Remington Consumer Products Ltd. [2006] Court of Appeal. In the High Court, Rimer LJ pointed out that Philips had, on the same facts, failed to persuade courts in France, Germany, and Italy, where, in each case, the Court ruled that the clover-leaf design was functional.
56. For example in Toy Corp. *v.* Plawner Toy Mfg. Corp., 685 F.2d 78, 216 U.S.P.Q. 102, (3d Cir. 1982) the shape and colour combinations of the 'rubic cube puzzle' constituted protectable trade dress; in Two Pesos Inc. *v.* Taco Cabana 120 L. Ed. 2d 615, 112 S. Ct. 2753, 23 U.S.P.Q.2d 1081 (1992) the detailed description of the theme of restaurant following was also considered protectable trade dress; in Application of David Crystal, Inc., 296 F.2d 771, 132 U.S.P.Q. 1 (1961) two coloured lines on socks were found not inherently distinctive and not registerable in the absence of distinctiveness acquired through use; in Re Dassler, 134 U.S.P.Q. 265 (TTAB 1962) the three Adidas lines have been found to have acquired distinctiveness through use.
57. For example, in Brunswick Corp. *v.* British Seagull, 35 F.3d 1527, 1532, 32 U.S.P.Q.2d 1120 (Fed. Cir. 1994) the colour 'black' was found to be functional for outboard boat motors: it decreased the apparent size of the motor and ensured compatibility with many different boat colours.
58. The Restatement (Third) of the Law of Unfair Competition, para. 17. According to McCarthy (1992: xx), functionality 'is a potent public policy, for it trumps all evidence of actual consumer identification of source and all evidence of actual consumer confusion caused by an imitator'.
59. US 844, 214 USPQ 1 (1982).
60. Majaro (1988: 6–7).
61. USLW 4172, 58 U.S.P.Q.2d 1001.
62. Dyson Ltd. *v.* Registrar of Trade Marks (Case-C321/03) [2007] E.T.M.R. 34.
63. Ibid,, paras 19–20.

64. Ibid., at para. 28.
65. Ibid., at para. 37.
66. See for example, Davis (2003).

BIBLIOGRAPHY

Aaker, D. and E. Joachimsthaler (2000) *Brand Leadership*, New York: The Free Press.
American Law Institute (1993) *Restatement (Third) of the Law of Unfair Competition*, Washington: American Law Institute.
Blackett, T. (1998) *Trademarks*, Basingstoke: Macmillan Press.
Brown, R. S., Jr. (1948) 'Advertising and the public interest: Legal protection of trade symbols', first published in *Yale Law Journal*, 57: 165–205; reprinted in (1999) *Yale Law Journal*, 108: 1619–1659.
Buerkle, T. (1999) 'US firm to pay $6.5 billion to bolster presence in Europe: Ford secures deal to buy Volvo cars', *International Herald Tribune*, 29 January 1999.
Carty, H. (2002) 'Registered trade marks and permissible comparative advertising' *European Intellectual Property Review*, 24(6): 294–300.
Cornish, W. and D. Llewelyn (2007) *Intellectual Property: Patents, Copyright, Trade Secrets, Trade Marks and Allied Rights* 6th edition, London: Sweet & Maxwell.
Davis, J. (2003) 'To protect or serve? European trade mark law and the decline of the public interest', *European Intellectual Property Review*, 25(4): 180–187.
Davis, J. (2006) 'The value of trade marks: Economic assets and cultural icons', in Y. Gendreau (ed.), *Bridging Aesthetics and Economics*, Montreal: Editions Themis: 97–126.
De Chernatony, L. and F. D. Riley (1997) 'Brand consultants' perspective on the value of the "brand"', *Marketing and Research Today*, 25(1): 45–52.
Dogan, S. L. and M. Lemley (2004) 'Trademarks and consumer search costs on the internet', *Houston Law Review*, 41: 777–838.
Firth, A., H. Gredley and S. Maniatis (2001) 'Shapes as trade marks: Public policy, functional considerations and consumer protection', *European Intellectual Property Review*, 23(2): 86–99.
Gaibraith, R. (2007) 'Private equity firms ready to cash in on luxury brands', *International Herald Tribune*, 27 September 2007.
Goodyear, M. (1996) 'Divided by a common language: Diversity and deception in the world of global marketing', *Journal of the Market Research Society*, 38(2): 105–122.
Haigh, D. (1998) *Brand Valuation: Understanding, Exploiting and Communicating Brand Values*, London: Financial Times.
Howell, C. (2007) 'Case comment: Intel: A mark of distinction?', *European Intellectual Property Review*, 29(11): 441–445.
Jacoby, J., A. Handlin and A. Simonson (1994) 'Survey evidence in deceptive advertising cases under the Lanham Act: An historical review of comments from the bench', *Trademark Mark Reporter*, 84: 541.
Landes, W. M. and R. A. Posner (1987) 'Trademark Law: An economic perspective', *Journal of Law and Economics*, 30(2): 265–309.
Lindemann, J. (2003) 'Brand valuation', in R. Clifton and J. Simmons (eds.), *Brands and Branding*, Princeton: Bloomberg Press.
Litman, J. (1999) 'Breakfast with Batman: The public interest in the advertising age', *Yale Law Journal*, 108: 1717–1735.

Llewelyn, D. (1999), 'The use of competitors' trade marks in advertising: Honest, fair or not?', in E. Barendt, E. and A. Firth (eds.), *Yearbook of Copyright and Media Law*, 1999, Oxford: Oxford University Press: 67–68.

Maniatis, S. (1997) 'Competition and the economics of trade marks', in A. Sterling (ed.), *Perspectives on Intellectual Property (Vol. 2): Intellectual Property & Market Freedom*, London: Sweet and Maxwell.

Majaro, S. (1988) *The Creative Gap: Managing Ideas for Profit*, London: Longman.

McAuley, T. (2003) 'Brand family values'. Available HTTP: <http://www.cfo.com>, accessed 31 December 2003.

McCarthy, T. (1992) *McCarthy on Trademarks and Unfair Competition*, St. Paul: West.

Mudambi, S. M., P. Doyle and V. Wong (1997) 'The exploration of branding in industrial markets', *Industrial Marketing Management*, 24: 433–446.

Muthukrishnan, A. V. and L. Wathieu (2007) *Ambiguity Aversion and the Power of Established Brands*, EMST Working Paper 07–005, Berlin: European School of Management and Technology.

Nelson, P. (1974) 'Advertising as information', *Journal of Political Economy*, 82: 729–754.

Paba, S. (1986) '"Brand-naming" as an entry strategy in the European white goods industry', *Cambridge Journal of Economics*, 10: 305–318.

Paba, S. (1991) 'Brand reputation, efficiency and the concentration process: A case study', *Cambridge Journal of Economics*, 15: 21–43.

Richardson, M. (2000) 'Australia intellectual property law: The form/function dilemma—A case study of the boundaries of trade mark law and design law', *European Intellectual Property Review*, 22(7): 314–319.

Schecter, F. I. (1927) 'The rational basis of trade-mark protection', *Harvard Law Review*, XL: 813–833.

Simon, I. (2006a) 'Dilution in the United States and the European Union, and beyond: Part I: International obligations and basic definitions', *Journal of Intellectual Property Law and Practice*, 1(6): 406–412.

Simon, I. (2006b) 'Dilution in the United States and the European Union, and beyond: Part II: Testing for blurring', *Journal of Intellectual Property Law and Practice*, 1(10): 649–659.

Smith, S. (2003) 'The brand experience', in R. Clifton and J. Simmons (eds.), *Brands and Branding*, Princeton: Bloomberg: 97–112.

Suthersanen, U. (2003) 'The European Court of Justice in Philips *v.* Remington—Trade marks and market freedom', *Intellectual Property Quarterly*, 7: 257–283.

Teather, D. and J. Treanor (2007) 'Private equity: The human cost', *Guardian Online*. Available HTTP: <http://www.guardian.co.uk/business/2007/feb/23/privateequity1>, accessed February 2007.

Thomas, G. (1989) 'Advertising in consumer goods industries: Durability, economies of scale and heterogeneity', *Journal of Law and Economics*, 32: 163–193.

Tollington, T. (2001) 'The separable nature of brands as assets: The United Kingdom legal and accounting perspective', *European Intellectual Property Review*, 23(1): 6–13.

William, T. and A. Castelli (2007) 'BMW among parties looking at Ford's Volvo cars, sources say', *Financial Times*, 25 May 2007.

Part III
Building Brands

7   Brands in Chains[1]

Paul Duguid

Typical brand wars of the industrial era include titanic confrontations such as GM *v.* Ford *v.* Chrysler or, in consumer goods, Pepsi *v.* Coke. In the late 1990s, the 'new economy' sector of personal computers (PC) produced a comparably aggressive war in which Microsoft, Intel, and Dell poured millions into their advertising budgets in the hope of being recognized as the premier PC brand. A moment's reflection reveals something distinctly different about that last grouping. Although certainly another battle of giants, it was, in one way at least, quite unlike the battle between the 'big three' car manufacturers, for Microsoft provides software and Intel provides microprocessors for Dell computers. These three live in the same supply chains; GM, Ford, and Chrysler do not. Microsoft *v.* Intel *v.* Dell was, nonetheless, a brand war, this chapter argues, because brands play an important role in the 'vertical' competition (Bresnahan and Richards 1999) between complementary firms within a supply chain. Within chains, that is, firms that must cooperate often engage in a struggle against one another both to control and to resist being controlled. Thus, certain supply chains may be quite as predatory as the food chain, for the spoils from these 'zero sum' supply chain struggles are significant. For the victor, they may produce increasing returns; for the loser diminishing returns. This chapter sets out to explain how these struggles develop and what part brands play in them.[2]

In the car industry, it would be absurd for the suppliers to wage a brand war against the car companies. In the PC world, things are evidently different. Yet, vertical competitions between partners who must cooperate are not another unprecedented outcome of the 'digital revolution'. On the contrary, such struggles have intriguing historical precedents. If we have failed to notice contemporary vertical brand wars, it may be because we have failed to see the historical ones. And the historical wars have been hard to see because we tend to take both supply chains and brands as relatively modern phenomena. 'Modern' brands are said to have arisen with the Chandlerian, hierarchical corporation (Wilkins 1994); the supply chain with its fall (Womack, Jones and Roos 1991). In what follows, I assume that both brands and chains are older and more connected than is generally assumed. A look at historical examples suggests that vertical struggles over branding or naming are likely to be particularly fierce in disaggregated supply chains that emerge as previously stable institutional arrangements collapse, especially in cases where resolving quality is an important but problematic issue. The PC chain meets both those conditions.

To make my case, I rely on three vignettes drawn from across a rather *longue durée*. I first explore the struggle in the PC chain a little further. This example shows that, even when struggles in chains are acknowledged, the contribution of brands is generally overlooked. I then look at the much earlier struggles of the book supply chain before modern copyright (roughly 1500–1710) and suggest that the emergence of the author's name as a kind of brand of authenticity was the surprising outcome of a vertical struggle. From there, I go to the supply chain for wine in the eighteenth and nineteenth century and argue that the label on the bottle was the field for a fierce vertical skirmish. By this odd route, I return to the PC chain to explore its genesis and development a little more closely. In conclusion, I argue that, although the differences between my cases in time and type are stark, a set of common issues clusters around the challenge of how—and by whom—quality is signalled to consumers. Comparing the three, we can see ways in which, within chains of complex goods (goods whose quality is not easily assessed by the buyer at the moment of purchase), there are struggles among the links to be the one that stamps quality, reliability, authenticity, and the like on the chain as a whole. In some cases, an institution plays the branding role and submerges rivalry by taking the major links inside a hierarchical organization. Without such an institution, chains have to achieve the same result. One way for this to happen is for one link to dominate. Thus, one way to see vertical struggles emerging is to look at situations in which hierarchical organizations, for one reason or another, collapse. This is a common element in the examples I have chosen.

STRUGGLES IN THE PC CHAIN

Supply chains readily appear as, on the one hand, revolutionary (Womack et al. 1991), and on the other, equitable arrangements of the modern economy. Fruin claims that chains offer 'the benefits of vertical integration without the disadvantages' (Fruin 1992: 259). Fruin's rather idyllic picture raises the question of whether such supply chains have simply made disadvantages disappear and, if not, where do they go?[3]

As Langlois (1992) notes, supply chains are critical to the production and distribution of the PC. That there may be disadvantages seems particularly likely in the case of these chains. Moore's (1965) 'law', for instance, suggesting that the cost of computers halves every 18 months, implies that the risk of holding PC inventory is potentially disastrous. And major high-tech firms have come close to disaster through poor inventory management.

Dell stumbled badly when it found itself overstocked with underperforming chips in 1989 (Koehn 2001). The same year, AMD, a chip-making rival to Intel, was similarly caught and pummelled for holding depreciating inventory. Even Cisco, a poster child of the 'network organization' (Castells 2002), was forced to face down embarrassment and write down $2.25 billion of excess inventory in 2001. 'Any strategy decreasing the holding period for inventory', Curry and Kenney argue about the PC sector, 'makes an immediate and significant contribution to profitability' (Curry and Kenney 2004: 124). One successful strategy involves persuading others to hold inventory for you. Koehn (2001) applauds Dell's ability to do this, but she does not explain who holds inventory for Dell, nor, given the loss-making potential of inventories, why they hold it. As the major firms pass high-risk inventory into the warehouses and onto the books of their suppliers (who nonetheless must supply parts 'just in time'), it would seem that some links in a chain are more powerful than others.

Furthermore, although some firms shed risk, they, nonetheless, manage to hold onto returns. Take, for example, one critically important component of the PC chain, hard disk development and production. The disk sector would figure high in any technological meritocracy. McKendrick describes it as 'among the most technologically innovative industries of the last fifty years', and the disks themselves as 'among the most valuable and technologically dynamic components of the computers that Dell and other PC manufacturers make' (McKendrick 2004: 142). In 2000, the last year of the 'dot com' boom, the six major suppliers of this central component for the PC collectively made 196 million disks, according to McKendrick. More remarkably, however, they collectively made no profit. By contrast, Dell reported profit margins of 7, Intel 13, and Microsoft 31 per cent. Indeed, Curry and Kenney report that Microsoft and Intel, alone, 'capture as much profit as all the other firms in the PC industry do' (Curry and Kenney 2004: 132).

Disk drive manufacturers remain subordinate partners in the chain. Their history of greater losses and lesser profits through bad times and good suggests, in response to Fruin's sunnier picture, that disadvantages are less likely to disappear than to be displaced along the supply chain to weaker partners. These end up carrying the depreciating inventory, idle capacity, and thinner margins for stronger partners, who capture the chain's profits. 'Virtual' integration, as Dell calls it—invoking one of those magical dot com terms—may not make the problems of vertical integration completely disappear. It merely puts them, from Dell's perspective, out of sight and off the balance sheet.

The disproportionate profitability of certain links in the PC chain and the inequitable distribution of risk and return suggests that power, too, is not evenly distributed among the partners in a supply chain. This is not entirely surprising. Chains, by definition, are not perfect markets, a standard mechanism for apportioning risk. Richardson (1972) noted how, supposedly, market relations can, in practice, be much closer to conventional hierarchical control (or 'direction' as he put it) than to the market. Richardson is relatively silent, however, on what can make the sorts of relations found in supply chains tilt from market towards direction (or vice versa). In certain chains, I suggest, brands help to allocate power.

Yet, even when supply-chain tensions are acknowledged, brands are not part of conventional explanations. Supply chain dominance by Intel and Microsoft, for example, is explained by Gawer and Cusumano (2002) as 'platform leadership' in a technological meritocracy. Such an explanation makes the billions Intel spends on marketing seem utterly wasteful. Certainly, when Intel introduced its brand, many thought the idea absurd. Yet, as I try to show in what follows, Intel's marketing largesse may have been the firm's wisest investment since developing the microprocessor. In a world where technological absolutes like the gigahertz and megahertz have become puzzlingly variable and, more generally, where signalling superior quality to the consumer is an art, it may be the art of branding, as much as technological merit, that wins.

At this point, you might ask yourself if you know who made the disk drive in your PC.[4] But before we look further into PC technology, I want first to look back to earlier technologies of the book and the bottle, where the currency of names is better recognized and the distribution of power underwent significant historical shifts.

BOOKS IN CHAINS, 1500–1710

The great Whig historian, Macaulay, saw the end of press licensing in 1694/5, as a critical moment in the march of democratic progress: 'What a revolution they were making, what a power they were calling into existence', he wrote of Parliament as it unleashed the press. The event itself lacked commensurate grandeur: Macaulay had to confess, 'On the great question of principle . . . not a word was said' (Macaulay 1969 [1855]: IV, 122–123). Indeed, the event was less the triumph of good over evil than a standoff, following the collapse of its old regulatory structure, among what Williams (1961) describes as 'residual, dominant, and emergent' forces— a standoff, that is, between old and new links in the chain that brought books into production and out to the market.

By the 1690s, rapid developments in the press, both as a technology and as an institution, had left most interested parties—religious, political, industrial, and cultural, as well as 'the reading nation' (St. Clair 2004)—unsure where their interests lay. Among the rising 'interests' of the day, parliamentary politicians, who had the power to reimpose the old press restraints, recognized that all political quarrels—theirs, as well as those of their enemies—were mediated through the press (or pressed through the media) and if controls would work to their advantage while they were 'in', controls would be to their disadvantage when they were 'out'. At the same time, the Stationers' Company, hitherto the government's proxy means of press control, was having trouble subduing rebellion against what Milton called 'the old *patentees* and *monopolizers*' (Milton 1956: 505). Old settlements were coming apart under new pressures and, with most parties less willing to concede defeat than claim victory in what probably appeared as a zero-sum fight *avant la lettre*, print regulation entered an interregnum that lasted until 1709/10.[5]

Since Gutenberg, and until this point, governments throughout Europe attempting to control the press had usually co-opted printers to help them. The English Crown granted its first press patent in 1518, but, progressively overwhelmed by the growth in patent application, delegated controls. In 1557, the Crown chartered the Stationers' Company to regulate 'the mystery and art of stationery' (Blagden 1960: 19). Children of Adam Smith, we often think of the division of labour as a progressive affair—the solitary pin maker becoming an extended pin factory. In fact, new technologies often concatenate preexisting practices into new networks. This was the case with printing. The Company formalized a set of guild relations extending across the book trades and back well before the era of print. The new settlement included, as Johns has showed, 'binders, stitchers, concealers, sellers, publishers, and dispersers' (Johns 1998: 159), who had worked with 'scriveners' and 'writers' long before printing. On the other hand, those who did try vertical integration with the help of the new technology soon turned to chains. Caxton, the first English printer, had also been publisher, importer, and seller of his books. But as Blagden argues, 'economic pressure forced all but the wealthiest printers to limit their activities' (Blagden 1960: 24) and to work cooperatively within chains, which, at first, the printers with their new technologies more or less controlled.

Soon after the chartering of the Stationers' Company, individual stationers were granted patents not merely over individual books, but over classes of books—law books for one, psalters for another, music for a third, and so on. Such properties were valuable and, here and elsewhere, a market quickly developed trading rights that reflected the supply chain in books. A printer might hold the printing right but sell the right to the 'publisher's profit' to an 'undertaker', who might cede distribution rights to a bookseller and network of chapmen. As rights devolved and rents accrued, the Company developed significant internal tensions among the different trades over how profits were dispersed. Holding uneasy relations together, however, was the collective and extremely lucrative Company 'stock', in which members could buy shares and, occasionally, buy off dissent with a subcontract or a grant for the 'benefit of the poore' (Blagden 1960: 75). The Company controlled the stock, but with returns as high as 12 per cent over many years, challenges inevitably arose over who controlled the Company (St. Clair 2004: 59). In time, despite their name, the booksellers absorbed the publishing role of 'undertakers', yet kept a grip on the distribution network. So doing, they presented their rivals for control, the once powerful printers, with something of a supply monopoly and a distribution monopsony. The Company consequently presided over a growing rivalry and needed both its rents and political power to control the tensions.

The onset of the English Civil War (1641–1642), ending licensing and the old monopolies, disturbed this arrangement. Printers found new sources of capital and copy from the proliferating opposition groups and built their own distribution networks of hawkers and mercuries to circumvent the booksellers and their chapmen. But Parliament—as fearful of radicals as of Cavaliers—soon restored the old privileges. With these, the prior settlement returned, giving control over the trade primarily to the booksellers. The Licencing Act [1662], which followed the restoration of the monarchy, managed to maintain the trade's power and subdue its internal struggle, but the Act had to be renewed every five years, so when Parliament failed to renew it in the tense political struggles from 1679 to 1685, during which the king learned to use the unlicensed press in his favour much as it had been used against him earlier (Harris 2005), the settlement was upset once again. At the low end of the market, a flurry of newspaper and ballad publishing developed outside the control of the Company and Parliament. But at the high end, entrepreneurial booksellers, learning perhaps from the resurgence of the printers in 1642, developed a different tactic that relied less on the statutes of the old Company. In particular, they formed strong financial alliances, or 'congers', to buy up rights in copy, to control distribution, and to project themselves as the public face of respectable, quality publishing. Once again, master printers faced a future as journeymen if they did not stand up to the booksellers and make their mark.

Though the printer was instrumental to the process of publishing (Maruca 2007), the printer's name dropped from significance on title pages with increasing frequency, and was rolled into the phrase 'printed for'.[6] The word *printer* came to designate the job of a mere mechanic, the word *bookseller* came to designate little more than the seller of books, and the word *publisher* was reserved for a new link that mediated between printer and bookseller and, directly or indirectly, represented the text to the reading public. By the end of the seventeenth century, congers of bookseller–publishers controlled the most lucrative 'copies' and, in the marketplace of books, represented in their names quality to the public. Jacob Tonson advanced his famous 'list' of great writers, from Benn, Congreve, and Dryden, among the living, to Jonson, Milton, and Shakespeare, among the dead, with his family name. With it thus well established, he could then use his name to provide warrants to the public for less famous authors and stables of anonymous editors and translators. The maverick publisher and editor John Dunton had once written about Richard Chiswell that 'His NAME at the Bottom of a Title Page, does sufficiently recommend the Book' (quoted in Johns 1998: 147). This sort of branding was not limited to warranting reliable editions of 'quality' literature. At the more dubious end of the trade, publishers signalled different kinds of literature—salutary, salubrious, and salacious—to different niches. In the early years of the eighteenth century, the dubious Edmund Curll had, as a recent biography has noted, 'worked to develop [his] modest toehold into something like a brand name, using energy and initiative to surf the wave of literary and political events, inciting and profiting from controversies political and local, packaging every kind of textual scrap into what he hoped would prove desirable commodities' (Baines and Rogers 2007: 24).

In this complex chain of cultural production, the author seems surprisingly unimportant. Indeed, once the copy was surrendered, the author, in general, made little further contribution. Except for the classical authors and the most famous of contemporary names, authors were generally 'fee-paid contractors' (St. Clair 2004: 145) to the booksellers—to whom even the famous authors were significantly beholden. 'The Stationers made "Shakespeare"', Erne reminds us, and lesser authors generally felt lucky to be used, let alone made (Erne 2003: 73). Given their profession, authors were not, of course, entirely silent about their subordination.[7] George Wither (1624) launched a suitably withering early attack on the system, and in 1644 the poet John Milton raised the authors' flag again in *Areopagitica* (1956), another high point in the defense of authorship. This appeared without the name of printer or bookseller on the title page. When Milton portrays the Catholic authors as pressed beneath the weight of licenses, it's not hard to sense that he feels the weight of the booksellers pressing at the bottom of English title pages: 'Sometimes 5 *Imprimaturs* are seen together dialogue-wise in the Piatza of one Title page, completing and ducking each to the other with their shav'n reverences, whether the Author, who stands by in perplexity at the foot of his Epistle, shall to the Presse or to the spunge' (Milton 1956: 469).

Authors were not to stand by for much longer, though their final, central role was more thrust upon them than achieved by their own hand. As the printers and booksellers fought one another to a standstill, the author, to the surprise of many (authors included), emerged with the prize from the Statute of Anne [1709/10] as the presumptive bearer of copyright. But much as the end of licensing was anticlimatic, so was the emergence of the author. Though authorial rights were championed by such as Locke, Defoe, and Addison, and naturalized by history, the Statute was less the recognition of the significant signifying name in the chain than the acceptance of a compromise candidate in the battle waged by the Crown, Parliament, publishers, booksellers, and printers to regain control over printing. Each was probably more determined that their opponent would lose than that they would win. The publisher–booksellers, in particular, felt less threatened by victory for their subordinate partner, the author, who was beholden to them for their fame, than by the return of either licensing or the Company. To resolve the struggles that had raged within and over the print supply chain since 1694/5 and so to help stabilize the chain once again, power devolved to a new and comparatively neutral figure. To most contemporaries, the author did not seem then, as he or she does today, the rightful owner of this property. (Attorney General Thurlow would sum up the 'Statute of Anne' when arguing the famous case of Donaldson *v.* Beckett [1774] as 'a new law to give learned men a property they had not had before'; quoted in Loewenstein (2002: 15).) Rather, this copyright-owning author was little more than 'an instrumental convenience in regulatory struggles carried on within the book trade' (Lowenstein 2002: 49). The author, as Chartier concludes, was a proxy deployed by the booksellers:

> The only way that the booksellers . . . could reassert their traditional ownership was to plead for the recognition of the author's perpetual right . . . Thus, they had to invent the author as proprietor of his works.
>
> Chartier (2003): 17

Though given title to a key asset in the chain, the author's name did not immediately rise to authenticate the chain in the way it does today. Booksellers were given continuing rights in the copy they already held. That of dead authors did not expire for 21 years; that of the living was renewable for two terms of 14. And following 1731 and 1738, many booksellers simply ignored the Statute of Anne and the author, claiming that common law rights made their copy 'eterne' (as Shakespeare had once hinted) and relying on congers and capital to help enforce their case (Deazley 2005). It took the (surprisingly narrow) decision in Donaldson *v.* Beckett, a battle among booksellers, to deny this claim. But by then, the publishers had turned once again to their collaborative congers, raising through them large sums to publish fine editions whose claim to 'quality'—to be complete, correct, authentic, or authoritative—was, in part, an attempt to stamp the publishers' old authority on the chain in spite of the authors' due or the public domain, and so to retain control of a disaggregated chain.

The strategy met with a certain success, though with the rise of Romanticism it became increasingly difficult to erase those authors' names that had, in Shakespeare's words, 'become a brand'.[8] Even today, the struggle between author and publisher remains one that is resolved differently in different chains. Publishers are still instrumental in the achievement of celebrity, making names; though, in most cases, once that is achieved, the author takes over the signifying power (hence publishers' contracts tend to include first-refusal on succeeding works), an intricate and unstable relationship suitably captured in the intricate prose of Henry James:

> He was Lambert Strether because he was on the cover, whereas it should have been for anything like glory, that he was on the cover because he was Lambert Strether.
>
> James (1962 [1903]): 54

It may seem like postmodern nihilism to deny authors their due as the creator of the work of art and so as the dispositive name in this cultural supply chain. Yet, we do not need to move far from the novel and the monograph to see how limited the author's warrant is. Most of those who cannot remember the name of the disk drive in their computer probably cannot remember the author of the last film they saw or television programme they watched. Though these forms are close to books in the way they are created, produced, and distributed, the author's warrant rarely extends to them.[9] In these chains, actors, networks, production companies, or performers often provide the name that brands and, by extension, controls the chain. Indeed, a struggle over who controls the chain in Hollywood precipitated the writers' strike of 2008—and it is a fitting reminder of a struggle extending back to the early modern period that the writers' union is still called a 'guild' (Cieply 2008).

Overall, the example of publishing suggests that when relatively stable, integrated, but also lucrative, settlements like the Stationers' Company fall apart, disaggregated supply chains will develop. And when quality is a problematic issue in these chains (over, in this instance, what is a reliable, trustworthy text), battles will develop over who can best assure the consumer and, in so doing, brand the chain. The battles can be fierce because the victor tends to accumulate rents commensurate with recognition. Out of this struggle in the book chain, the modern concept of the author, which seems quite natural and obvious today, emerged as an important, though not necessarily dominant, signifier. The struggle, I've suggested, is a 'zero sum' game, because those who do not control the chain will tend to be subordinated and controlled by those who do. Something similar, as we shall see, happened in the otherwise dissimilar chain that brought wine to British consumers in the eighteenth and nineteenth century.

WINE: TRANSNATIONAL TRADE IN CHAINS, 1700–1880

In 1874, an English journalist writing about the wine trade suggested that 1860 was the year of the 'disestablishment' of port wine (Turner 1874: 598), acknowledging in the comment that Portuguese wine in general, and port wine in particular, had benefited greatly from British foreign policy. As policy changed, so the wine trade was forced to change too.[10] Port's establishment had lasted a long time and produced a lucrative international trade. Its disestablishment led to long-distance fights among what had formerly been relatively quiescent trading partners.

The chain was set up at the end of the seventeenth century as souring Anglo-French relations led to repeated embargoes against French wine in England.[11] As a wine-producing country possessing good relations with the British government and good access for British merchant vessels, Portugal was an obvious place to turn to meet demand. It was always likely that a fickle market would turn back to French wine whenever peace was restored, but diplomacy and politics gave it a surer foothold. In 1702/3, the Methuen treaties between Britain and Portugal sought to lure the latter into alliance against France. The third, commercial treaty promised that Portuguese wines would be taxed at a rate one-third that of French wines. In return, the Portuguese agreed not to inhibit imports of English woollens with sumptuary laws. This treaty was threatened in 1713, when the British and French negotiated their own commercial treaty. An Anglo–French treaty seemed likely to succeed until it was pointed out that such an agreement would negate the Methuen Treaty. To the extent that negation threatened Portuguese wine, the loss of the treaty was not politically significant. But when the Portuguese hinted that they would retaliate by blocking English wool, Portuguese wine found it had widespread support, from England's landholding sheep barons to shepherds, wool carders, and stockingers. The Anglo–French commercial treaty was defeated. In the process, wearing wool hats and drinking port wine became patriotic, anti-French symbols.[12] Port became 'the Englishman's wine', embraced even by Jonathan Swift, who encouraged true patriots to

> Bravely despise *Champagne* at Court
> And choose to dine at home with port.
> Swift (1937) vol. II: 487

When port's reputation fell in the 1750s, the Portuguese government moved quickly to stabilize this important trade. In 1756, it created a quasi-government monopoly, the Wine Company, to oversee port production and exports. This was a remarkable body with powers not only to search and seize (much like the Stationers), but also to confiscate and exile (and, *in extremis*, to hang). The Wine Company demarcated a port wine region and set controls over every link of the wine chain from the planting of vines to the export of wine. So doing, in tandem with the Methuen Treaty, the Wine Company helped to secure an international supply chain in which Portuguese farmers grew the wine, British merchants exported it, and wine merchants in England imported and distributed it. Though the British complained about the Wine Company, which undoubtedly was draconian and capricious, under its rule they nonetheless managed to form a small, tight oligarchy that controlled up to 80 per cent of the market for English wines. Under Company rule, the wine regained its reputation and its hold on the British market.[13]

This wine supply chain worked effectively until the Napoleonic Wars. During this period, shipping was disrupted, but the greater threat came in the rapprochement between Britain and France that followed. Developing closer relations with France, Britain no longer needed Portugal as either a diplomatic or a trading partner. French and Spanish wine began to rival Portuguese wine in the British market, with the help of new advertising and marketing techniques. In 1834, following the Liberal victory in the Portuguese Civil War, the long unravelling of the Wine Company's power began, leading to its final dissolution in the 1860s. An increase of competition in Britain accompanied a loss of regulation in Portugal.

As wine consumption in Britain grew and the market expanded, the gullibility of new wine drinkers met the cupidity of wine merchants. Wine in general, and port in particular, were threatened by fabrications. Wine claiming to be port came not only from southern France and southern Spain, but also from the East End of London, where dreadful concoctions of spirits and colouring, occasionally spiced with alum and sulphuric acid, entered the market. Unscrupulous merchants found it easy and profitable to pass off elaborate but cheap confections as simple, but expensive, wines. High-end wines can make judging quality and price difficult.[14] Port, in particular, is problematic, because it is hard to predict how young or recently bottled wines, which tend to be harsh and crude, will taste when they are settled and ready for drinking. The better it tastes when young, the more reason to be suspicious; though, of course, wine that tastes foul may remain foul. As the great scientist Robert Boyle suggested, even sophisticated consumers may need an expert to judge for them: 'Epicures themselves in the choice of Wines, do oftentimes desire the Skillfull to Tast these Liquors for them, and relye more on the Palates of Others than their own' (Boyle, *Papers*, quoted in Shapin 1994: 219). The role of the experts was, then, a powerful one, and brokers who were as honest as they were skilful were hard to find. Even in the trade, skill was contentious, as demonstrated by the following note of 1793 from a wine exporter in Porto to an English wine merchant who had complained about a consignment of wine:

> The wines you mentioned could only at present be fit to put in the bottle not to use. We therefore persuade ourselves that the judgment found was premature. . . . We therefore request of you to suspend your opinion until they have had more time to mature.[15]

In the early nineteenth century, with new merchants setting up all the time, not only was skill elusive, as this letter suggests, so was honesty. Wine merchants formed a suspect profession. In 1815, one member of the port trade called them the 'most rotten set in London'. 'No branch of trade is prone to the practice of more chicanery and fraud than that of wine dealing', he continued, pointing out that the trade was prominent among lists of gazetted bankrupts.[16]

Faced with a growing crisis of quality, the port trade needed a means both to control its supply chains (particularly those links that were engaged in the fabrications) and to signal quality and reliability to consumers if it was to survive. Traditionally, wine was sold under the name of the merchant, who, by default, branded the wine. From the seventeenth to the early nineteenth century, it is overwhelmingly the merchant's name that appears in advertisements for wine. Changes in advertising practices for alcohol during the nineteenth century suggest that these names no long carried weight. Wine merchants tried to bolster their own names with others that were more reliable. After soliciting testimony from customers and scientists, they turned to their suppliers, whose reputation seemed less tarnished.

Since the early eighteenth century, wine had been advertised as 'neat as imported', to indicate that the importer had not blended the wine when it was received.[17] Blending could be legitimate (port, after all, is a blend of wine and spirits), but the distinction between blending and adulteration was often a fine one. The claim 'neat as imported', occurring repeatedly in eighteenth-century advertisements, suggests that customers preferred wine merchants to leave what they received alone. By implication, it seems that the consumer had more faith in the honesty of the exporter than in the importer. Faced with a lack of confidence from their customers, British wine merchants seem to have put forward the names of these previously unknown, and so unsullied, suppliers to shore up credibility. As one London wine merchant stated abjectly in testimony about the genuineness of his wine before a parliamentary committee, 'We rely upon the respectability of the house that ships them; we have no right to argue anything else' (House of Commons 1852: 440). Before too long, even quality merchants—those that served the carriage trade and were reluctant to advertise at all—started using the names of their suppliers. Hedges and Butler, a venerable merchant, began to note, for example, that the port it sold was 'Sandeman's shipping'.[18] But, in highlighting their suppliers' names, the wine merchants were simultaneously subordinating their own. With Sandeman's name as a warrant, consumers might now shop for Sandeman's wherever it could be found, thereby undermining not merely Hedges and Butler's clout, but also its very purpose in advertising. Rising from obscurity to prominence, though not through their own entrepreneurial activity . . . these new names (like the authors' names a century before) unsettled the established balance of power in the old chain and set newly identified links against old.

As they saw their names subordinate the formerly dominant British retailers downstream, the exporters also discovered that the way port was made helped them to resist subordination by all but the most powerful names from upstream. Most port reached Britain as a blend created by the exporters from the output from several producers. Thus, although the producer's name possessed a lot of authority in French wine, the process of blending in Portugal effectively dissolved the names of the port producers and gave distinction to the name of the exporter. The resistance to blending in England also put power in the hands of the exporter. Sandeman's 1834 was distinct from Offley's 1834, because Sandeman had blended it. Although those who liked Sandeman's blend were no longer confined to Hedges and Butler, they were confined to Sandeman. Against this strong point of the chain, only very well-established wine producers in Portugal or wine merchants in Britain managed successfully to oppose their own name.

In sum, as the institutions that helped construct the port-wine supply chain crumbled, actors in the chain itself—faced not only with their 'disestablishment' but also with aggressive competition from champagne, burgundy, Bordeaux, and sherry—struggled for their collective survival. Collective danger did not produce a wholly cooperative response, however. Rather, it revealed internal tensions over names and trademarks, which the courts in Britain, and eventually Parliament, were increasingly willing to protect. Brands became a means for one firm in the chain to subordinate, in a quasi-hierarchical fashion, other links, even though they had no formal control over them. All but the best retailers in England were forced to advertise others' names, and thereby subordinate their own, while paying for the privilege. At the other end of the chain, all but the best wine growers in Portugal gradually became contract grape farmers, whose produce was bought one year and disdained the next.

The rise to prominence of the export names represents a critical shift in signifying power, which had previously rested almost entirely with wine merchants. Gradually, this power was transferred up the chain to their historically more reliable suppliers, the exporters, who, in turn, subordinated their suppliers, the winemakers in inland Portugal.[19] The geographic distribution here indicates how the power inherent in a trademark can work along supply chains and over geographic distances, allowing some to dictate terms—in a way closer to 'direction' than to the market nexus, as Richardson (1972) puts it—to other links over which they have no formal control and from whom they are separated by large distances. The power of names to signal quality and exert authority across distances became particularly clear in the nineteenth century.

One problem with this argument is that 'modern brands' have not yet appeared in economic–historical theory. In the Chandlerian tradition, brands are purported to be the product of the modern corporations that arose towards the very end of the nineteenth century, after the landmark trademark legislation of the 1860s and '70s, and supply chains are generally deemed to arise with the fall of the Chandlerian organization.[20] Of course, supply chains did not only succeed the integration of business organizations, they also preceded it. And legislation did not so much bring modern branding practices into being as respond to practices that had become well established through the support of common and equity law. Equity courts, in particular, had acknowledged a right to trademarks for some time before laws were written. A detailed look at court cases reveals two intriguing points. First, in 'reported' trademark cases (that is, in the precedent-setting cases), alcohol is second only to medicines in the number of cases fought. (As medicines in the nineteenth century were usually laced with alcohol, it may be fairer to lump the two into a single category.) Thus, it would not be unreasonable to assume that alcohol cases represent dominant trends in case-made law. Second, a review of alcohol trademark cases of the third-quarter of the century reveals that a minority (seven out of 60) were canonical brand fights between like companies (Duguid 2003b). Bass did not fight with Guinness, Veuve Clicquot did not fight with Moët and Chandon, Hennessey did not fight with Martell, though all these companies litigated actively over marks—Hennessey, more than any firm from any sector. Rather, they fought with their suppliers and their distributors up and down their supply chains. Not just instruments of horizontal competition, alcohol brands were deployed in vertical struggles.[21]

It is unsurprising, then, to discover that when a rogue exporter threatened the port chain in the 1880s, British importers with well-established brand names, who should have been competing with one another, joined together (almost like the booksellers of the seventeenth century, or, as we shall see, Microsoft's antitrust opponents in the twentieth) to quash the threat that came from a supplier, with whom they would normally be expected to cooperate.[22]

In the wine trade, then, as in the book trade, the disruption of a settled system of provision—the Stationers' Company and the Wine Company—led to the development of a chain with more autonomous links than before. Within both sectors, links in the chain fought with one another to become the name by which the chain, as a whole, was recognized and its quality guaranteed. Those that won were in a position to dominate the chain as a whole and extend control over long distances and disparate players.

THE PC CHAIN

Do these stories of earlier supply chains have any bearing on modern technology chains like the PC supply chain? Does the packaging of wine have much to do with the packaging of chips? To address these questions, we need to understand a little more about the emergence of the PC chain.

In the 1970, larger than all its competitors combined, IBM dominated the US and computer market in a quasi-monopolistic fashion. In 1993, it sustained not only its first ever annual deficit, but at $5 billion, the largest loss in industrial history up to that time (Ferguson and Morris 1994). In the years between, its de facto monopoly had crumbled and a series of disaggregated supply chains replaced its hierarchical dominance. Like the firm itself, IBM's technology had also been closely bundled. Its remarkably successful 360 series held together hardware, central processing unit (CPU), operating system (OS) and applications. Most of its competitors were reduced to making 'IBM compatible' peripherals, a strategy that allowed IBM to lead and the competitors to follow, picking up crumbs that fell from the rich firm's table.

IBM's hierarchical strategy, however, best served a market dominated by firms just like itself and machines like those it sold. By the 1970s, Digital Equipment Corporation (DEC) created a new market with its VAX lines of minicomputers. These were favoured more by research labs and universities, a niche IBM mostly ignored, than by vertically integrated businesses, the niche IBM served. The VAX, like the 360, was more or less an all-in-one, all-or-nothing machine, bundling hardware, including the CVAX CPU, and its proprietary VMS operating system. Many DEC users, however, particularly those at universities, preferred the UNIX operating system, developed at AT&T, but advanced with the help of major universities.[23] By the early 1980s, as many as one in four of the VAX machines was running UNIX and, on top of it, third-party software (Sturgeon 2002). Around the same time, SUN's SPARC stations soon became popular, not only because of the SPARC RISC processor, but also because its proprietary UNIX OS, Solaris, allowed access to the growing library of UNIX software applications. Simultaneously, the personal computer was developing, and its manufacturers encouraged—indeed relied on—third-party software (such as, for Apple, the very successful VisiCalc), while relying on others to supply the CPU at the heart of the machine. The seams in the bundle that had sustained IBM and DEC were slowly coming apart. The era of the modular computer, built in an extended supply chain, was beginning (Langlois 1992).

Industry insiders at first regarded the PC as little more than a 'toy', but the rapid growth of a market for these cheap and relatively versatile machines made many, and particularly IBM, reconsider. A latecomer to this market, IBM decided to accelerate its entry by outsourcing the CPU (to Intel) and the OS (to the fledgling Microsoft). More used to doing everything in house, IBM management nonetheless relied, in part, on its copyright-protected ROM-BIOS chip to hold the chain together. Control of the BIOS, the critical link between the CPU and the rest of the hardware, it was assumed, would prevent anyone else in the chain from coordinating the hardware, the CPU, and the operating system. It would also prevent anyone else from building a rival, but compatible, BIOS. Thus, the rights in the BIOS and trademark-protected brand, it was thought, would allow IBM to retain control over its fledgling partners in the new supply chain and its lucrative market.

At first, the strategy was heralded as a remarkable success in 'complementary assets' and as a prototype for the future (Teece 1986). The commercial success of IBM's PC was less a tribute to the machine, however (it was not particularly innovative or powerful), and more to the firm's corporate brand. This helped to push the IBM PC into firms interested in PCs but suspicious of the 'home-brew' hobbyists and garage-bred entrepreneurs. American folklore said that 'nobody ever lost their job by buying IBM', and purchasing managers asked to buy these new machines seemed willing to buy IBM-branded PCs where they were unwilling to buy those of, for instance, Apple, a firm founded by long-hairs and phone *phreaks*. Moreover, a powerful advertising campaign helped to make the terms "IBM PC" and "PC" interchangeable. By the mid-1980s, for all but enthusiasts and hobbyists, a personal computer meant an IBM-branded PC. If you bought one of those, you had one of the world's most storied technology companies behind you.

This settlement all fell apart in 1982, when Compaq famously reverse-engineered IBM's BIOS without, the courts ruled over IBM's protests, infringing the company's critical intellectual property. When IBM failed to prevent an alternative BIOS from working with the Intel CPU and Microsoft OS, the door was left open for manufacturers to make PCs or 'IBM clones' without using any IBM technology. Powerful but not agile (which is why it outsourced the PC in the first place), IBM confronted a series of finely divided and rapidly evolving supply chains addressing a series of finely divided and rapidly evolving niches.

Using the same CPU and same OS, the 'clones' effectively worked as an IBM PC. Thus, clone makers who used that CPU and OS, which Intel and Microsoft proved willing to supply, managed, to a significant degree, to appropriate the benefits of the IBM brand—an assurance of quality—without having to defer to the brand holder. Cloned computers became known as 'IBM compatible PCs', and then just 'PCs', suggesting now that anything an IBM could do, a clone could do too, but more cheaply. With this shift came a fundamental transfer of signifying power. The Microsoft DOS and the Intel 8086 chip, previously subordinate to IBM's brand and familiar only to enthusiasts, now became the essential ingredients of a PC, and the term *PC*, itself, became 'semigeneric'. The previously little-known Intel and Microsoft, to whom IBM had inadvertently devolved power as the booksellers had to authors and the English wine merchants to previously unknown exporters, became, by the second half of the 1980s, the principal guarantors of what was 'compatible', and hence of quality, to the PC supply chain. To signal whether a particular bland white box was reliable and to assuage the doubts of purchasing managers, the critical indicators became 'Microsoft' and 'Intel', brands that had received their power from IBM, but now operated independent of it. As Andrew Grove, the CEO of Intel, later acknowledged, 'by choosing to base [the PC] on Intel's technology, [IBM] made Intel's microprocessors preeminent' (Grove 1997: 14). The shift gave these two new firms extraordinary, quasi-monopolistic powers, which both learned to wield over others, such as the disk drive manufacturers, in the supply chain.

Such power changed their competitive outlook. Intel undoubtedly worried about AMD, Zylog, and other chip makers, and devoted a good deal of money to keeping them at bay, principally by keeping them in court. But in competition for supply chain domination, its major competitor was Microsoft. Microsoft paid even less attention than Intel to its 'direct' competitors in the operating system market, CP/M, Apple, and even IBM's own OS/2. But it paid a lot of attention to Intel. And like Intel, it also paid a good deal of attention to the major hardware suppliers, the OEMs (Original Equipment Manufacturers), happy while these were in disarray, and concerned when one predominated, as Compaq did at first and Dell later. The major struggle in the PC world, then, was waged less between like firms in different supply chains than between complementary firms up and down the same chain. Weapons included technological development, IP protection, and marketing strategies.

Brands were a surprising weapon in what is generally thought of as a war of technological or 'platform' superiority. Intel stumbled upon the power of its brand in an early supply chain skirmish. When OEMs were slow to use the new 386 chip, Intel introduced its 'Red X' campaign. Advertisements showed the number '286' with a red 'X' through it and '386' uncrossed beside. AMD called the campaign 'trash marketing'; others simply thought it a waste of money. But in drawing attention to the CPU (or 'chip' as it was popularly known), Intel produced enough pressure among consumers to force the OEMs to upgrade. The achievement was a surprise to Intel, whose vice-president and director of marketing, Denis Carter, confessed:

> I didn't really know what a brand was. But it became evident that we had created a brand and that it made a difference in consumers' purchase plans.[24]

In 1991, AMD broke Intel's lock on the 386 supply chain by producing its own 386 chip, which was highly regarded. Intel responded, in part, by pushing out new chips (the 486 and the Pentium I and II), but also by redeploying the 'accidental brand' in its new 'Intel Inside' campaign. This was actually a 'co-campaign', which invited OEMs to advertise their use of Intel and share the cost of marketing. Some were sceptical; the most powerful, Compaq, initially refused; but many realized that, in the short term at least, Intel's brand would help move their relatively indistinguishable boxes.

In the long run, however, the OEMs became Intel dependent: once you have persuaded customers that 'Intel Inside' is a guarantee of the quality of your product, it becomes hard to take the label off. Or, as Grove put it, the campaign 'established a mindset in computer users that they were, in fact, Intel's customers, even though they didn't actually buy anything from us' (Grove 1997: 67).[25] Like Hedges and Butler selling Sandeman's port, Compaq found itself selling 'Intel machines'. Pushing its own label onto OEMs' products, Intel diluted the relative power of the OEMs' own names in the process of strengthening its own. In 1994, after his company had joined the campaign, a Compaq executive acknowledged that the 'Intel Inside' advertising campaign was 'promoting the semiconductor company at the expense of Compaq's brand'.[26] And, we might add, at the expense of Compaq's bank account: not only had Intel placed a rope around Compaq's neck, it had beguiled Compaq into helping to pay for the noose.[27]

While deploying its brand to control the OEMs, Intel inevitably had to resist being controlled by the other major brander in the PC supply chain, Microsoft. The fabled WINTEL *entente* has not been particularly *cordiale*. Over the years, Intel has tried to promote other operating systems (such as Linux, which was originally written for the x86 chip), to appropriate some of Microsoft's domain by, among other things, including some signal processing capabilities in its chips, promoting 'Viiv' as the chip-based fulcrum for the digital home, and (perhaps here with a sense of humour about the reliability of Microsoft) offering its own antivirus protection. But, above all, Intel has resisted subordination by promoting its brand ferociously, spending $3.4 billion in the first five years of the 'Intel inside' campaign alone. By 1993, a couple of years after people were asking why a chip needed a brand, Intel was one of the strongest corporate brands in the world. That year, the magazine *Financial World* ranked it behind only Marlboro and Coca-Cola, and ahead of Kellogg, Nestlé, and Kodak. Considering the age of those brands and the relative youth of Intel, the achievement was remarkable. Technical explanations for Intel's dominance make the effort seem wasteful. Yet the value of this accidental brand becomes apparent whenever Microsoft looms over its partners in the chain.

Microsoft has a particularly potent combination of intellectual property, including its copyrights, patents, and trademarks. This gives it extensive ability to control the chains they find themselves in, an ability that is reflected in its remarkable, disproportionate margins in a chain that is continually being squeezed ever tighter. Indeed, though it was billed in terms of conventional anticompetitive behavior, the celebrated 'Microsoft trial' must be seen in the light of its dominance over the supply chain and stranglehold over complementary assets that Microsoft does not own. It was, to a significant degree, Microsoft's partners within the PC chain, not its competitors, that persuaded the US government (and later the European Union) to try to limit Microsoft's power (Auletta 2001). From the trial documents came abundant evidence of Microsoft using any means at its disposal to maintain tight control over the PC chain. Branding was only one among several, but it was an important one. With the development of Windows 95, Microsoft increased its control over whose brand would appear on the desktop, in part, by designing their software to prevent users 'booting' multiple OSes. (This was aimed, in particular, at IBM's competing OS/2.) The company also exerted itself to prevent OEMs from interfering with the appearance of the Microsoft desktop and, in particular, its Internet Explorer logo. Though Microsoft had no hierarchical authority over these OEMs, they complied as if they were a subordinate part of the same organization. Microsoft's pressure went up and down the chain. To weaken the power of Intel's brand, Microsoft provided warrants for competing CPUs to make it clear that a computer could still be a PC without Intel inside—as long as it ran Windows. (It also provided OEM warrants to prevent Compaq from looming too large.) Again, Microsoft fought to prevent Intel from incorporating into its processors, as previously noted, some of the functionality that was previously carried out by Microsoft's operating system. Microsoft achieved its end in part by threatening Intel directly and in part by using its control over the OEMs to persuade them not to buy chips with the new signal processing capability.

Unsurprisingly, then, the Microsoft trial was remarkable for the number of witnesses that the government called, against Microsoft, who were less direct competitors than cooperating partners in Microsoft supply chains. Witnesses came from major partners: Intel, who provide CPUs designed around Microsoft OSes; Apple, who relies on Microsoft to provide the 'Office' suite for Apple's OS; and HP and IBM, both OEMs relying on the Microsoft OS. Given Microsoft's power and ruthlessness, of course, many up and down the supply chain would not testify. David Boise, the lead attorney prosecuting Microsoft joked, 'It has been very difficult to convince an OEM to appear in court without a hood' (Auletta 2001: 254).

Of the big three branders in the PC world, Dell is perhaps the most interesting. Intel has copyright and patent protection. Microsoft gains significant protection from copyright in the code of its OS. Dell, however, has almost no IP protection for its technology (as opposed to its business processes) and has several major rivals, including IBM, Hewlett-Packard (which now owns Compaq), Sony, and Gateway, as well as numerous 'white box' assemblers. What it trades on, to a significant degree, is its trademark and brand (Koehn 2001). This is always diluted by the need to carry Intel and Microsoft logos on its products. Dell tries hard to do without both, offering first PCs with 'Motif', its open source OS distribution, and later the PC E510n, without any OS loaded at all. Dell has further trimmed itself down so that—a little like Nike—its most important assets are its brand and reputation, which, supported by remarkably efficient business processes, manage to keep it from being completely subordinated by the WINTEL duopoly. And while keeping those at bay, the Dell brand subordinates suppliers along its Texas-to-Thailand chain who know that their best chance of getting into the market is through Dell. Dell's market recognition gives it power, which it uses ruthlessly to pass risks onto, and drive down margins for, what are politely called its 'partners'.

In all, the PC supply chain, like the book chain and the wine chain before it, contains internal competitive battles that are as fierce as, and sometimes fiercer than, the external, horizontal competitions in which the links must also engage. (Microsoft, after all, retains comparatively cordial relations with Apple.) The aggressiveness of the competition suggests that it take some power to keep particular PC chains relatively stable. In considering how IP figures in this fight, no one should underestimate the power of copyrights and patents held by Microsoft and Intel, but, given that Dell has little of either, that Intel and Microsoft invest heavily in marketing, and that IBM was let down by the faith it put in copyright and patents to maintain control of the PC, it is equally important not to overlook the role that their trademarks and brands play too.

Further, the role of brands in this chain helps to emphasize two points about modern chains. First, even in PC and similar hi-tech chains, technological merit alone does not win the day. Gawer and Cusumano (2002) trace 'platform leadership' to persistent and impressive research. But Intel holds off AMD, which often produces better chips, in part through its 'Intel Inside' campaign, with which it grasps OEMs like Dell by the throat (and warns them off AMD) while simultaneously keeping Microsoft's embrace from turning to suffocation. For Microsoft, 'positive network externalities' have undoubtedly been critically important, but those network effects are lent support by the ubiquity of the brand. Certainly, some buy the brand because of the network, but others join the network because of the brand. Second, a look at the PC chain helps to show that, in newly developing supply chains, neither who brands, nor where in the chain brand dominance can arise, is predetermined. Over time, it may be that one position will typically dominate—much as the OEMs dominate the automobile chains—but where that will be, and whose brand will count, can rarely be determined in advance.

Brands, then, have many distinctive aspects; among these is their signaling power, which is capable of acting across distances. As noted, brands have helped firms, though connected neither institutionally nor—in the case of port's London-to-Portugal or Dell's Texas-to-Thailand chains—geographically, to dominate others. Hence, where the Chandlerians bundle them into hierarchies, brands perhaps only show the extent of their 'vertical' power in vertically disaggregated chains of the sort that existed as much before as after the Chandlerian moment. As modern supply chains spread out across the globe in attempts to arbitrage weight and wages (so Dell's lightest work is done in Burma and Vietnam, the heaviest in Mexico) the firm or location that brands the chain gets to pass many of the disadvantages of hierarchy (such as manufacturing, stockholding and decreasing returns) onto others while keeping the advantages (market recognition, increasing returns) for itself.

CONCLUSION: QUALITY CONTROL

These three vignettes reveal very different industries in very different times. They, nonetheless, share one thing: the challenge of quality. In each of the three cases, the objects that enter the market give consumers the difficult task of assessing whether the object is of sufficient quality to be worth buying. Let me present the common issues.

Books, which need to be sold before being read, for once read they have lost the centre of their value, need someone to warrant the content. Without this, the customer is buying a pig in a poke. At the beginning of the seventeenth century, however, as the bookselling cartel crumbled, the supply chain left open the question of who would warrant—the bookseller, the publisher, the printer, the author, or, indeed, someone else. Wine, particularly complex wines whose quality only emerges over time, also needs, as Robert Boyle noticed, someone to vouch for it and to justify the price. It is this 'someone' whose name tends to end up on the label. The newly disestablished supply chain of the nineteenth century did not have a natural candidate. There was one unlikely link: the retailers who had, for the most part, lost their credibility. So a search went on for a new champion and a struggle emerged around the search. Finally, with the PC, the general customer and purchasing managers faced a challenge, made more demanding by the continuous evolution of the machines, in deciding which, among the relatively expensive and untried tools on offer, was reliable. Again, which point in the chain could brand was open, and, to some extent, has remained open, with the three dominant points—the CPU, the OS and the OEM—battling with one another in vertical competition.[28]

As their stories are told here, these examples also have in common the collapse of large institutions. These moments of transformation are not necessary conditions for vertical competition; these fights go on all the time. But disintegration of a hierarchical structure tends to bring new chains, and so new fights, into being (we are witnessing such a chain of events with the collapse of the phone carriers and the rise of the phone makers and OSes such as Android). If you want to understand vertical fights and how they develop, such moments of disintegration provide useful cases to study, as this chapter has attempted to show. The institutional connection is relatively easy to understand. As Arrow (1984) and Akerlof (1970) make clear, monopoly-like institutions play an important role in assuring quality, whether of second-hand cars or (though they don't always like the comparison) 'doctors, lawyers, and barbers' (Akerlof 1970: 500). When they collapse, as did the Stationers' Company, the Wine Company, and IBM's PC division, a vertical fight will develop among the survivors over who will play the branding role and deal with the complexities of quality. One reason, then, that the vertical component of branding has been overlooked is that business and economic history have tended to explore brands in the context of large, vertically integrated institutions. Where an institution provides the brand, while subduing vertical tensions through internal, hierarchical power, brands will have no vertical part to play. They emerge in the absence of such institutions, when several links have the possibility of branding the chain of which they are a part. These fights, as I have suggested, precede 'modern brands'; indeed, they were a critical part of the formation of modern branding case law. Many such fights, however, were soon subsumed by vertical organizations. It is not surprising that they are becoming noticeable once again as hierarchical organizations are dissolving into vertical supply chains.

NOTES

1. Versions of the argument in this chapter were presented at the seminar CONDOR at the *École Polytechnique*, the annual meeting of the Association of Business Historians, and at an economic history seminar at the Wharton School. I'm grateful to both audiences for helpful comments, particularly to

Andrew Godley who followed up with incisive comments, not all of which I have been able to address. I'm also grateful to Hervé Dumez and Daniel Raff for the invitation to Paris and Wharton, respectively, and to Bill Sherman and my colleagues, Teresa da Silva Lopes and John Mercer, for careful reading and helpful suggestions.

2. None of this argument challenges standard assumptions about the conventional, horizontal battles between brands. It merely suggests that, in certain circumstances, branding has a vertical component that is easily overlooked.

3. Notions of 'platform leadership', frictionless markets, and perfect information that have accompanied 'new economy' discussions have played an important part in painting supply chain relations as close to egalitarian. A quick look at the frequency of the term *supply chain* in twentieth-century newspapers—it appears around 1916, reaches one peak in 1942, another in the early 1950s, and a third in the mid 1960s, before the term is absorbed by the business literature—reminds us that the concept is originally a military one. It comes from the world of command and control and logistics, where direction and hierarchy, not markets and egalitarianism, reign. The quietist tone of the supply chain literature is not echoed in the 'commodity chain' approach. See, for instance, Gereffi and Korniewicz (1994), Dicken, Olds and Yeung (2001), or Raikes Friis Jensen and Ponte (2000). However, developed in the tradition of Wallerstein, the commodity chain approach frames power relations in the political–diplomatic terms of a global centre and periphery, paying less attention to other, disaggregated forms of control, such as the ones I examine here. See Hopkins and Wallerstein (1986).

4. A moment's thought tells most but the geeks that we don't know or care who makes the disk in our PC (or phone or music player); another moment's thought, however, reveals to all but the geeks (who tend to be more conscious about backups) that the hard disk is the most valuable component of our PC. Corrupt software and processors can be easily replaced. Lost work on a crashed disk cannot. The anonymity of such an important component would be puzzling were it not for the aggressive fight to be identified that other components in the chain have waged. Those fights have been costly, but the rewards have been commensurate.

5. An unfortunate number of events recorded in this section occurred between January and March. In the era under discussion, England celebrated the New Year on 25 March. Consequently, what we would today call January 1695, people alive at the time would have thought of as January 1694. Hence the numerous virgules for that period of the year.

6. The lengthening chain, shifting powers and projected names over this period can be briefly illustrated in successive title pages and shifting prepositions in Samuel Daniels's *History*. At different times, the name of author, the printer, or the bookseller is presented at the foot of the opening page as the warrant for the title above. The book first appeared in 1613, as 'by Samuel Daniel' and printed for the Company of Stationers. A 1621 edition was merely by 'S.D.' and was printed by Okes. Another was printed by Okes for the bookseller Waterson, who in 1634 gave the printing to a different printer, Cotes. The 1685 edition, however, is printed by F. Leach for Richard Chiswell, Benjamin Tooke, and Thomas Sawbridge (who now owned the copy), and is to be sold by William Whitwood. At this point, a collaborative group of booksellers, who would be expected to compete, had formed an alliance to own the copy and subordinate the other crafts (printing, distribution, and even authorship), from whom the group, nonetheless, expected cooperation.

7. The 'stigma of print' prevented the more aristocratic writers from using their power and authority on behalf of authors.

8. For Shakespeare on eternal copy, see *Macbeth* Act 3, scene 2, and on author as brand, see Sonnet 111, though in the latter, clearly he was using the notion as a liability, like a criminal brand, not an asset.

9. Encyclopedias and romantic novels, at different ends of the book's spectrum, show how variable the notion of the author can be. Wikipedia and Harlequin romances have, in their different ways, taken advantage of the idea that the author need not be a single person. Encyclopedias have also proved to be adept at absorbing an authorial name such as Grove, Pears, or Chambers into collective production. The competition between authors and publishers over warranting often reemerges. A recent comment on the remarkable success of Penguin Books noted that (Allen Lane the founder)

> was a shrewd promoter of his company, and by creating a uniform line of books, he defied the conventional wisdom that readers don't care who publishes what they read. The well-designed series advertised itself far more than it advertised its writers. (Weisberg 2005)

10. Port wine was produced in the Douro Valley in the north of Portugal and exported through the entrepôt of Oporto (or *Porto* to the Portuguese), hence its name.

11. French wine was prohibited between 1668–1669, between 1678–1685, and from 1691 (with intermittent gaps) to the peace of Utrecht (Francis 1972).

12. This argument is laid out more fully in Duguid (2003a).

13. This argument is laid out more fully in Duguid (2005).

14. Plassmen, O'Doherty, Shiv and Rangel (2008) suggest that with wine, judgments of price and quality can be strangely intertwined.

15. Outgoing letter from Offley & Co, Oporto, to Thomas Harridge, 6 May 1793. Archive of the House of Sandeman, Vila Nova de Gaia, Portugal.

16. Incoming letter from T. H. Hunt, Maisonette, to Hunt & Co, Oporto, 25 October 1815. Archive of Hunt, Newman, Roope, Vila Nova de Gaia, Portugal.

17. In 1711, Daniel Defoe, who had been a wine importer, noted in his *Review*, 'Infinite Frauds and Cheats of the Wine-Trade will be discover'd, and I hope for the future, prevented; for if once we can come to a usage of drinking our Wines neat as they come from the Country where they grow, all the vile Practices of Brewing and Mixing Wines, either by the Vintners or Merchants, will die of Course' (Defoe, 1938 [1711]: 207).

18. Sandeman was a relatively new exporter that had rapidly grown into one of the largest. For the details of this argument, see Duguid (2003b).

19. It would be a mistake to suggest that this was a universal trend. What I have described affected the higher-end wines primarily. The new retail outlets— Victoria Wine and Gilbeys, for instance—were able to create retail brands for middle-class markets as certain new wine bars—Bodega, for instance— were able to brand the chain for lower-middle class markets. (We see a similar strategy to Bodega's in 'buyers' own brands' today.) The wine labelled Victoria, Gilbeys, Bodega, or Sandeman could, in fact, be the same wine. More generally, then, what link controls a particular chain is likely to depend on what niche the chain ends in. It can be equally important to a high-end brand not to get caught in the wrong niche. Sandeman, for instance, did provide wine to lower quality outlets (including Gilbeys and Victoria), but it made sure its name was kept off any labels.

20. For histories of branding in the Chandlerian tradition, see Chandler (1990), Church (1999), Fitzgerald (1995), Fullerton and Low (1994), Koehn (2001), Laird (1998), Strasser (1989), Tedlow (1990), and Wilkins (1992; 1994).

21. Nor are these attempts to control the chain through the name on a bottle a nineteenth-century phenomenon. It is evident in the voluminous litigation of Coca-Cola, which has fought mightily over the years with its bottlers, using its brand name to control their freedom (Hayes 2004). It is equally evident in the merger of Gillette and Procter and Gamble, who have combined forces in a modern pharmaceutical conger, to prevent themselves from being subordinated by Wal-Mart, which is not, ostensibly, a direct competitor, but rather an important supply chain partner (Hayes 2005). The struggle is primarily over what names will appear on the Wal-Mart shelves. (For a related argument, see Miskell, this volume.)
22. Support for the argument in this paragraph and the evidence on which the earlier claims about advertising are based can be found in Duguid (2003b).
23. Anti-monopolistic supervision by the Department of Justice prevented AT&T from developing a line of computers in which it might have bundled UNIX. Indeed, supervision probably prevented AT&T from understanding what it had in UNIX, and helped to unbundle the computer business.
24. 'Accidental Advertising Campaigns', *Financial Times* 17 Oct 1997: 12.
25. The effects of the advertising were almost as accidental as the brand itself. Grove also acknowledges that several of the beneficial consequences of this campaign were 'an attitude change ... we actually stimulated, but one whose impact we at Intel did not fully comprehend' (Grove 1997: 67). This particular asset turned briefly into a liability when problems arose with the IBM Pentium chip, and OEM customers began to act as if, indeed, they were Intel's customers. In a similar way, Microsoft's attempt to brand the PC chain with its "Vista Ready" claim may prove a liability, given that many machines so labelled seem more equipped to crawl or stall Vista than to run it.
26. 'Computer Giants Clash Over Strategy: Compaq Attacks Intel Over Advertising Campaign.' *Financial Times* 12 Sept 1994: 1.
27. When Apple computers decided to use Intel chips, it was clear from very early on that Apple, always conscious of its brand, was not going to allow 'Intel Inside' to be scrawled on its computers. It has managed to treat Intel as a valuable component, but one that has no branding effect on the OEM product. Apple seems to be trying to play a similar role with telephone carriers such as AT&T in the United States and Orange in France. Where once people shopped for the network and accepted the phone, now they are encouraged to shop for the phone and accept the network. Meanwhile, Apple has fought very hard to control what other components (particularly any with branding potential) may be added to the iPhone.
28. If, as I have suggested, business and economic theory have had difficulty in seeing the role of brands in chains, it may be because economics has never found dealing with the question of quality easy. Early in the discipline's history, Adam Smith acknowledged his discomfort: 'Quality is so disputable a matter', he wrote, 'that I look upon all information of this kind [i.e., about quality] as somewhat uncertain' (Smith, 1937 [1776]: 244). More recently, Stigler noted bluntly, 'quality has not yet been successfully specified by economics, and this elusiveness extends to all problems in which it enters' (Stigler, 1961: 224). It is not clear that the discipline has advanced a great deal with the problem since.

BIBLIOGRAPHY

Akerlof, G. (1970) 'The market for lemons: Quality, uncertainty, and the market mechanism', *Quarterly Journal of Economics,* 84: 488–500.

Arrow, K. (1984) 'Information and economic behavior' in K. Arrow (1984) *Collected Papers,* Cambridge, MA: Harvard University Press, pp. 136–152.

Auletta, K. (2001) *World War 3.0: Microsoft vs. the U.S. Government and the Battle to Rule the Digital Age,* New York: Broadway Books.

Baines, P. and P. Rogers (2007) *Edmund Curll, Bookseller,* Oxford: Clarendon Press.

Blagden, C. (1960) *The Stationers' Company: A History, 1403–1959,* London: George Allen & Unwin.

Bresnahan, T. and J. Richards (1999) 'Local and global competition in information technology', *Journal of the Japanese and International Economies,* 13: 336–371.

Chandler, A. (1990) *Scale and Scope: The Dynamics of American Capitalism,* Cambridge, MA: Cambridge University Press.

Castells, M. (2002) *The Internet Galaxy: Reflections on Internet, Business, and Society,* New York: Oxford University Press.

Chartier, R. (2003) 'Foucault's chiasmus: Authorship between science and literature in the seventeenth and eighteenth centuries' in M. Biagioli and P. Galison (eds.) *Scientific Authorship: Credit and Intellectual Property in Science,* New York: Routledge, pp. 13–32.

Church, R. (1999) 'New perspectives on the history of products, firms, marketing, and consumers in Britain and the United States since the mid-nineteenth century', *Economic History Review,* 52: 405–435.

Cieply, M. (2007) 'Writers begins strike as talks break off', *New York Times,* November 5. Available HTTP: <http://www.nytimes.com/2007/11/05/business/media/05strike.html >(accessed 14 January 2008)

Curry, J. and M. Kenney (2004) 'The organizational and geographic configuration of the personal computer value chain' in M. Kenney and R. Florida (eds.) *Locating Global Advantage: Industry Dynamics in the International Economy,* Stanford, CA: Stanford University Press, pp. 113–141.

Deazley, R. (2005) *On the Origin of the Right to Copy: Charting the Movement of Copyright Law in Eighteenth-Century Britain (1695–1775),* Oxford: Hart.

Defoe, D. (1938 [1711]) *Defoe's Review,* New York: Columbia University Press.

Dicken, P., K. Olds and H. Yeung (2001) 'Chains and networks, territories and scales: Towards a relational framework for analysing the global economy', *Global Networks,* 1 (2001): 89–112.

Duguid, P. (2003a) 'The making of Methuen: The commercial treaty in the English imagination', *História, Revista da Faculdade de Letras,* 3(4): 9–36

Duguid, P. (2003b) 'Developing the brand: The case of alcohol, 1800–1880', *Enterprise & Society,* 4(3): 405–441.

Duguid, P. (2005) 'Networks and knowledge: The beginning and end of the port commodity chain, 1703–1860', *Business History Review,* 79 (Autumn 2005): 493–526.

Erne, L. (2004) *Shakespeare as Literary Dramatist,* Cambridge, UK: Cambridge University Press.

Ferguson, C. and C. Morris (1994) *Computer Wars: The Fall of IBM and the Future of Global Technology,* New York: Times Books.

Fitzgerald, R. (1995) *Rowntree and the Marketing Revolution, 1862–1969,* Cambridge, UK: Cambridge University Press.

Francis, A. (1972) *The Wine Trade,* London: A. & C. Black.

Fruin, W. (1992) *The Japanese Enterprise System: Competitive Strategies and Cooperative Structures,* New York: Oxford University Press.

Fullerton, G. and R. Low (1994) 'Brands, brand management, and the brand manager system: A critical–historical evaluation', *Journal of Marketing Research,* 31: 173–190.

Gawer, A. and Cusamano, M. (2002) *Platform Leadership: How Intel, Microsoft, and Cisco Drive Industry Innovation,* Boston, MA: Harvard Business School Press.
Gereffi, G. and M. Korniewicz (eds.) (1994) *Commodity Chains and Global Capitalism,* Westport, CT: Praeger.
Grove, A. (1997). *Only the Paranoid Survive,* London: HarperCollins.
Harris, T. (2005) *Restoration: Charles II and his Kingdoms, 1660–1685,* London: Allen Lane.
Hayes, C. (2004) *The Real Thing: Truth and Power at the Coca-Cola Company,* New York: Random House.
Hayes, C. (2005) 'A household giant in the store: What's behind the Procter deal? Wal-mart', *New York Times,* 29 January.
Hopkins, T. and I. Wallerstein (1986) 'Commodity chains in the world-economy prior to 1800', *Review* 10: 159.
House of Commons (1852) *Minutes of Evidence Taken Before the Select Committee on Import Duties in Wine,* London: House of Commons.
James, H. (1962 [1903]) *The Ambassadors,* New York: New American Library.
Johns, A. (1998) *The Nature of the Book: Print and Knowledge in the Making,* Chicago: University of Chicago Press.
Koehn, N. (2001) *Brand New: How Entrepreneurs Earned Consumers' Trust From Wedgwood to Dell,* Boston: Harvard Business School Press.
Laird, P. (1998) *Advertising in Progress: American Business and the Rise of Consumer Marketing,* Baltimore, MD: Johns Hopkins University Press.
Langlois, R. (1992) 'External economies and economic progress: The case of the microcomputer industry', *Business History Review,* 66(1): 1–50.
Loewenstein, J. (2002) *The Author's Due: Printing and the Prehistory of Copyright,* Chicago: University of Chicago Press.
Macaulay, T. (1969 [1855]) *History of England: From the Accession of James II.* 4 vols., London: J. M. Dent.
Maruca, L. (2007) *The Work of Print: The English Text Trades, 1660–1760.* Seattle: University of Washington Press.
McKendrick, D. (2004) 'Leveraging locations: Hard disk drive producers in international competition' in M. Kenney and R. Florida (eds.) *Locating Global Advantage: Industry Dynamics in the International Economy,* Stanford, CA: Stanford University Press, pp. 142–174.
Milton, J. (1956) Paradise Lost *and Selected Poetry and* Prose, New York: Rinehart & Co.
Moore, G. (1965) 'Cramming more components onto integrated circuits', *Electronics* 8 (April 19): 4–7.
Plassmen, H., J. O'Doherty, B. Shiv and A. Rangel (2008) 'Marketing actions can modulate neural representations of experienced pleasantness', *Proceedings of the National Academy of Sciences,* 18 January.
Raikes, P. M., Friis Jensen and S. Ponte (2000) 'Global commodity chain analysis and the French filière approach: Comparison and critique', *Economy and Society,* 3: 390–417.
Richardson, G. (1972) 'The organization of industry', *The Economic Journal,* 82(327): 883–896.
Rooney, P. (2002) 'XP services stalled', *CRN* 1017: 14–18.
Shapin, S. (1994) *A Social History of Truth: Civility and Science in Seventeenth-Century England,* Chicago: University of Chicago Press.
Smith, A. (1937 [1776]) *An Inquiry into the Nature and Causes of the Wealth of Nations,* New York: Modern Library, 1937.
St. Clair, W. (2004) *The Reading Nation in the Romantic Period,* Cambridge, UK: Cambridge University Press.

Stigler, G. (1961) 'The economics of information', *Journal of Political Economy*, 69(3): 213–225.

Strasser, S. (1989) *Satisfaction Guaranteed: The Making of the American Mass Market*, New York: Pantheon.

Sturgeon, T. (2002) 'Modular production networks: A new model of industrial organization', *Industrial and Corporate Change*, 11(3): 451–496.

Swift, J. (1937) 'On the Irish-Club,' in H. Williams (ed.) *The Poems of Jonathan Swift*, 3 vols., Oxford: Oxford University Press.

Tedlow, R. (1990) *New and Improved: The Story of Mass Marketing in America*, New York: Basic Books.

Teece, D. (1986) 'Profiting from technological innovation: Implications for integration, collaboration, licensing, and public policy', *Research Policy*, 15: 285–305.

Turner, M. (1874) 'Wine and wine-merchants', *New Quarterly Magazine*: 595–619

Weisberg, J. 2005. 'March of the penguins', *Slate* 10 November. Available HTTP: <http://www.slate.com/id/2129497/entry/2129501/> (accessed 14 January 2008)

Wilkins, M. (1992) 'The neglected intangible asset: The influence of the trade mark on the rise of the modern corporation,' *Business History*, 34: 66–99.

———. (1994) 'When and why brand names in food and drink' in G. Jones and N. Morgan (eds.), *Adding Value: Brands and Marketing in Food and Drink*, London: Routledge, pp. 15–40.

Williams, R. (1961) *The Long Revolution*, London: Chatto & Windus.

Wither, G. (1624) *The Schollers Purgator Discovered in the Stationers Commonwealth*, London.

Womack, J., T. Jones, T. D. and Roos (1991) *The Machine That Changed the World: How Japan's Secret Weapon in the Global Auto Wars Will Revolutionize Western Industry*, New York: Harper Perennial.

8 Turning Trademarks into Brands

How Advertising Agencies Practiced and Conceptualized Branding, 1890–1930

Stefan Schwarzkopf

> There is no doubt that if this country wants to maintain their posi-
> tion in the world markets 'branded goods' is the only method as a
> hall-mark of quality. . . . The private trade-mark is the keystone in
> modern commerce.
>
> *Advertiser's Weekly*, August 29 1918[1]

In late August 1918, the British trade journal *Advertiser's Weekly* predicted
that the future of world commerce belonged to the branded commodity that
was protected by a registered trademark. Although the previously quoted
article used the terms *brand* and *trademark* as virtually synonymous, modern trademark law argues that trademarks are essentially pieces of intellectual property and, as such, are part of the legal realm, whereas brands are
trademarks that have been loaded with social and cultural meaning (Phillips 2003; George 2006). Trademarks are a type of intellectual property.
They consist of names, words, phrases, designs, images, or a combination
of these to exclusively identify the commercial source of a product or service. A brand, in turn, is a trademark that has been 'released' to compete
in the socio-cultural sphere of the market. Whereas a trademark is a purely
legal entity operating in a commercial context, the brand is a 'cross-over'
concept:

> It is an image or a message which is embodied in icons which are pro-
> tected by trade marks, while being embedded in cultural as well as
> commercial contexts. Checks on the abuse of trade mark monopolies
> will not be brought to bear on abuses of the power exerted by the
> owner of a brand image (Phillips 2003: 658).

This understanding of the relationship between trademarks and brands
is supported by de Chernatony and Macdonald (2003) and Aaker (1997;
2002), who argued that being a legal instrument—in form of a protected
trademark—is just one aspect of the multiple functions of a brand. A brand

is much more than merely a 'legally defensible proprietary name' (Lopes 2007: 5) and it serves more than as a differentiating device, indicating source: brands are essentially identity systems, encompassing a personality, a relationship, and an image in consumers' minds. Schultz's model of corporate branding sees the function of a trademark in facilitating brand awareness and recognition, 'encouraging consumers to hold special expectations about the promises of the brand—whether it is a promise of special quality, unique experience, or personal identity' (2005: 25–6).

Brands and branded products have existed since at least the early modern period, and the late eighteenth and early nineteenth centuries saw a proliferation of such goods, which began to be promoted through various advertising tools such as leaflets and bills, trade cards, or advertisements in magazines and newspapers (McKendrick 1960; McKendrick et al. 1982; Breen 1988; Berg 1994; Strachan 2003). The mid-nineteenth century somewhat interrupted and revolutionized the continuous growth of branding and marketing communication in two aspects. On the one hand, laws emerged in Britain and in the United States that commodified the knowledge of the commercial source of a product, by reinventing branded goods as trademarks (Sherman and Bently 1999; Duguid 2003; Andersen 2006). On the other hand, there emerged advertising agencies that began to assume an increasingly powerful mediating role between branded goods and their consumers. From the mid-nineteenth century, advertising agencies performed the role of charging and loading trademarked goods with meaningful and often purely symbolic connotations to aid consumer decision-making in the marketplace. Agencies, for example, began to decide which information about a product should be presented to consumers in what kind of way (Lash and Urry 1994; Brierley 2002; Lury 2004; McFall 2004; Leiss et al. 2005; Arvidsson 2006).

Marketing historians have traditionally focused on how advertising agencies promoted particular products, created specific campaigns, or built particular product images for soaps, cigarettes, or cars. In addition, business historians acknowledge the role that advertising agencies played in externalizing marketing as a management function, by creating a body of specialized knowledge about markets and consumers (Chandler 1990; Wilson and Thompson 2006). However, little is known about how the advertising industry, in general, developed a conceptual understanding of the branding process during the past century. Given that brands are embodied and externalized forms of knowledge about the consumer decision-making process and the competitive advantage of a product, there is surprisingly little research on when and how advertising agencies first developed this knowledge and how agency professionals rationalized and conceptualized the process of turning their clients' intellectual property, i.e. trademarks, into meaningful and collectively shared symbols, i.e. brands (e.g. Wilkins 1992; but see Fullerton and Low 1994; Lopes and Casson 2007).

Interbrand's Tom Blackett (2003: 15), for example, writes that:

Hand in hand with the introduction of brands came early trade mark legislation. This allowed the owners of these brands to protect them in law. The birth of advertising agencies such as J. Walter Thompson and N.W. Ayer in the late nineteenth century gave further impetus to the development of brands.

This statement is typical of contemporary popular knowledge in that it is unspecific at best, and chronologically wrong at worst, since the two agencies named here, and many others, existed before the introduction of trademark law in the United States and the United Kingdom. As shown by Nevett (1982), the business model of the advertising agency as a mediator in the marketplace between media, advertiser, and consumer had emerged in Britain as early as the 1830s. Elsewhere, Blackett (1998) writes that advertising agencies do not enjoy developing brand names and find the legal aspects of trademarks irksome and a threat to their creativity. He also advised that agencies should leave the choice of brand names to their clients and specialist branding consultancies like Interbrand, Landor, or Wolff Olins. This statement further reduces the roles and functions of advertising agencies in the making of brands by artificially separating the trademark function of a brand from its various social, communicative, and symbolic functions (Bussey 2006). Although Schechter's (1925) seminal study on the historical foundations of trademark law acknowledged the role of advertising in creating and maintaining goodwill behind a trademark, there seems to be no consistent body of historical knowledge on the exact role of advertising agencies in the process of managing a trademark's augmentation to a key symbolic element of marketing strategy.

This chapter has, therefore, two aims. It first traces the work of advertising agencies in turning trademarks into brands between the late nineteenth century and the interwar period. It mainly draws on the papers of American agencies such as N. W. Ayer and J. Walter Thompson (JWT) and their work for the owners of global brands like Lever. Second, the chapter attempts to identify forms of shared knowledge and practices that the advertising industry drew on when augmenting trademarks to successful brands. This body of knowledge and practices did not only consist of creative skills in visualizing and personalizing an otherwise abstract or intangible trademark. It also contained increasingly formalized approaches to market research, which helped advertisers decide which information about a product was to be presented to consumers, how, and through which media channels. Following Miller and Rose (1997) and, most recently, Pettit (2007), this chapter thus studies how advertising agencies' knowledge about trademarks, brands, and consumers' psychology contributed to the 'assemblage of the subject of consumption' (Miller and Rose 1997) during those decades that preceded the post-war age of mass affluence.

In the transatlantic marketplace (North America and Britain), marketers acquired competitive advantages by developing a scientific 'culture' of branding—one that looked beyond the mere visually attractive presentation of trademarks and logos (Kreshel 1990). The study presented in the following shows that this culture, fostered by the competitive position of manufacturers of similar products and the competition of large, international advertising agencies for clients, fuelled innovations in the conceptualization of the branding process. Major intellectual innovations in branding, embodied in the concepts of brand personality, brand image, brand identity, relationship marketing to foster brand bonding, the idea of the lifestyle brand and lifestyle research, the idea that brands need rejuvenation through line extensions, and the idea of the global brand, had all become practical knowledge, which means implicit and tacit knowledge, within the advertising industry before the golden age of post-war affluence between the mid-1950s and the mid-1970s. It was during these two decades that most of the tacit knowledge about consumers and brands was turned into conceptual (explicit) knowledge and became codified, for example, in marketing textbooks or seminal marketing science papers by Theodore Levitt, Sidney Levy, Neil Borden, and others (Jones and Monieson 1990; Shaw and Goodrich 2005; Tadajewski and Jones 2008). Thus, I argue that the idea that advertising had to build up the total value (equity) of the brand in the mind of consumers, rather than simply put a sign, symbol, product, slogan, etc. (trademark) in front of them, and that consumers see brands holistically as promises of quality and individual fulfilment, was first developed tacitly in daily agency practice and only later conceptualized.

ADVERTISING BECOMES BRAND MANAGEMENT

At the heart of a brand is, of course, the legal concept of the defensible trademark, which is distinct and recognizable to all distribution channel members from the wholesaler to the end-consumer. This was recognized early on by British manufacturers in the fast-moving consumer goods sector, such as Bass, Wills, Lea and Perrins, and Lever. After the 1862 Merchandise Marks Act and the 1875 Trade Marks Registration Act were instituted, a plethora of branded and mass-produced consumer goods appeared, offering consistent quality and identical shape and size (Patent Office 1976; Mendenhall 1989). Trademarked commodities appealed to consumers because they made quality and price comparisons easier, and thus facilitated decision-making. They appealed to the retailer because some of them were prepackaged and standardized, and therefore had a longer shelf-life. They also reduced the need for skilled salesmen and increased the speed of consumer through-put in the shop. Products like Lever's wrapped and branded Sunlight soap, Bass beer with its red triangle, or Lyle's Golden Syrup with its distinct lion symbol suited the emerging chains of retailers (multiples) such as Maypole's, Lipton's, and Sainsbury's, which were based on the proposition to consumers that standardized goods produced under a trademark offered reliable quality, and secure and traceable origins, as well as consistently low prices (Fraser 1981; Corley 1987; Jones and Morgan 1993; Benson 1994; Church and Clark 2000; Church and Clark 2003; Fitzgerald 2005).

As shown by Tedlow (1990), Friedman (2004), and others, the late nineteenth and early twentieth centuries were characterized by an approach to marketing communication mainly in form of mass promotion, with the aim of selling. Rather than focussing on long-term brand loyalty, marketing communication was supposed to generate product recognition through reiterating advertising messages and offering short-term incentives to buyers (Fraser 1981; Church 2000). Wills, for example, offered cigarette cards from 1887 to give additional reasons for customers to purchase their cigarette brands. Thomas Barrett promoted Pear's soap by adapting John Millais' painting of a little boy as the famous "Bubble" poster in 1886, which was reprinted and distributed in millions of copies. Barrett's dictum that any fool could make soap but it took a clever man to sell it summarized the outlook of the late Victorian generation of marketers (Nevett 1982; Goodall 1986; Richards 1990). Mass promotion as the main marketing tool became outdated during the early twentieth century, when certain brand names had become firmly established in the minds of their target audiences and ever more competitor products offered similar product quality at a comparable price. As the distinctiveness of particular products became unrecognizable and whole segments of the consumer market began to develop new types of needs, marketers realized that the purely sales-oriented outlook on the market had to be replaced by a philosophy that had, at its heart, a meaningful brand that was able to establish a long-term relationship between manufacturer, distributor, salesman, and consumer (Friedman 2004). In other words, mass promotion in a mature market became a cost factor for companies like Lever, Cadbury, Rowntree, Wills, or Colman's, which spent thousands of pounds per annum on advertising even before the turn of the last century. At that moment in time, the brand and its manageable and communicable meanings—not the trademark itself—became the most important asset of a company.

Advertising agencies came into this process at a relatively late stage. Although large-scale British agencies, such as Mather and Crowther (founded in 1850), Sells (1869), Smiths (1878), T. B. Browne (1872), the London Press Exchange (1892), and S. H. Benson (1893), and American agencies, such as J. Walter Thompson (1864), N. W. Ayer (1869), Lord and Thomas (1873), and McCann-Erickson (1902/1912), had existed since around the 1850s and '60s, it was not until the First World War that advertising professionals adopted a strategic brand- and value-focused outlook on campaign planning. Before that, most agencies contended themselves with simply placing their clients' advertisements in print media and the agencies' technical expertise stemmed mostly from an in-depth knowledge of available newspapers and magazines and their (estimated) circulation, as well as from knowledge about the printing process, such as block making, engraving, etc., and the management of poster campaigns (Schwarzkopf 2005). The key expertise of an agent was the ability to secure the best rates for clients, or the knowledge of how to sell available newspaper space to new advertisers at a profit ('space farming').

When William Hesketh Lever worked on the idea of a branded and indi-vidually wrapped soap with scale-economies and national distribution, he initially got in touch with the Liverpool trademark and patent agent W. P. Thompson, who helped Lever design and register the 'Sunlight Soap' name in 1884 and the 'Lux' trade mark in 1900.[2] Advertising agents were rarely part of this technical process of actually 'branding' a product. A similar process took place, for example, in 1927 when the Hamburg-based merchant Karl Seyferth needed a trademark for his ice-cream and honey products. Seyferth advertised in the *Hamburger Fremdenblatt*, a liberal business paper, that he was looking for a trademark and received an offer from the export merchant and biscuit manufacturer, Viktor Langnese. Seyferth purchased the 'Langnese' name for 300 German Reichsmark and began to build up a successful company, which, in 1962, was incorporated into Unilever's multinational food Empire. Both Lever and Seyferth, in their attempts to create, buy, and register trademarks, were unable to draw on the services of the advertising agents of their day.

A noteworthy exception to this rule was Thomas Brooks Browne's advertising agency, founded in 1872 in London. T. B. Browne's quickly grew into one of Britain's largest agencies around 1900, and boasted of a very successful trademarks department established under a Mr. King, a qualified Patent Agent. By the 1920s, this department had become per-haps Britain's leading trademark agency, which served clients like Cad-bury Bros., Rowntree, J. S. Fry and Sons, Alfred Bird and Sons, McVitie and Price Ltd., Peek Frean and Co., Arthur Bell and Sons, Chivas Bros., Courtaulds, and many others. King later left the agency to form his own company, which became known as King's Patent Agency (Browne 1984). Browne's understanding of the role of the advertising agency in relation to the trademark and the brand, however, was limited. His agency offered to legally defend, but not necessarily to strategically build, the brand in the minds of consumers.[3]

One of the first American agencies to realize the responsibility of adver-tising as that of building a brand was the Philadelphia-based N. W. Ayer company (Hower 1949). In 1914 and 1915, the agency placed several adver-tisements in the US trade journal *Printer's Ink* to explain its services to pro-spective clients.[4] One of the advertisements exemplified that Ayer's, as an advertising agency and specialized service provider, did not only attractively visualize the trademark of their client but could attach vital social meaning to it. For the Roger Bros. company, the agency, for example, invented 'the 1847 girl' in order to visualize and, more importantly, symbolize the trade mark of '1847 Roger Bros. Silverware' (see figure 8.1).

Figure 8.1 N. W. Ayer invents 'The 1847 Girl'. Source: 1915 Agency Booklet, N. W. Ayer Advertising Agency Records, Archives Center, National Museum of American History, Behring Center, Smithsonian Institution.

This example shows that, by 1915, some agencies were aware that their expertise actually lay in developing brands by visualizing and personalizing an otherwise intangible trademark. The Ayer agency had thus recognized that the property protection that trademarks allowed was worth little if the product that carried the mark offered no physical and psychological benefits to consumers. Another Ayer agency house advertisement from 1923 explained the services the agency rendered to the American Fruit Growers Inc. and their 'Blue Goose' brand, which communicated the *meaning* of agricultural excellence and reliable quality of fruit and vegetables to the consumer: 'But a trade-mark, however beautiful, is not meant for decoration alone. It must be full of meaning to the people who buy' (see figure 8.2).

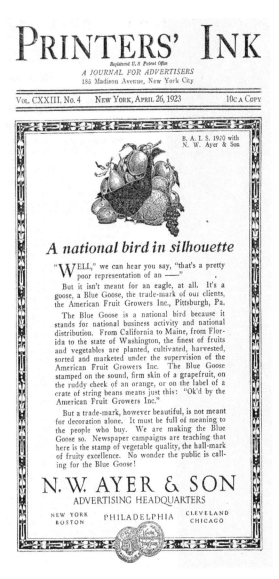

Figure 8.2 1923 N. W. Ayer trade advertisement. Source: *Printer's Ink*, April 1923: 15, N. W. Ayer Advertising Agency Records, Archives Center, National Museum of American History, Behring Center, Smithsonian Institution.

A prime example for how advertising agencies from the 1910s began explicitly to focus on developing brand personality, brand image, and brand identity is the American J. Walter Thompson company (JWT). Founded in 1864, it became the largest US agency after it had been purchased by Stanley B. Resor in 1916. Between the interwar years and the 1960s, it was the largest and certainly most important among all international advertising agencies (West 1988; Silva 1996). As early as 1911, the agency offered a booklet of some 80 pages to its clients, under the title *Things to Know About Trade-Marks* (Thompson 1911). With this brochure, the agency positioned itself as a comprehensive advisor to manufacturers on all aspects of trademark law and registration. The booklet took the reader through all steps of how to apply for trademark registration, the various procedures at US Patent Offices, and trademark registration in foreign countries. It advised manufacturers, for example, that geographical names, shapes, colours, and materials were not registrable, and it also showed readers how to devise a well-recognizable trademark through the use of distinctive shapes, faces, colours, or words and slogans. The JWT agency even developed an early advertising and branding theory in the booklet—a theory that grew out of practical considerations and accumulated marketing experience with clients like Mennen's Talcum Powder, Woodbury Facial Soap, or Eastman Kodak cameras. For JWT, the most important business force was not the ability to produce at lower costs but the 'recognized distinction' (Thompson 1911: 10) of the product and the goodwill that it carried in the minds of millions of consumers: 'Advertising is a systematic method of creating Good Reputation' (ibid.). The advertised trademark thus allowed the manufacturer to directly link up with the end-consumer and cut out the jobber, wholesaler and retailer in his sales efforts: 'The trade-mark is the connecting link between the manufacturer and the ultimate consumer' (ibid. and figure 8.3).

Based on this knowledge, the JWT agency formulated a catalogue of advertising services that included advice on trademarks and their protection against infringement, but also on media and consumer research, campaign planning and creative execution. According to JWT, creativity did not only consist of visually 'attractive' advertising, but of the ability to 'create a desire for the advertised product' (see figure 8.4).

This is perhaps the first time that an agency stated that advertising services could not limit themselves to devising and registering a distinct trademark, publicizing it on a high-quality product, and then waiting for consumers to buy it. In the booklet, the agency clearly stated that brand-focused advertising did not only assure consumers about the sources and origins of a product—a function exercised by the trademark—but instead formed social desires. This assertion about the 'creation of desire' is a public admission by the agency that products are carriers of socially shared symbolic meanings that manifest themselves in cognitive and behavioural reactions that are guided by a multiplicity of motives, specifically including

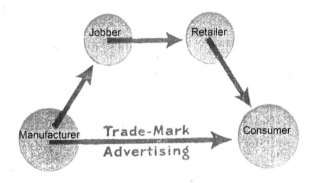

This looks like a problem in geometry, but it isn't.

This diagram shows at a glance how Trade-Mark Advertising draws a straight line between the manufacturer and the consumer.

The manufacturer who doesn't advertise has to depend on the jobber and the retailer. In the majority of cases his name never reaches the consumer. His trade is necessarily precarious, and he is constantly in danger of the kind of cut-throat competition that shaves the lowest margin of profit to nothing.

But the manufacturer who advertises has his name and the name of his goods on the lips of millions of people. The retailer who attempts to keep advertised goods from selling is like the man who cuts off his nose to spite his face. People will go elsewhere and get what they want.

We would like to talk with you about advertising. Among our clients are some of the largest and most successful advertisers in the United States. It will cost nothing to have a talk with us—and we may be able to suggest an idea or plan that will simplify your sales problem.

J. WALTER THOMPSON COMPANY

New York: 44 East 23rd Street
Boston: 201 Devonshire Street
Cincinnati: First National Bank Bldg.
St. Louis: Odd Fellows Bldg.

Chicago: The Rookery
Cleveland: Swetland Bldg.
Detroit: Trussed Concrete Bldg.
Toronto: Lumsden Bldg.

London: 33 Bedford St., Strand

Figure 8.3 J. Walter Thompson visualizes the role of the trademark (1911). Source: *Things to Know About Trade-Marks*, JWT Collection, The History of Advertising Trust Archive, Norwich.

The
J. W. T.
Advertising

Service

An advertising agency's claim to an advertiser's consideration must be based on the service that it gives.

Service consists of :—

1st.　Information as to advertising mediums, their circulations, rates and qualities.

2nd.　Advice resting on actual experience.

3rd.　Knowledge of commodities, their composition, prices and methods of sale.

4th.　Knowledge of merchandising conditions.

5th.　Knowledge of the buying public, its needs, its habits and its income.

6th.　The ability to plan advertising campaigns—that is, to grasp the whole subject and work out its details in conformity with a general principle.

7th.　Knowledge of trade-marks, their use in advertising, and methods of protecting them from infringement.

8th.　The ability to write advertising that will create a desire for the advertised product.

9th.　The artistic ability to make advertising attractive.

The service of the J. Walter Thompson Company covers all these functions of an advertising agency.

We have had a continuous experience of forty-six years in planning and carrying out advertising campaigns.

We have reached the stage of development where we know advertising as a swimmer knows the water.

Doesn't it seem good business to entrust your advertising to an agency that really knows ?

J. WALTER THOMPSON COMPANY

New York: 44 East 23rd Street　　　Chicago: The Rookery
Boston: 201 Devonshire Street　　　Cleveland: Swetland Bldg.
Cincinnati: First National Bank Bldg.　　Detroit: Trussed Concrete Bldg.
St. Louis: Odd Fellows Bldg.　　　Toronto: Lumsden Bldg.
London: 33 Bedford St., Strand

Figure 8.4　J. Walter Thompson explains the role of advertising agencies. Source: *Things to Know About Trade-Marks*, JWT Collection, The History of Advertising Trust Archive, Norwich.

emotions and social aspirations, and not only by a 'rational' cost-benefit assessment (Katona 1953; Lears 1983; O'Shaughnessy 2003).

By the early 1920s, JWT was beginning to notice that consumers' knowledge of trademarks did not necessarily translate into preference for a brand or the ability to distinguish between two types of cigarettes or chocolate.[5] Through its work for the Lever brand Lux, the JWT agency developed an early understanding of the fact that trademarks had to be charged with image, identity, and personality, and be built up into aspirational brands in order to achieve the aim of creating desire in consumers' minds.

Lever's Lux brand, for a new type of soap flakes, was launched in Britain in 1900 with the aim of providing a superior quality product that made the washing of laundry easier for women and allowed more delicate materials, especially wool, to keep in good shape for longer, since housewives using Lux flakes did not have to rub the textiles with a hard soap bar (see figures 8.5 and 8.6).

Figure 8.5 Lux packaging around 1910. Source: Unilever Archives, Unilever PLC.

Figure 8.6 Modernized Lux packaging around 1930. Source: Unilever Archives, Unilever PLC.

The product, with its distinctive brand name (derived from the Latin word for light, *lux*, which in English also suggested luxury) and packaging, was one of the first attempts at integrated marketing in Britain. All aspects of the marketing of the brand, the product development itself, the packaging, the advertising communication, the distribution methods and pricing, were integrated to establish Lux as an innovative, high-price, and high-value product. In 1906, Lever began to export Lux soap flakes to the United States, and later established a manufacturing plant there as well, to supply the US and the Canadian markets with the product. Intitially, the advertising expenditure was kept at a low rate, and Lux was positioned as an expensive product to be used for the washing of woollen garments, like blankets, jackets, and underwear ('Lux won't shrink woollens'). In 1915, the advertising account for Lux was handed over by the American Lever subsidiary to JWT. The agency suggested that the traditional positioning of Lux as a product for woollen garments should be widened so that consumers could see Lux as a product to be used for all fine fabrics in the household. But, crucially, for this to be effected the Lux brand had to be more closely associated and even become identical with the image of expensive clothing and upmarket fashion.[6] For Lever Brothers in the US, this strategy resulted in increased sales from 10,000 cases in 1915 to over one million cases in 1918 (Lovett 1970).

During the early 1920s, the JWT agency demonstrated a clear insight into how brands become part of social life and acquire new meanings and values in daily consumer practices. This insight was translated by the agency into various innovations in the communication and brand development of Lux. In 1924, for example, JWT invited American housewives to submit testimonials for Lux soap flakes. These letters, of which about 53,000 arrived at the JWT headquarters, were used by the agency to conduct a survey of consumer habits. It turned out that consumers had independently begun to use the flakes for the washing of their hands, for baths, for their babies, and for their hair, thus effectively creating brand extensions into new product lines (toilet soap, shampoo, etc.). These findings encouraged Lever Brothers in the United States to extend the brand and offer consumers a Lux Toilet Soap, which was launched on the American market in 1925, and three years later on the British market.[7] JWT used such consumer competitions and slogan contests to find out about the additional uses of the Lux brand in households and in order to create virtual bonds between the brand and a global collective of users.[8]

Through the close bonds that emerged between the brand and its devoted consumer community, the agency was able to spot new opportunities to create line extensions, and thus allow the brand to rejuvenate itself in the form of toilet soap, shampoo, and dishwashing flakes.[9] Between the 1920s and '50s, the agency continuously improved on the products that were put on the American market under the Lux brand umbrella. Before the Second World War, Lux shampoo and toilet soap were launched in the United States, as well as an improved form of Lux, 'Quick Lux'.[10] After the war, 'Lux Liquid' was launched in order to match a similar offering by Procter and Gamble in the new product category of washing-up liquids.[11]

The backdrop to JWT's constant activities in repositioning and reinventing the Lux brand was its recognition, at around 1920, that the product would attract a 'swarm of competitors' due to its superior quality and innovative production technology.[12] Thus, it was not the expectation of rising average incomes or other changes in the macro-marketing environment (demand structure) during the 1920s, but the realization that other firms might offer a similar product, which spurned staff at JWT to charge the Lux product with a sense of magic and mystery and make it identical with the idea of classy fashion.[13] The strategy to turn soap flakes into a magical and mysterious product in order to ward off identical competitor products supports Cano (2003), who argues that marketing practitioners followed competitor-based approaches to market segmentation and product positioning long before these terms were formally introduced into the marketing literature by Wendell Smith in 1956 (Smith 1956).

While Lever's American subsidiary with its agency JWT made great efforts in conquering the North American market for Lux, the British market became more receptive for the product as well. With medium advertising support by Lever at Port Sunlight, Lux kept being positioned in the minds of British consumers as a household product for woollen garments. The marketing activities by Lever in Britain—in marked contrast to the US—were heavily influenced by the fact that Lever tried to acquire a monopoly for soap products. By the end of the 1920s, the Lever group had acquired 49 soap-manufacturing companies and produced some 60 per cent of all soap consumed in the United Kingdom. Moreover, until the mid- and late 1920s, Lever in Britain had no major competitors, as Colgate-Palmolive only entered Britain in 1924 and Procter and Gamble followed in 1930 with the acquisition of Thomas Hedley Ltd (Wilson 1954; Edwards 1962; Wilson and Thomson 2006).

During the late 1920s, however, Lever's once comfortable position in the British market came under attack from foreign competitors. In 1924, Colgate's 'Palmolive Toilet Soap' was introduced in Britain supported by the American Lord and Thomas advertising agency. By the mid-1930s, Palmolive had diversified into shampoo, toilet soap, shaving cream, and face powder (*Statistical Review* 1937). Lever also suffered from its own diseconomies of scale, as the soap products manufactured by the combine incurred heavy advertising expenditure while competing for similar segments of the market. Lever's limitations in strategically positioning its own brands in the crowded British market became more and more apparent. By the late 1920s, Rinso, Persil, Sunlight Soap, Lifebuoy, the Monkey Brand, Pear's Soap, and Lux were all part of the Lever Empire. As low-involvement products, all these brands had to be heavily advertised in order to gain consumers' awareness and, thus, they consumed each others' market shares and incurred large advertising costs on Lever (cannibalization). This made it even more necessary to make the Lux brand identifiable and allow consumers to emotionally bond with a certain image and lifestyle that the brand projected. In a highly volatile market, the expensive quality product Lux had a difficult time in maintaining market share as competitors managed to copy the manufacturing process and thus offer flaked or grated

5

soaps. In response to these competitive pressures, Lever handed over the British advertising account for Lux to the JWT agency in 1927.

Faced with the challenges of the British market, the JWT agency attempted to revive Lux by drawing on its experiences with the brand on the American market since 1915. At the heart of the agency's strategy was to identify, through market and consumer research, the unique place that the brand could occupy in people's minds. By conducting extensive research surveys, JWT not only found out through which distribution channels women bought soap products, and which factors (water hardness, use of soda as substitute, high price, unwieldy package, unavailability in certain retail outlets) inhibited the acceptance of Lux among women,[14] it also recognized that their advertising for Lux had to tell a certain story about the brand that naturally connected the product to the attitudes, interests, and opinions of its target market. In their attempt to put advertising on a more 'scientific' base, JWT researchers and copywriters discovered that consumers' behavioural and psychic dispositions towards a brand were influenced by the images that a brand invoked in people's minds.

In this endeavour, the London JWT office was able to use the insights the agency had gained while working for Lux in the United States. In the more competitive US market, the agency had learned that the Lux brand was not only a trademark, but a collection of social attributes. This discovery had been summarized at a 1924 JWT account planning conference in New York, when a female copywriter described Lux in terms of its image and its brand personality:

> I think of Lux as a member of the lesser nobility. She is probably a Marquise. She is gay, spontaneous, care-free. If you met her in the flesh she would greet you with squeals of delight and trills of laughter. She had a home. . . . But her home gave her no anxiety. She whisked her handsome woolen blankets through the rich lather and out they come like new. Husband she must have had, but he never appears. Maybe he follows the sea or maybe he couldn't stand the pace.[15]

Through a careful analysis of the Lux 'personality' and the changes this 'person' went through, the JWT campaign planers also discovered that the brand needed to be rejuvenated in order to make 'her' more meaningful and relevant to her target audience. Although the early Lux was a carefree individualist who lived only for her lovely clothes, 'she' now discovered that 'her friends' needed Lux for dishwashing, too:

> For five long, happy years nothing happened to change her gay, whimsical clothes loving nature. Her sixth year started out happily enough, but she was suddenly forced to consider stern realities. Did competition stalk her trail? Did she really have secret troubles that she nobly concealed? . . . This phase lasted for two full years. And Lux has never

been quite the same since. She has lost some of her charm—there is no doubt about that. She has also become less of an individualist. Other people's problems affect her a bit . . . there is a strong inkling in her mind that she can not live by clothes alone. She must have a wider interest and she has found it in dishes. And how true she is to type. She doesn't talk about how clean she gets her dishes. Not at all. She is only interested in her own hands, the huzzy. At first she hypocritically preached economy, but this year she has thrown economy to the winds and stands forth blatantly on her platform of pride in her well-kept hands. A pride she is trying to impose upon her neighbors—she is endeavouring to threaten and to frighten them.[16]

These insights into the way consumers mentally construct an image of a brand were directly fed into the repositioning process that JWT attempted for Lux on the British market. Since the agency had come to realize that advertising was effectively an activity of strategically manipulating socially-shared symbols, it attempted to facilitate the market penetration of Lux by disconnecting it from the mental images of the housewife's 'slavery' and hard work and, instead, connect it to images of happiness and leisure. When JWT began to work on the account in Britain in 1927 it, therefore, recommended that Lux advertisements should be based on the theme of fashion. In order to increase the relevance and attractiveness of the brand, the London JWT office devised advertisements that conveyed news about the world of style, prestige, and glamour. The ultimate aim of the campaign was to turn the perception of the product from being 'simply a different kind of laundry soap' into a 'magical kind of product'.[17] The new Lux campaign that started in March 1928 in Britain broke with the traditions of soap advertising, which, until then, tended to stress formal product attributes in a 'slice-of-life' surrounding characterized by housewives shown at work in the kitchen or in the bathroom. In the new Lux campaign, the female reader was no longer confronted with real-life images of hard-working housewives, but instead with stylish, thin, modernist drawings of living fashion-dolls. In order to attach the unique selling proposition of Lux—keeping women's most treasured clothes like new—and in order to surround Lux with an air of distinguished lifestyle, JWT used designs and drawings that women recognized from retail and fashion advertising (See figure 8.7).

The key to this radical change was the ability of JWT copywriters to tap into their target group's attitudes, interests, and opinions. Using innovative market research and consumer analysis methods, JWT found out that the brand's target group was interested in news about fashion and read advertisements to gather information about lifestyle trends. JWT, therefore, decided to construct a new type of advertisement that proffered women's gossip, lifestyle advice, and fashion news.[18] The JWT brand planners used market research strategically to look deeper into the social and emotional worlds of their target group and found that the 'new woman' of the 1920s wanted

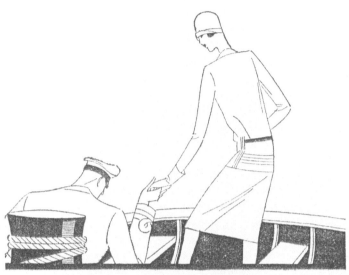

Rubbing shrinks jumpers;- makes them harsh, unlovely

Keep them like new . . right through the summer

Adorable—the new sports clothes! Crisp washing silks — woollens softer, finer than any you had before — slim tailored flannels . . . how to keep these lovely things fresh, trim, smart!

For if you rub them with bar soap you may ruin them at once — make them faded, unattractive.

Rubbing with bar soap wears out the frail silken threads, ruins flannels and woollens too—makes them shrink, grow harsh, unlovely. Lux makes all harmful rubbing unnecessary. Just whip its glistening flakes to a sparkling lather — and rinse each garment up and down, gently squeezing the bubbling, cleansing Lux suds through the fabric. Dirt and stains vanish like magic. In a few seconds your precious things are clean again — silks just as lovely, unfaded, woollens as soft and downy, as when they were new!

Directions for washing silks and woollens most successfully are given on every Lux packet.

Made by a 10-day process so costly none but Lever Brothers, the world's greatest soap-makers, could afford it, the snow-white Lux flakes are safe for washing any fabric water alone won't harm. Lux is sold only in the familiar blue packets.

Lx 501-247   LEVER BROTHERS LIMITED, PORT SUNLIGHT

Figure 8.7 Lux advertisement in *Home Notes*, August 1928. Source: Unilever Archives, Unilever PLC.

her clothes not just clean, but used them to prove herself in real life. JWT's advertisements presented Lux as a friend and lifestyle expert for its users and constructed an entirely new symbolic universe around the brand.

The agency thus reinvented Lux as one of Britain's first lifestyle brands, or what Douglas Holt called an 'identity brand' (Holt 2003: 3–14). The skilful design of the fashion-styled advertisements translated the tangible, unique selling proposition (USP) of Lux into an emotional selling proposition (ESP). While the communication of all other soap products told consumers what the product did to their clothing (cleaning) and how it helped women caring for their families ('Lifebuoy Soap for Health'; 'The shortest way on washing day: the Rinso way'; 'Sunlight: Not yet One and washing done'; 'Victory— won by Persil'), Lux advertising told female audiences what the product did for their personality. Unlike Rinso or Persil or the plethora of unbranded products that were available to British and American women, Lux became a brand that based its very identity on the narrative of transformation: Lux promised to turn a simple housewife into a style-savvy, adorable fashion-goddess. The key to this narrative were the findings of JWT's behaviour- and identity-oriented market research (Schwarzkopf 2009).

By the late 1920s, JWT had thus successfully personalized and largely emotionalized the Lux brand, both on the American and the British market. This assessment counters the assertion by Davies and Elliot (2006) that consumers in the interwar period used brands for rational decision-making. While the Lux brand communication always stressed the product's use value and its high quality, the advertising platform ran completely on the themes of romance, drama, and social excitement, and used the human interest story in order to breed familiarity with the consumer. Indeed, brand loyalty was created in a series of advertisements in which movie celebrities and famed novelists shared 'a secret' with female consumers—advertisements that seemed to say to young women that the Lux brand knew and understood them. During 1929, for example, American readers of women's magazines saw slogans such as '"Don't call it luck", says Elinor Glyn— famous authority on romance' or 'Beatrix Fairfax answers Cleveland girl's query: "How can I attract?"' Since Lux kept clothing fresh and colourful it 'brought romance into the lives of millions of girls'.[19] In order for the human touch to work, JWT exploited the idea of personifying the brand image to the full. In 1928, it first used the Hollywood star appeal for Lux Toilet Soap and in 1950 for Lux Flakes under the slogan '9 out of 10 screen stars use Lux'.[20]

FORMALIZATION OF BRAND MANAGEMENT IN LAW AND MARKETING THOUGHT

Innovations in understanding the relationship between consumers and brands were not necessarily limited to American agencies alone. During the 1920s, the British agency W. S. Crawford's Ltd., for example, began to talk about 'product personality', the 'advertising idea', and argued that in order to stimulate sales and create a 'buying habit', advertising had to 'build a definitive association of ideas round the goods' that advertising promoted (Schwarzkopf 2008).[21] For the purposes of this chapter, however, it is sufficient to establish that the previously described approaches of turning trademarks into image-laden brands were *practised* before brand management was formally established as a managerial technique at Procter and Gamble in 1931 (Fullerton and Low 1994; Dyer et al. 2004) and also before the idea entered marketing *theory* that advertising's central role was to develop a brand image at the corporate and/or product level (Meenaghan 1995). The JWT agency tried to formalize this approach during the 1920s and '30s, but focussed their efforts mostly on ways of turning creative copy writing into a more accountable and self-reflexive process (Cherington 1924; Webb Young 1940).

In Britain, too, advertising agencies and their clients began to recognize the value of powerful and emotive brands. One way of enhancing this power was, of course, to strengthen the legal protection that a registered trademark offered the brand in the competitive marketplace. Consequently, during the interwar years, British businesses began to mount pressure on successive governments to modernise the Trade Marks and Merchandise Marks Acts. In 1919–20, the Merchandise Marks Committee, and in 1933–34, the Departmental Committee on the Law and Practice relating to Trade Marks (Goschen Committee), paved the way for a strengthening of the trademark owner against nontraditional forms of infringement, which had emerged since the Victorian era. The Goschen Committee also recommended the relaxation of some of the restrictions on the assignment of trademarks and a facility for a person to register a trademark to be used by others under a 'registered user' provision (Merchandise Marks Committee 1920; Joint Trade Marks Committee 1933; Report of the Departmental Committee 1934). The ensuing trademark legislation under the 1937 and 1938 Trade Marks (Amendment) Acts provided for this recommendation by allowing for the assignment of a trademark in gross, i.e. without the underlying 'goodwill' that a trademark symbol, name, or slogan was associated with. According to the trademark lawyer, Dawson, this right 'reflected and facilitated the growing practice of corporate acquisition and restructuring and the fact that brands were fast becoming major commercial assets in their own right' (Dawson and Firth 2000: viii).

The new legislation furnished the advertising industry with an increased sense of importance. Before the 1930s, many British manufacturers and traders could claim that a product's quality reputation stemmed solely from the goodwill afforded by those who used it—just as good wine allegedly needed 'no bush'. The new trademark legislation, however, took into account that a brand's reputation could be quickly built up through the use of image-oriented advertising campaigns. This, in turn, accelerated the transition within the advertising industry away from a self-definition based on the idea of trademark publicity towards a professional identity based on building powerful brands (see figures 8.8 and 8.9).

As mentioned earlier, this understanding emerged slowly during the early 1920s, with advertising trade journals such as the *Advertiser's Weekly* telling its readers that trademarks needed to be developed into brands in order

"I AM A MODERN LOAF OF BREAD. I seldom grow old and crusty. People like me too well for that. At parties and picnics I am especially popular because I make such thin, unbroken sandwiches.

"My taste is delicious because I am made of the best flour, under hygienic conditions, in a sun-lit bakery.

"You cannot buy better nourishment than me. I am full of health-giving cereals, proteins, vitamins and phosphates. Children are very fond of me, and I of them. I make the *staff of life* more sustaining than ever. And you can have me for a few pennies."

Selling might be simpler if bread could speak. As it is, it must be advertised. How may advertisements speak for the product, effectively, warmly, and without waste of money?

That, we submit, involves abilities as specialized in their way as the baking of the bread itself.

It means finding out what manner of people use most bread, and when, and why. *What influence should the trend toward smaller families have in the size of a loaf? How many like crust? Soft bread? Wholewheat bread? Milk rolls? Why?*

It means finding out what are housewives' buying habits. And where do they buy? *At the door? Or at a shop? Do they specify a brand? Or take what is given them?*

It means framing a message to them that arouses desire — desire that the product will satisfy. *What is this message? How may it best be presented?* Of two good ways of presenting an idea, one often proves three times as profitable as the other. *How shall we choose?* Individual judgment is dangerous — and costly.

We, as advertising agents, set ourselves the task of finding out the answers to these cardinal questions before we plan our clients' advertising or write their advertisements.

We believe that this care in approaching our clients' problems explains, in part, why they have obtained substantial sales increases even during the depression.

J. WALTER THOMPSON COMPANY LIMITED
Incorporated Practitioners in Advertising · *BUSH HOUSE, ALDWYCH, LONDON, W.C.2*

Among our clients are: CALVERTS · COURTAULDS · HORLICK'S · HUDSON'S (RINSO) · KRAFT CHEESE
KODAK · LEVER BROTHERS (LUX, LUX TOILET SOAP) · LLOYDS BANK · POND'S · ROWNTREE'S

Figure 8.8   1934 J. Walter Thompson trade advertisement. Source: JWT Collection, The History of Advertising Trust Archive, Norwich.

Figure 8.9   1939 London Press Exchange trade advertisements. Source: LPE Collection, The History of Advertising Trust Archive, Norwich.

to make products stand out like 'lone stars on a night-sky'.[22] By the late 1930s, even the most traditional members of the industry had understood that, although trafficking in trademarks themselves was still an offence under the law, the reputation associated with image-laden and socially highly symbolic trademarks had become what Earl Loreburn called a 'marketable commodity'.[23]

This recognition expressed itself in a series of new texts for the British advertising industry, which acknowledged that the task of agencies was not only to help their clients with publicizing a trademark that indicated the commercial source of a product but also to create and manage symbolic and socially shared meanings that brands are based on. Arnold Plant, Professor of Business Administration at the London School of Economics, was one of the first who conducted consistent research in Britain into the macroeconomic effects and advantages to individual consumers of branded household goods. Even in 1937, he noted that 'the introduction of brands implies a doubt in the mind of the manufacturer whether he can otherwise continuously hold the market' and that branding 'was not universally believed by manufacturers to be the best way of selling their output' (Plant 1937: 305–6). In his report, he also found that some 50 per cent of products stocked by British grocers were still unbranded. Notwithstanding the wide-spread scepticism against brands in the British retail environment noted by Plant, 1920s and '30s business handbooks began to teach that all marketing activity had its final objective in creating competitive brands (Chisholm 1924: 44; 53). In June 1939, the *Daily Mail* told its readers that advertising and consumers could work hand-in-hand through the provision of and demand for standardized, high-quality, and branded goods: 'Fish, Bananas, fancy ties . . . they are all branded now. Just as hall-mark identifies silver, the brand name of the manufacturer speaks for the quality of his product' (Anon. 1939: vii).

The interwar period turns out to be a period in which advertising agencies moved much more into the centre ground of the complex interplay between manufacturers, and distributors' marketing decisions, the communication of branded products and consumer behaviour in the marketplace. The renewed emphasis on flexible and competitive trademark legislation in the 1930s made itself felt in the advertising industry and lent more authority to those agencies that argued that meaningful brands that tapped into the lifestyle of their targeted audiences were the most important intangible assets of a company, in addition to tangibles such as capital, buildings, machinery, and infrastructure (Wilkins 1992). In a series of newspaper advertisements, the two largest advertising agencies in London at that time, JWT and the London Press Exchange, visualized the meaning of brands to companies and the market, as well as the crucial role of advertising agencies in that complex relationship. The agencies' advertisements, for example, told the story of a nonbranded loaf of bread that wondered by whom it would be bought or showed brands who got lost because they lacked an advertising agency that showed them the right 'way to the market place'. During the 1930s, the Advertising Association issued propaganda brochures and posters that called on consumers to trust branded goods and brand names because 'There is safety in a brand name'. In 1940, the Advertising Association published posters calling on manufacturers to keep on advertising to avoid losing 'brand goodwill', and it reminded consumers, retailers, and manufacturers that the 'trade mark guarantees value'.[24]

CONCLUSION

Advertising agencies' role in the making of brands radically changed during the first half of the twentieth century. During much of the nineteenth century, advertising limited itself to publicizing a trademark within a framework of mass promotion as the main communication aim. Little attention was paid to the idea of the symbolic and emotional capacities of brands in building consumer loyalty and forming certain consumer identities. The self-definition of the advertising agency's work changed at around the time of the First World War. During the early 1920s, advertising practitioners discovered the advantages of the proactive and planned creation of brands with unique image and personality. By the late 1920s and early '30s, some agencies and their corporate clients, like Unilever and Procter and Gamble, had begun to develop a practical understanding of how advertising could build brands, and also recognized that brands and their communication need careful management in an increasingly competitive environment.

There is evidence that this transformation was influenced by changes in trademark law, which increased the focus within the advertising industry on creating brand equity through large-scale and long-term advertising campaigns. The perennial search within the industry for clearer ideas and definitions of the brand was fed by the need to make the marketing communications process more efficient and accountable. This need, in turn, was fuelled by the competition between advertising agencies for clients and the competition for consumers among manufacturers of similar products.

It was not before the mid-1950s, however, and the arrival of David Ogilvy on Madison Avenue, that the idea of the brand image became a common staple within the global advertising industry (Fox 1984; Millman 1988; Haygood 2007; Tungate 2007). A British immigrant to the US, Ogilvy, had read about the notion that a brand held holistic and personal characteristics in a *Harvard Business Review* article by Sidney Levy and Burleigh Gardner in March 1955 (Gardner and Levy 1955; Mitchell 1959; Levy 2003). The article, under the title 'The product and the brand', was a revelation for Ogilvy and the rest of the advertising world because it made explicit what many of the more innovative agencies, such as Lord and Thomas, J. Walter Thompson, or W. S. Crawford, had practised for at least three decades. This practice was summarised by Ogilvy in his agency's creative credo: 'Every advertisement is part of the long-term investment in the personality of the brand'.[25]

This study reminds marketing historians that the conceptualization of the branding process in marketing theory followed its emergence in practice, not vice versa. This puts a question mark behind approaches to marketing history as a purely intellectual exercise that only looks at the development of explicitly formalized and published knowledge, and ignores social practices and repertoires of implicit knowledge within advertising agencies as the earliest branding laboratories. Briefs and company memos at advertising agencies' archives leave no doubt about that: they show that, by the 1920s, both agencies and their clients were highly self-reflective and fully aware of the fact that the advertising process was essentially about building (brand) images for trademarked products through conscious manipulation and deployment of symbols that resonated with targeted consumers.

NOTES

1. 'National Trademark inimical to established brands', *Advertiser's Weekly* (August 29 1918): 464–5.
2. 'The history of Lux Flakes', *Lever Standard* 22 (October 1950): 3–8. Thompson was then perhaps Britain's best-known trade mark and patent agent. See

W. P. Thompson, 'Trade-Marks in China', *The Times* (6 September 1904): 6 and W. P. Thompson, 'The Patents Act', *The Times* (21 May 1909): 19.

3. See T. B. Browne papers at History of Advertising Trust Archive, Norwich, AdAg B3, and 'Inventions and designs: New Patent Act', *The Times* (12 October 1932): 7.

4. 'The Show window of an advertising agency' (1914/15), N. W. Ayer Collection, Box 3, Series 16, Washington Smithsonian Museum.

5. 'The value of a Trade mark', pp. 1–2, and 'Test and testers', p. 6, *JWT News Bulletin*, No. 91 (16 October 1922).

6. *Account Histories: Lever Brother Company—Lux*, 11 February 1926, Folder Lever Brothers (1916–1959), and *Lux Flakes Account History (1926–1950)*, 21 September 1950, Folder Lever Brothers, Lux Case History (1923–1973), both in JWT Information Center Records, Box 5 (J. Walter Thompson Archive, Hartman Center, Duke University).

7. Ibid., and *Lux 1928/1939*, 1939, JWT Account Files, Box 687 (JWT Collection, HAT Archive).

8. *All Over the World They Use it!*, 1923, Folder Lever Brothers (1916–1959), and *Account Histories: Lever Brother Company—Lux*, 11 February 1926, Folder Lever Brothers (1916–1959), both in JWT Information Center Records, Box 5 (JWT Archive, Duke University).

9. *Lux for Dishwashing, Questionnaire by Mail*, September 1923, Folder Lever Brothers (1916–1959), in JWT Information Center Records, Box 5 (JWT Archive, Duke University).

10. *Lux Flakes Account History (1926–1950)*, 21 September 1950, Folder Lever Brothers, in JWT Information Center Records, Box 5 (JWT Archive, Duke University).

11. *Case Report on Lux Liquid*, 1956, Folder Lever Brothers, Lux Liquid, Case History in JWT Information Center Records, Box 5 (JWT Archive, Duke University).

12. *Creative Staff Meeting*, 25 May 1932: 4, Folder Lever Brothers (1916–1959), in JWT Information Center Records, Box 5 (JWT Archive, Duke University).

13. *Lux Advertising During 1928*, 1928, JWT Account Files, Box 687, JWT Collection, History of Advertising Trust Archive, Norwich and *Creative Staff Meeting*, 1932 (JWT Archive, Duke University).

14. *Lux England 1928*, 1927, JWT Account Files, Box 687, and *Summary of Investigation*, 1930, Box 693, both JWT Collection, HAT Archive.

15. *Conference Miss Flemming*, 21 February 1924: 1, Folder Lever Brothers (1916–1959), JWT Information Center Records, Box 5 (JWT Archive, Duke University).

16. Ibid.: 2.

17. *Lux Press Campaign*, 1927, and *Lux Advertising During 1928*, 1928: 1, both JWT Account Files, Box 687 (JWT Collection, HAT Archive).

18. *Advance Fashion News* (Published by the Lux Educational Bureau in Co-operation with Harper's Bazaar, 1932–1934), JWT Account Files, Manila Box Series, Box 10; *Gossip Style* advertising, 1930, JWT Account Files, Box 693, and *Lux Press Campaign*, 1927, all JWT Collection, HAT Archive.

19. *Advertisement Proofs*, 1929, Folder Lever Lux Flakes, JWT Domestic Advertisements Collection, Box LB 7 (JWT Archive, Duke University).

20. *Tie-up of Lux Toilet Soap With the Cinema Industry*, 4 January 1933, JWT Account Files, Box 690, *Interim Report on Post-War Planning for the Advertising and Merchandising of Lux Toilet Soap*, March 1944, JWT Account Files, Box 689, both JWT Collection, HAT Archive; 'Lever Brothers—Lux Flakes: JWT Campaign of the Week', *J.W.T. News* IV, No. 52 (1949): 3.

21. '3-point-advertising', *Advertiser's Weekly* (9 January 1920): 29.
22. 'Why branded goods sell', *Advertiser's Weekly* (16 April 1920): 61–2.
23. Earl Loreburn L.C., House of Lords ruling in the case Bowden Wire Ltd. *v.* Bowden Brake Co. Ltd. (1914) 31 R.P.C. 385, p. 392.
24. Advertising Association papers 13/1/1 (1934) and 13/1/6 (1940), Advertising Association Collection, HAT Archive.
25. 'The image and the brand: A new approach to creative operations' (4 October 1955), Speech given at AAAA Luncheon in Chicago, Box 78, Folder: Speeches 1954–56, David Ogilvy Papers, Library of Congress, Washington.

BIBLIOGRAPHY

Aaker, D. (1997) 'Dimensions of brand personality', *Journal of Marketing Research*, 34 (2): 347–56.
Aaker, D. (2002) *Building Strong Brands*, Simon & Schuster: London.
Andersen, B. (2006) *Intellectual Property Rights: Innovation, Governance and the Institutional Environment*, Cheltenham: Edward Elgar.
Anon. (1939) 'They are all branded now', *Daily Mail* 19 June: vii (Supplement).
Arvidsson, A. (2006) *Brands: Meaning and Value in Media Culture*, Abingdon, Oxon: Routledge.
Benson, J. (1994) *The Rise of Consumer Society in Britain: 1880–1980*, London: Longman.
Berg, M. (1994) *The Age of Manufactures, 1700–1820: Industry, Innovation and Work in Britain*, London: Routledge.
Blackett, T. (1998) *Trademarks*, Basingstoke: Macmillan Business.
———. (2003) 'What is a brand?', in R. Clifton, J. Simmons (eds.), *Brands and Branding*, London: Profile Books, pp. 13–25.
Breen, T. H. (1988) '"Baubles of Britain": The American and consumer revolution of the eighteenth century', *Past and Present*, 119 (May): 73–104.
Brierley, S. (2002) *The Advertising Handbook*, Abingdon, Oxon: Routledge.
Browne, R. B. (1984) *T. B. Browne Ltd.: The First 100 Years*, London: privately printed.
Bussey, N. (2006) 'Do brand consultancies offer value?', *Campaign* (4 August).
Cano, C. (2003) 'The recent evolution of market segmentation concepts and thoughts primarily by marketing academics', in E. Shaw (ed.) *The Romance of Marketing History: Proceedings of the 11th Conference on Historical Analysis and Research in Marketing (CHARM)*. Boca Ranton, FL: AHRIM.
Chandler, A. (1990) *Scale and Scope: The Dynamics of Industrial Capitalism*, Cambridge, MA.: Belknap.
Cherington, P. (1924) *The Consumer Looks at Advertising*, New York: Harper.
Chisholm, C. (1924) *Marketing and Merchandising*, London: Modern Business Institute.
Church, R. (2000) 'Advertising consumer goods in nineteenth-century Britain: reinterpretations', *Economic History Review*, 53 (4): 621–45.
Church, R. and C. Clark (2000) 'The origins of competitive advantage in the marketing of branded packaged goods: Colman's and Reckitt's in Victorian Britain', *Journal of Industrial History*, 3 (2): 98–119.
———. (2003) 'Purposive strategy or serendipity? Development and diversification in three consumer product companies, 1918–39: J. & J. Colman, Reckitt & Son, and Lever Bros./Unilever', *Business History*, 45 (1): 23–59.
Corley, T. A. B. (1987) 'Consumer marketing in Britain, 1914–1960', *Business History*, 29: 65–83.

Davies, A. and R. Elliot (2006) 'The evolution of the empowered consumer', *European Journal of Marketing*, 40 (9/10): 1106–21.

Dawson, N. and A. Firth (eds.) (2000), *Trade Marks Retrospective*, London: Sweet & Maxwell.

de Chernatony, L. and M. MacDonald (2003) *Creating Powerful Brands in Consumer, Service and Industrial Markets*, Oxford: Elsevier.

Duguid, P. (2003) Developing the brand: The case of alcohol, 1800–1880', *Enterprise & Society*, 4 (3): 405–41.

Dyer, D. et al. (2004) *Rising Tide: Lessons from 165 Years of Brand Building at Procter & Gamble*, Boston, MA: Harvard Business School Press.

Edwards, H. R. (1962) *Competition and Monopoly in the British Soap Industry*, Oxford: Oxford University Press.

Fitzgerald, R. (2005) 'Products, firms and consumption: Cadbury and the development of marketing, 1900–1939', *Business History*, 47 (4): 511–31.

Fox, S. J. (1984) *The Mirror Makers: A History of American Advertising and its Creators*, New York: Mirror.

Fraser, H. (1981) *The Coming of the Mass Market, 1850–1914*, London: Macmillan.

Friedman, W. (2004) *Birth of a Salesman: The Transformation of Selling in America*, Cambridge, MA: Harvard University Press.

Fullerton, R. and G. Low (1994) 'Brands, brand management and the brand manager system: A critical–historical evaluation', *Journal of Marketing Research*, 31 (May): 173–90.

Gardner, B. and S. Levy (1955) 'The product and the brand', *Harvard Business Review*, 33: 33–9.

George, A. (2006) 'Brand rules: When branding lore meets trade mark law', *Journal of Brand Management*, 13 (3): 215–32.

Goodall, F. (1986) 'Marketing consumer products before 1914: Rowntrees and Elect Cocoa', in R. P. T. Davenport-Hines (ed.), *Markets and Bagmen: Studies in the History of Marketing and British Industrial Performance, 1830–1939*, Aldershot: Gower, pp. 16–56.

Haygood, D. (2007) 'David Ogilvy versus Rosser Reeves and their "competing" advertising philosophies: the real story', in B. Branchik (ed.), *Marketing History at the Center. Proceedings of the 13ᵗʰ Conference on Historical Analysis and Research in Marketing (CHARM)*, Durham, NC: AHRIM: pp. 105–14.

Holt, D. (2003) 'What becomes an icon most?', *Harvard Business Review*, 81: 43–9.

Hower, R. (1949) *The History of an Advertising Agency: N W Ayer & Son at Work, 1969–1949*, Cambridge, MA: Harvard University Press.

Joint Trade Marks Committee (1933) *Memorandum on British Trade Mark Law*, London: HMSO.

Jones, D. G. B. and D. Monieson (1990) 'Early development of the philosophy of marketing thought', *Journal of Marketing*, 54: 102–113.

Jones, G. (2005) *Renewing Unilever: Transformation and Tradition*, Oxford: Oxford University Press.

Jones, G. and N. J. Morgan (eds.) (1993) *Adding Value: Brands and Marketing in Food and Drink*, London: Routledge.

Katona, G. (1953) 'Rational behaviour and economic behavior', *Psychological Review*, 60: 307–18.

Kreshel, P. (1990) 'The "culture" of J. Walter Thompson, 1915–1925', *Public Relations Review*, 16 (3): 80–93.

Lash, S. and J. Urry (1994) *Economies of Signs and Space*, London: Sage.

Lears, T. J. Jackson (1983) 'From salvation to self-realization: Advertising and the therapeutic roots of the consumer culture, 1880–1930', in R. Wightman Fox and T. J. Jackson Lears (eds.) *The Culture of Consumption: Critical Essays in American History*, 1880–1980, New York: Pantheon Books, pp. 1–38.

Leiss, W., S. Kline, S. Jhally and J. Botterill (2005) *Social Communication in Advertising: Consumption in the Mediated Marketplace*, Abingdon, Oxon: Routledge.

Levy, S. (2003) 'Roots of marketing and consumer research at the University of Chicago', *Consumption, Markets and Culture*, 6 (2): 99–110.

Lopes, T. (2007) *Global Brands: The Evolution of Multinationals in Alcoholic Beverages*, New York: Cambridge University Press.

Lopes, T. and M. Casson (2007) 'Entrepreneurship and the development of global brands', *Business History Review*, 81 (Winter 2007): 651–80.

Lovett, R. (1970) 'Francis A. Countway and "the Lever way"', *Harvard Library Bulletin* 18 (1): 84–93.

Lury, C. (2004) *Brands: The Global Logos of the Global Economy*, Abingdon, Oxon: Routledge.

McFall, L. (2004) *Advertising: A Cultural Economy*, London: Sage.

McKendrick, N. (1960) 'Josiah Wedgwood: An eighteenth-century entrepreneur in salesmanship and marketing techniques', *Economic History Review*, 12 (3): 408–33.

McKendrick, N., J. Brewer and J. Plumber (1982) *The Birth of a Consumer Society: The Commercialization of Eighteenth-Century England*, London: Europa.

Meenaghan, T. (1995) 'The role of advertising in brand image development', *Journal of Product & Brand Management*, 4 (4): 23–34.

Mendenhall, J. (1989) *British Trademarks of the 1920s and 1930s*, San Francisco: Chronicle Books.

Merchandise Marks Committee (1920) *Report to the Board of Trade of the Merchandise Marks Committee (Cmd. 760)*, London: HMSO.

Miller, P. and N. Rose (1997) 'Mobilizing the consumer: Assembling the subject of consumption', *Theory, Culture and Society*, 14(1): 1–36.

Millman, N. (1988) *Emperors of Adland: Inside the Advertising Revolution*, New York: Warner.

Mitchell, A. (1959) *The Brand Image and Advertising Effectiveness* (ATV Series of Technical Research Studies, No. 1), London: ATV.

Nevett, T. (1982) *Advertising in Britain: A History*, London: Heinemann.

O'Shaughnessy, J (2003) *The Marketing Power of Emotions*, Oxford: Oxford University Press.

Patent Office (1976) *A Century of Trade Marks*, London: HMSO.

Pettit, M. (2007), 'The unwary purchaser: Consumer psychology and the regulation of commerce in America', *Journal of the History of the Behavioural Sciences* 43 (4): 379–99.

Phillips, J. (2003) *Trade Mark Law: A Practical Anatomy*, Oxford: Oxford University Press.

Plant, A. (1937) 'The distribution of proprietary articles', in A. Plant (ed.), *Some Modern Problems: Series of Studies*, London: Longman's, pp. 302–36.

Report of the Departmental Committee on the Law and Practice Relating to Trade Marks (Cmd. 4568) (1934), London: HMSO.

Richards, T. (1990) *The Commodity Culture of Victorian Britain: Advertising and Spectacle, 1851–1914*, Stanford, CA: Stanford University Press.

Schechter, F. (1925) *The Historical Foundations of the Law Relating to Trade-Marks*, New York: University of Columbia Press.

Schultz, M. (2005) 'A cross-disciplinary perspective on corporate branding', in M. Schultz, Y. Mi Antorini, and F. F. Csaba (eds.), *Corporate Branding: Purpose, People, Process*. Copenhagen: Copenhagen Business School Press, pp. 23–55.

Schwarzkopf, S. (2005) 'Sources for the history of advertising in the United Kingdom: The records of advertising agencies and related advertising material at the History of Advertising Trust', *Business Archives*, 90: 25–36.

———. (2008) 'Creativity, capital and tacit knowledge: The Crawford agency and British advertising in the interwar years', *Journal of Cultural Economy*, 1: 181–97.

———. (2009) 'Discovering the consumer: Market research, product innovation and the creation of brand loyalty in Britain and the United States in the interwar years', *Journal of Macromarketing*, 29 (1):8–20.

Shaw, E. and K. Goodrich (2005) 'Marketing strategy: From the history of a concept to the development of a conceptual framework', in L. C. Neilson (ed.), *The Future of Marketing's Past: Proceedings of the 12ᵗʰ Conference on Historical Analysis and Research in Marketing (CHARM)*, Long Beach, CA: AHRIM: pp. 265–74.

Sherman, B. and L. Bently (1999) *The Making of Modern Intellectual Property Law: The British Experience, 1760–1911*, Cambridge: Cambridge University Press.

Silva, J. (1996) 'The marketing complex: The J. Walter Thompson company, 1916–1929', *Essays in Economic and Business History*, 14: 207–18.

Smith, W. (1956) 'Product differentiation and market segmentation as alternative marketing strategies', *Journal of Marketing* 21: 3–8.

Statistical Review of Press Advertising (1937) (1) (October): 154–157.

Strachan, J. (2003) *Advertising and satirical culture in the romantic period*, Cambridge, UK: Cambridge University Press.

Tedlow, R. (1990) *New and Improved: The Story of Mass Marketing in America*, New York: Basic Books.

Tadajewski, M. and D. G. B. Jones (2008) 'The history of marketing thought', in M. Tadajewski and D. G. B. Jones (eds.) *The History of Marketing Thought*: Vol. 1. London: Sage, pp. xviiii–xlii.

Thompson, J. Walter Co. (eds.) (1911) *Things to Know About Trade-Marks: A Manual of Trade-Mark Information*, New York: J. Walter Thompson Co.

Tungate, M. (2007) *Adland: A Global History of Advertising*, London: Kogan Page.

Webb Young, J. (1940) *A Technique for Producing Ideas*, Chicago: Advertising Publications.

West, D. (1988) 'Multinational competition in the British advertising agency business, 1936–87', *Business History Review*, 62: 467–501.

Wilkins, M (1992) 'The neglected intangible asset: The influence of the trade mark on the rise of the modern corporation', *Business History* 34 (1): 66–95.

Wilson, C. (1954), *The History of Unilever*, 2 vols., London: Cassell.

Wilson, J. and A. Thomson (2006) *The Making of Modern Management: British Management in Historical Perspective*, Oxford: Oxford University Press.

9 Corporate Brand Building
Shell-Mex Ltd. in the Interwar Period

Michael Heller

The history of corporate branding and its contribution to the marketing process, although flourishing in the United States, barely exists in Britain (Zunz 1990; Marchand 1998; Bird 1999; Lipartito and Sicilia 2004). Corporate branding encompasses the processes by which an organization, as a whole, is branded and its name then used to support its product brands. The process has many benefits. The corporate brand can endorse product brands, providing indications of trust, reputation, and recognition, and making powerful associations with innovation, public service, and national characteristics. Corporate brands act as effective platforms for brand stretching and brand extensions and provide a sense of *gestalt* for those brands that operate in diverse, and seemingly unassociated, categories. In addition, corporate branding is important for an organization's reputation, image, and public acceptance. In this way corporate branding is closely allied to public relations. Brands do not operate in a vacuum, subject simply to the vagaries of supply and demand in the market place. Brands, and the organizations behind them, exist in complex social environments and have to garner trust and acceptance amongst the various publics with whom they interact to survive and thrive. The benefit that individual product brands provide through their enhanced recognition, trust, and imputed characteristics often depends on public goodwill towards their parent, corporate brands.

In the United States, important work has been done on corporate branding by Marchand (1998) and Bird (1999). Marchand demonstrates how major American corporations such as AT&T, General Motors, and Ford invested heavily between 1900 and 1950 in promoting their corporate image in an attempt to obtain public acceptance and trust. His starting point was the resistance and opposition to the rapid growth of American corporations at the end of the nineteenth century by disaffected liberals, journalists, regional businessmen, trade unionists, and other groups. Such groups portrayed the new corporate behemoths as monopolistic, bullying, uncaring, and soulless.

To counter such claims, American business developed corporate identities that emphasized their public service, their patriotism, and their humanness.

Key to this was an association of the American way of life with corporate America. Bird's (1999) analysis follows a similar line of argument, though it focuses on the 1930s to '50s and the opposition of American corporations to what they saw as excessive government regulation and interference, from Roosevelt's New Deal. Bird shows how American corporations harnessed the new media of radio, film, and television to create a new dramatic language that emphasized that business, and not government, was responsible for 'better living' in the United States. Entertainment via corporate-sponsored radio programmes, films, and television shows became a powerful agent for developing corporate legitimacy and supremacy. Big business battled the US government by switching its arguments from the political to the cultural. A key point in both authors' arguments is that corporate identity-building and branding became powerful supports for the products and services of big business.

In Britain, similar research is lacking. Although prominent major British concerns such as ICI, Boots, Lever Brothers, Pilkington, and Wills developed their corporate identities over this period, emphasizing their public service to the nation, there have been no historical studies dedicated to this subject, nor analysis of how corporate branding assisted these firms' marketing operations (LeMahieu 1988; Fitzgerald 1995). Although Saler (1999) has carried out an important study of the use of avant-garde art by the London Underground in the 1920s and '30s, on which this chapter draws, his principle focus is on art, rather than the organization. In a previous study of the Prudential Assurance Company (Heller 2007), I have argued that this major life insurance company attempted to develop its corporate brand and identity through its contribution to public health in Britain in the first half of the twentieth century, and through its role in the administration of the National Insurance Acts between 1911 and 1947. By its association with health and the welfare of the British nation, the Prudential was able to use its corporate brand to help distinguish its various insurance products and to develop important distribution channels, which gave it competitive advantage. Such corporate branding was also important in developing an internal culture that assisted the company in attracting and retaining a dedicated workforce and in enhancing employee commitment, which further assisted its brands.

In this chapter, I make a similar argument about Shell-Mex, the British arm of the oil and petroleum giant Royal Dutch Shell. I examine how Shell-Mex, in the interwar period, developed its organizational identity and image through a careful and systematic process of corporate brand building that had manifold benefits for its various product and service brands. Shell-Mex is known, during this period, for its sponsoring of art and artists for publicity purposes (LeMahieu 1988; Hewitt 1992). Much of the academic attention given to Shell, however, focuses primarily, like Saler's (1999) work on the London Underground, on art and Shell's role as a sponsor of the arts, rather than on art's role within the company's overall marketing and branding strategy. As this chapter argues, the role of art within Shell can be studied from a perspective of corporate brand building and, so, in relation to other components of this programme, such as Shell's films; its publications, including road guides; its development of an internal culture; and its self-acclaimed public service to motoring, international transport, the British Empire, and the English countryside. This chapter demonstrates that through this corporate brand building, Shell was able to distinguish its product from its competitors and create strong links with customers, not simply by emphasizing the quality and functionality of its product, but also by creating powerful associations with the English countryside, modernity, and aesthetic beauty, none of which had direct links with petrol. Moreover, it did this through the use of an integrated communication model, using several communication media. The press, posters, booklets, art, exhibitions, guides, and films were all used under the guise of advertising, public relations, personal selling, and even direct marketing programmes to build Shell's brand in the United Kingdom. Finally, the chapter will discuss how Shell's corporate brand building formed an important component of its public relations policy. Public relations, a corporate strategy very much in its infancy during the interwar period, was important for the company in its contribution to corporate identity, its legitimization of the organization and its activities, and for its contribution to forging relations with Shell-Mex's publics.

SHELL-MEX LIMITED: AN OVERVIEW

The parent company of Shell-Mex, Royal Dutch Shell, was born out of the merger, in 1907, of the Royal Dutch Petroleum Company of Holland and the Shell Transport and Trading Company of the United Kingdom (Howarth 1997; Howarth et al. 2007). Both companies had been founded in the 1890s and had originally concentrated on the lucrative market for kerosene, which was then a popular household fuel used in lighting, cooking, and heating. By the interwar period, the organization had developed into a major vertically integrated multinational oil company with global interests in exploration, drilling, production, refining, shipping, distribution, marketing, and related services. Its products included oil, kerosene, petrol, heating fuels, and hydrocarbon chemicals, with principal markets in the transport sectors of motor vehicles, aviation, and shipping. In Britain during the interwar period, the public face of the company was Shell-Mex, a distribution and marketing company born out of the acquisition by Shell, in 1921, of Mexican Eagle. In 1931, as a result of the economic crisis and overcapacity in the global oil industry, the company merged with BP, the marketing and distribution arm of the Anglo-Persian Oil Company (APOC), to create the joint marketing venture Shell-Mex and BP Ltd. Within the concern, Shell held 60 per cent of the shares and APOC 40 per cent. This company, with its iconic headquarters, Shell-Mex House in central London, was responsible for the sustained, path-breaking, and highly creative augmentation of the Shell brand in the UK in the 1920s and '30s, which is the subject of this chapter.

In relation to the market for oil products in the United Kingdom, and particularly regarding the rapidly growing motor spirit sector, Shell-Mex was a member of a triumvirate that dominated the industry. The other two members were Anglo-American and associated companies that belonged to the American Standard Oil and BP, which, as noted, belonged to APOC. These three companies controlled around 70 per cent of the market for motor spirit in Britain (Ferrier 1986).[1] The remainder of the market was divided among smaller firms, which competed on price, rather than brand. Amongst the three (and later two) dominant companies, collusive marketing agreements were reached throughout the 1920s and '30s in relation to market share quotas, distribution, prices, and expenditure on advertising. The three parent companies reached a similar global pact in 1928. Such restrictive marketing arrangements were common in nearly all sectors in Britain amongst the major producers at the time.

In the 1930s, Shell-Mex commanded around 26 per cent of total spirit sales in Britain. This compared to 29 per cent for Anglo-American and 13 per cent for BP. In 1939, Shell-Mex and BP Ltd had an allocation of 35 per cent of the total in the UK (Ferrier 1986: 48).[2] During the difficult economic conditions of the 1930s, Shell-Mex increased profits marginally.[3] The contribution of advertising, publicity, and marketing to this cannot be quantified, but it was regarded as central to market success by Shell. As Ferrier (1986) has noted, brand recognition and customer loyalty were crucial in the competitive market for motor spirit. The multiple market agreements between the major oil firms in the interwar period highlighted advertising and marketing, and great attention and detail went into its control.[4] The remainder of this chapter focuses on how Shell-Mex built up its corporate brand by a process of internal marketing within the company, its sponsorship of road and air travel, its harnessing of contemporary art to promote the company, and its development of *The Shell County Guides*.

INTERNAL MARKETING

Internal marketing is the process of marketing to employees within the organization (Varey and Lewis 2000). The phenomenon can take several forms and have different aims. In relation to brand building, it is the process of instilling the values of the brand within employees, who, it is hoped, will then act as brand ambassadors to external publics. It is particularly important in service industries. Employees must first imbue the values, benefits, and associations of the brand before these can be passed onto the customer.

This 'buying in' of corporate values was evident in Shell's establishment and commitment to building up a strong internal organizational structure and concomitant culture. As Gospel's (1992) and Fitzgerald's (1995) work has noted, in the case of capital intensive firms such as Shell, which had invested heavily in plant, machinery, and industrial processes, there was an organizational imperative to build up strong internal structures, bureaucracies and labour management processes. Shell invested heavily in industrial welfare to maintain worker loyalty, attract and retain key workers, and establish, in the parlance of the time, *esprit de corps*, to motivate employees and meld them into the beliefs, practices and values of the organization. This was felt not simply to have internal benefits for the organization but also external ones. In addition, company magazines were felt to act as important links between the internal organization and important publics outside the organization, such as customers and shareholders. As R. Pugh, General Manager of Factory Services and Utilities Ltd., commented in 1932 at the eleventh conference of editors of works magazines organized by the Industrial Welfare Society (of which Shell was a member), 'the employee's magazine is passing through a stage in which it is becoming the organ of the internal and external relations of the firm'.[5]

The principal medium of internal marketing for Shell in the UK was its house journal. The company had originally started a company magazine in 1914, called the *St. Helen's Court Bulletin*, after the then headquarters of the company in Britain. The original purpose of the magazine was to enable staff in the organization to receive news of their colleagues and friends who had joined the military, and for the latter to obtain news of Shell.[6] A new magazine appeared in 1921, called *The Pipeline*, which in 1934 was renamed *The Shell Magazine*. This magazine was one of many in the sprawling Royal Dutch Shell company. In the United States, for example, there were several magazines for its east and west coast operations, including *Sign of the Shell* and *The Shell Globe*.[7] In the United Kingdom, under its chairman Sir Robert Waley Cohen, the company was an advocate of the multiple benefits of in-house journals. Shell-Mex was an active member of the Industrial Welfare Society, which held annual conferences for the chief editors of company magazines. At the 1934 conference, for example, Waley Cohen was quoted as stating that, 'the House Magazine was a valuable link between the leaders of commerce and industry and their employees, and served to maintain the human touch which, he thought would other wise perhaps be lost in the increasing momentum of modern progress'.[8]

Determining the actual popularity of the magazine within Shell is difficult, and there is always the danger in any analysis of assuming that simply because the magazine existed and was supported by management that it was read by employees, was taken seriously, and achieved its organizational goals. One way to estimate its significance is to note that sales of *The Pipeline* grew from 2,000 in 1921 to 12,000 in 1937, with subscribers reported in every country in which Shell operated.[9] The problem here is establishing how many people actually worked for Shell and, of these, how many could speak English. Although the first reliable figure in 1935 gave a total company employment of 180,400 people, it must be emphasized that the majority of these would have been periphery workers in secondary and temporary positions (Howarth et al. 2007). Core workers (whom the magazine was aimed at) probably stood at something near a quarter of this, and if one considers that more than one individual was likely to have read each magazine, then these figures show a relatively wide readership. The fact that it was sold, at a price of 2d in 1934, rather than simply forced upon employees, also suggests that these figures are meaningful. That a magazine established for the period was revived in 1921 is further testament to its popularity. In addition, much of the content of the magazine was contributed by employees, rather than management, which accounts for the diverse range of subjects and the sense of spontaneity that is still apparent today.

The magazine also has a certain sense of popular appeal. Sport was an important component in the magazine; physical recreation was seen as a key part of industrial welfare amongst large-scale organizations in the UK during this period and was promoted for its contribution to building up *esprit de corps* (Heller 2008). The discourse around sport within Shell certainly confirms this.[10] Finally, we should avoid projecting our distrustful and jaundiced attitudes towards labour relations in large-scale employers, engendered by contemporary job insecurity, anomie, and instrumentalism, onto the organization of 70 or 80 years ago. Many of the employees of Shell-Mex and the wider Royal Dutch Shell were, as Whyte observed 50 years ago, 'organizational men' (Whyte 1956). These were individuals who had life-long careers at Shell. Many had personal connections with the company and would send their children into it. Employees at this time were more 'corporate', and in such a milieu corporate messages may have been more meaningful.

The Pipeline and its successor were products of the late-Victorian journalistic construct of education, information, and entertainment, which, in the 1920s and '30s, was symbolized in Britain by the BBC (Scannell and Cardiff 1991). Serious articles on the crisis in the Gold Standard stood beside company announcements, and news of the organization sat next to monthly features on films, books, music, and radio programmes. As Waley Cohen's previous quotation indicates, the magazine was seen by the company and its management as serving several important functions within the organization.[11] It was thought to create a sense of unity in a disparate organizational structure where units were spread out across the country and the globe. It acted as a means of communication between management and employees and among employees themselves, and was a key element in the construction of an organizational culture in Shell.[12]

Amongst these various roles, the magazine informed and promoted the manifold products and services of the company to its readers. On one level, the magazine educated Shell's employees about the many products provided by the company. One full-page announcement in *The Pipeline* in 1931 asked its readers if they knew all of Shell's products. 'I hope', wrote F. L. Halford, the general manager of Shell-Mex, 'the members of the Shell organization besides always using our products will never lose an opportunity of recommending them to their friends.' Beneath was a list of Shell's various products, including 'Shelltox' for killing insects, and Mexpahlte, an asphalt used in road construction.[13] Regular articles appeared in the magazine on Shell products and their multiple benefits, and on Shell's activities in marketing, advertising, and trade exhibitions. In addition, the journal often ran articles on the oil industry in general and on production processes.

Shell's house journal did not only concern itself with what the company made and which services it provided. It also informed Shell's employees of the company's advertising, publicity, and marketing. There were frequent articles, for example, on the company's numerous exhibitions and publications.[14] On a broader level, it attempted to inculcate in its workers the values and vision of the organization, which played such an important role in transforming its goods from commodities into brands. Many of the corporate values and associations that were transferred to Shell's brands were broadcast to Shell's staff via the magazine. It highlighted, for example, Shell's role in developing air travel, and associated this with the strengthening of Empire through travel and communication; and it drew on another of Shell's publications, *Shell Aviation News*, excerpts of which appeared regularly in its house magazine.[15] The social benefits of Shell's products were a constant theme of the magazine. One of the key associations of Shell's corporate brand—that the company did not simply produce petrol or oils, but rather positive experiences such as travel, adventure, and speed—filled its pages. Without a core workforce who held and imbued the values and associations of the organization, it is difficult to see how the brand could have functioned or been taken seriously in its external markets. Consequently, internal marketing was a key component in Shell-Mex's corporate brand building.

ROAD AND AIR: TRAVEL AND SPEED

Harp (2001) has noted that the French tyre maker, Michelin, did not so much market tyres as promote travel, destinations, and an entire way of life. Organizations such as Shell, Michelin, Dunlop, and Imperial Airways had to first create the desire and need to travel, whether on land or air via the new technology of internal combustion engines, if they were to create a demand for their products. To generate demand for these new industries, production, advertising, and distribution were often inseparable (Harp 2001: 16). The need to create markets for new products partially explains why so many of these 'new' industries were so creative in their publicity and marketing. Many of these organizations associated their products with modernity and speed. The sponsorship of races and record breaking journeys became a major marketing tool. Not only did this association embellish and reinforce the powerful associations connected with these products, but it also demonstrated their quality and reliability and earned valuable marketing exposure for their brands.

Shell was at the forefront of such marketing tactics in Britain. From its beginnings, much of the company's publicity focused on car racing and land speed records.[16] During the interwar period, the company also moved into aviation and sponsored record-breaking global flights. In 1925, for example, it sponsored the Chief of the Italian Air Staff, Marchese de Pinedo, in a record flight from Rome to Australia and back Pinedo flew a record-breaking 34,000 miles (see figures 9.1 and 9.2).

On his homeward trip from Bangkok to Taranto, he flew 6,400 miles in 10 consecutive days, a long-distance speed record. It was noted in the promotional literature that,

> The aviator and his engineer attribute their success in large measure to the fact that they were able to obtain Shell spirit at every stop. They had no engine trouble'.[17]

Pinedo promised his fellow aviators that if they used Shell motor spirit, their engines would run smoothly and they could, too, go around the world many times.[18] This was celebrity endorsement at its very best.

Sponsorship of flights within the British Empire was a favourite for Shell. Such marketing activities gave the organization imperial and patriotic appeal, something important for winning the UK market for a company that was only 40 per cent British. Flights from far-flung corners of the Empire, such as Australia, Canada, and Africa, were valued as much for strengthening the bonds of empire as for furthering the cause of aviation.

Figures 9.1 and 9.2 Chief of the Italian Air Staff, Marchese de Pinedo, in a record-breaking flight from Rome to Australia, 1925. Source: Royal Dutch Shell PLC Archives. Reproduced by kind permission of Royal Dutch Shell PLC.

Good examples of this sponsorship were the flights of H. F. Broadbent from Australia to England and H. L. Brook from South Africa to England, both in the first week of May 1937. Both were record-breaking flights: Broadbent reached London within 6 days and 11 hours, taking 26 hours off the previous record, and Brook flew to England in 4 days and 18 minutes, 16 hours faster than the previous record holder. He also broke the unofficial record for the 'out and back' trip. Both flights used Shell Aviation Spirit and both records gained large exposure in the national press and were used by Shell for publicity purposes.[19]

The degree of skill and control with which Shell controlled these media events provides marketing historians with one of the earliest examples of commercial PR in Britain through the use of press releases. In 1931, Shell brought out *Shell Aviation News*. The magazine grew out of the circular flight letter of the Aviation Department and was originally a typed document. By 1933, it had gained print status and was produced monthly. The journal was for internal use, though it could be subscribed to privately—a technique Shell regularly used in its publicity. The journal provided important information about aviation for Shell employees, helping to develop 'airmindedness' within the Shell organization (a good example of internal marketing). It was also used for press releases with the intention of supporting sales and promoting aviation.[20] It is in this latter role that the magazine followed Broadbent's and Brook's records. News and information appeared for both in the May 1937 edition of the magazine.[21] This information was principally factual, with routes and times of the journey and comparisons with previous records given. In addition, some of the difficulties encountered by Brook in his flight were briefly summarized. *The Times* and *Telegraph* clearly based their reports on these press releases.[22] Although reports in the *Daily Mail* and *Daily Express*, the two most widely read newspapers in Britain, focused more on the human-interest stories of the flight, such as how the pilots stayed awake or the activities of their wives, they, too, contained information from *Shell Aviation News*.[23] In all these newspapers, a large customized advert for Brook endorsing Shell appeared, and in the *Telegraph* and *Aeroplane* magazine a similar advert appeared for Broadbent (see figures 9.3 and 9.4).

The marketing and PR was extremely sophisticated for the period. Shell partially sponsored the flights, helped to create the news stories in national daily press through press releases from its own aviation journal, and then placed carefully tailored adverts of the pilots endorsing their products in the same newspaper. Shell was, thus, not merely passively benefiting from the publicity generated from these records, but was active in the creation of these news events. Through such activities, Shell was able to build its brand by a clear association of its organization and product with the achievement, speed, endurance, and path-breaking accomplishments of these record holders.

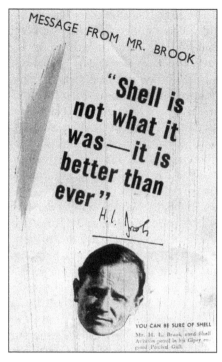

Figures 9.3 and 9.4 Brook and Broadbent advertisements. Sources: Daily Telegraph, 4 May 1937 and Daily Telegraph, 6 May 1937. British Library Board. All rights reserved.

International air travel was impossible without logistical facilities such as fuelling depots, service stations, and information on routes and local environs, and Shell was active in developing all of these. The company was one of the 15 founding members, for example, of the International Air Traffic Association in 1919, a date associated with the birth of commercial aviation in Britain and its Empire.

In the 1934 article, 'Aviation and the Shell Company', Shell outlined its activities in laying the foundation of an international aviation fuel distribution system, which by 1934 served 2,500 aerodromes and seaplane stations worldwide.[24] Noting that 'the delivery of gasoline and oil to an aircraft does not depend solely on stocks being available at aerodromes', the article outlined in detail how Shell had developed an infrastructure that distilled, distributed, and stored aviation fuel and developed a ground organization to serve the needs of pilots. The organization had developed electrically powered refuelling trucks that could fill planes quickly and efficiently, thus making journey times shorter. For sea-planes, which were commonly used in civil aviation in the 1930s, it had developed tank boats and motor launches equipped with fuel pumps. The company also had a network of Shell Aircraft Service Stations where pilots could buy supplies; have maintenance work performed; and find facilities for writing up log books, plotting courses, eating, washing, and even sleeping. The stations also assisted in bureaucratic work involved in visas and passports. Finally, Shell also assisted international civil aviation by developing what it called, 'a wealth of information on aerodromes, routes, flying and meteorological conditions, etc., which has been collected over a number of years and is at the disposal of any pilot'.[25] Just as it was doing for roads in Britain with its *County Guides* (discussed in the following), Shell was making aviation possible not simply through its supply of fuel but also by its facilitation of information essential to safe and speedy travel.

Shell was keen to publicize this work. Publicity had the triple benefit of raising the profile of air travel, of making it more popular, and of boosting the reputation of the company. In the 1930s, the company did this primarily through the medium of film.[26] Under its head of publicity, Jack Beddington, Shell had, in 1934, established a film unit that made documentaries covering oil products and the services of the organization (Artmonsky 2006). Shell documentaries, such as *Seven Point Service* (1935) and *Power Unit* (1937), were usually shown in cinemas across the nation as the short film before the main showing. They broadcast not only Shell's products and services, but, perhaps more important, the Shell company to millions across the United Kingdom. In the 1930s, Shell made two major aviation documentaries, *Contact* (1933) and *Airport* (1935).[27]

Contact perfectly exemplifies the attempts of Shell to promote air travel amongst the British public and to demonstrate its associations with the company. In the words of its maker and producer, Paul Rotha, the 20-minute documentary, 'spoke of Man's new conquest of space and time with emphasis laid on the closer communication between peoples made possible by air travel, especially by airmail' (Rotha 1973: 72). The film was funded entirely by Shell-Mex but was a collaborative project of the oil company with Imperial Airways, something that would be repeated in *Airport*. Beddington insisted that there be no direct reference to Shell, whether through the use of logos or insignia. The company was not even mentioned in the film titles. As Rotha recalls, Beddington emphasized that the film was not meant to be considered as a piece of advertisement, and in the filmmaker's opinion, 'This was public relations at its best and most imaginative' (Rotha 1973: 72). *Contact* stands out as one of the most remarkable British documentaries of the interwar period, along works such as *Drifters* and *Night Mail* (Rotha 1973; LeMahieu 1988; Aitken 1990).

As Rotha (1973) notes, *Contact* premiered at the Dorchester Hotel in July 1933 before the Prince of Wales, the Prime Minster, the Cabinet, prominent economists, and newspapermen, and was met by them with repeated applause. It played in West End cinemas in London for nine weeks and was then shown in more than 1,500 film houses in Britain. The film received good reviews in the national press and was even entered in the Venice Film Festival. Shell did not receive a penny from its investments, but Rotha reports that Beddington was more than satisfied by the prestige gained by the film. He also recalled that, despite the latter's insistence, it soon became widely known following *Contact*'s release that Shell had backed the documentary.

In a narrow marketing sense, Shell had little to gain from its public proclamation of its work in international civil aviation. All but the very richest were precluded from this novel form of transportation, and would be until long after the Second World War. Yet the benefits to Shell were not directly monetary but, rather, organizational and more particularly in terms of brand. By associating itself with aviation through its investment and sponsorship, Shell gained wide public exposure, which kept its corporate brand constantly in the public eye. It was able to portray itself as a responsible corporate body that augmented its reputation not simply amongst customers but also among the media, politicians, its workforce, and the general public. Finally, the Shell corporate brand was able to promulgate traits such as service, progress, modernity, and the exotic over its entire range of brands.

SHELL AND MODERN ART

Perhaps the most discussed and well-known of Shell's brand building efforts in the interwar period was its sponsorship of modern art in Britain. This has received academic attention, and Shell's art is still popular amongst the public today (LeMahieu 1988; Hewitt 1992). Exhibitions of Shell art are still shown across Britain, and prints and catalogues of its posters are still purchased, particularly from Beaulieu Motor Museum in Hampshire, the home of the Shell art collection (Shell UK Ltd 1998). Shell's sponsorship of modern art started under Beddington. Leading British modern and avant garde artists such as Paul Nash, McKnight Kauffer, Rex Whistler, Duncan Grant, and Graham Sutherland were commissioned by Shell to produce paintings that figured in national campaigns over the period, such as 'See Britain First on Shell' (see figure 9.5) and its long running series, 'You can be sure of Shell'. These paintings were primarily depictions of the British countryside and famous landmarks, such as Stonehenge and Bodiam Castle. Another series was 'These Men Use Shell', which used modern and often abstract art to portray a diverse range of professions from architects to farmers to racing car drivers (see figure 9.6). In addition, these campaigns did not publicize a particular product or service, but rather promoted the company as a whole, and its corporate brand. The popularity of the company's exhibitions and discussion in the press and journals indicates a strong association over the period between modern art and Shell.

Figure 9.5   'See Britain First on Shell' campaign. 'Stonehenge' by Edward McKnight Kauffer, 1931. Shell Art Collection. Copyright © Simon Rendall.

Figure 9.6   'These Men Use Shell' campaign. 'Journalists' by Hans Schleger (ZERO), 1938. Shell Art Collection. Reproduced by kind persission of Pat Shleger.

The use of modern art to publicize a corporation in Britain originated with the London Underground, under its publicity director, Frank Pick (Saler 1999). Pick began a revolution in corporate advertising in the inter-war period not simply by his use and patronage of modern, serious art but also by his insistence that corporations had a duty in their advertising to treat the public both responsibly and seriously in their use of publicity, and also to educate them in appreciating modern painting and design.

Shell's use of modern art followed in the tradition of Pick. As the architect and public figure Clough William Ellis commented in his opening of the first Shell exhibition of its press and pictorial advertising at the New Burlington Gardens in 1931,

> There is advertising and advertising—the Shell sort and the other. The intelligent, the discreet and the witty way which is Shell's, the blatant, the unmannerly method which is the method of the anti-social num-skulls who quaintly imagine that to arrest attention is the same as to attract.
>
> Too much of our publicity is Mad Dog publicity—it startles and offends us instead of winning our goodwill by its ingratiating tact.[28]

Shell's relationship with Clough William Ellis is itself significant. Ellis was an active public campaigner and founding member of Council for the Preservation of Rural England (CPRE), a movement that Shell sponsored (Ellis 1928). A major campaign of the CPRE during this period was against advertising along rural roads and in villages (a common practice at the time), which the CPRE argued to be leading to the spoilation of the natural beauty of the British countryside. By removing its publicity from country areas and, instead, placing its artistic advertisements (which themselves depicted rural Britain) on its three thousand petrol tankers that daily traversed the nation, Shell was thus able to strengthen its image as a responsible organization and, in the process, enhance its strong associations with nature and rural Britain. This association is clearly demonstrated in the introduction to Shell's catalogue for its 1931 exhibition by Robert Byron (Shell-Mex Ltd 1931). Entitled 'Responsible Publicity', it argued that Shell's use of advertising was salutary in the tastefulness of its content, its respect for and efforts to improve its audience, its care for the countryside, and its depiction of rural England in a genuine and aesthetic manner.

Shell's use of modern art in its publicity and its depiction of rural Britain won it widespread acclaim and gave its corporate brand massive exposure. Its exhibitions, first at New Burlington Gardens and later at Shell-Mex House, became regular public events that attracted thousands of visitors and were widely reported and favourably commented upon in the press.[29] They were opened by important public figures such as Ellis; Sir Kenneth Clark, director of the National Gallery; and the poet T. S. Eliot. All praised the corporation in their introductory speeches.[30] Exhibitions of Shell art and advertising were regularly held in regional galleries across Britain, and its posters rapidly became collector items, available by subscription from Shell or through its popular published catalogue collections.[31] The company also gave gifts to the Victorian and Albert Museum Department of Circulation, which lent art to colleges and schools (Artmonsky 2006). Such patronage of the arts, and the cultural partnerships that this engendered, gave the company a distinct identity and fostered strong associations of the corporate brand in the popular mind with taste, nature, authenticity, and Britain.

The techniques that Shell used in its publicity were intentional. LeMahieu (1988) has argued that during the interwar period, American advertising methods were introduced and disseminated in Britain. Amongst these was the use of behavioural psychology and, in particular, the cultivation by advertisers of associations between ideas and products in the minds of the public. LeMahieu quotes, for example, T. Russell, who argued in his work, *Commercial Advertising*, published in 1919, that, 'If the announcements of a firm are habitually artistic and beautiful the firm becomes cumulatively associated in the public mind with ideas of refinement and good taste' (LeMahieu 1988: 162). These arguments were openly expressed in Shell's publicity campaigns. Robert Byron, for example, argued in the opening lines of his introduction for the 1931 Shell Exhibition that,

> The principles of successful advertising are as numerous as those of psychology. Each advertisement must caress some instinct, sentimental, logical, or otherwise, which is shared by a large body of persons.
> (Shell-Mex Ltd 1931: 2)

Similarly, Cyril Connolly, in his article on Shell's 1934 exhibition, 'The New Medici', observed, 'The advertising by association of ideas is particularly apparent in the series "Artists, archaeologists, architects, etc., prefer Shell", where the emblems of distinction, the insignia of specialization in each art suggest a corresponding excellence, just as intricate as the product' (Connolly 1934: 2). Shell's brand building was intentional and systemic, its techniques as modern as those of the art it utilized.

THE SHELL COUNTY GUIDES

In 1934, Shell-Mex brought out the first of its *Shell County Guides* for Cornwall published by the Architectural Press (Betjeman 1934). By 1939, 13 guides had been printed; the series was overseen by the future poet laureate John Betjeman, who wrote the first guides, for Cornwall and for Devon, and then edited and selected the authors for subsequent counties. These tended to be artistic and literary figures, such as John Nash and Robert Byron, who were friends of Betjeman and Beddington and often produced work for Shell. Around 50 pages long, the guides served a practical purpose for motorists and were promoted by the company. But like so many of Shell's publications and films, they were primarily marketing tools. Betjeman reflected later on that,

> The Guides in those days were not expected to pay. They were prestige advertising subsidized by Shell. There were no publishers' contracts and the whole thing was done on a personal basis because Beddioleman [Beddington] and subsequently William Scuddamore Mitchell and I and the printers all knew each other. (Artmonsky 2006: 50)

By 1934, the road guide was already an established genre. Shell, however, brought to the guides a creative novelty and individuality that distinguished them from what was then available. Its guides were as much pieces of artwork as they were practical tools for motorists. Each one was richly decorated with photographs, artwork, poetry, and even music. Although each guide had a certain uniform structure, with sections on areas such as history and sport, maps, and a gazetteer, they were also highly idiosyncratic, according to the whims of the individual author. Betjeman's guide to Devon, for example, was filled with amusing excerpts on popular customs, superstitions, local dialects, and etymologies, giving the guide a very personal and local feel. Sharp's guide to Northumberland and Durham had sheet music throughout of local folk songs, and John Nash's work on Buckinghamshire contained many landscape paintings of the county by various artists (Betjeman 1936; Nash 1937; Sharp 1937). Shell tried to distinguish the guides from other contemporary offerings by focusing on the beauty and character of Britain's counties, rather than channelling its readers towards popular recreation and tourist areas. As Betjeman wrote in 1937,

> The Shell Road Guides had at once to be critical and selective. They had to illustrate places other than the well-known beauty spots and to mention the disregarded and fast disappearing Georgian landscape of England; churches with box pews and West Galleries, handsome provincial streets of the late Georgian era; impressive mills in industrial towns; horrifying villas in overrated 'resorts' had to be touched upon. These things, for various reasons left out by other guides, are featured in the Shell Guides. (Green 1994: 139)

In all of the guides, there was no advertising for Shell except in the final page, which featured one of the company's *jeu de mot* topographical adverts for the relevant county. The company was not advertising petrol, itself, but rather Britain with a heavy focus on the rural. As Bernstein argued in his introduction to the 1992 *Shell Poster Book*, Shell advertised destination rather than product; it promoted motoring rather than oil; and it promised the joy and freedom of motoring rather than quality or technical distinction

(Shell UK Limited 1992: 2). Yet in so doing, the company embellished its corporate identity which guaranteed its products and services. As in its posters, it brought taste and finesse to its brand, which served to distinguish Shell from its competitors. In its county guides, it further reinforced its strong association, as seen by its work with the CPRE and in its publicity, with the British countryside (Hewitt 1992).

During the period, older concepts of civilization, liberties, progress, and even empire gave way to a more parochial and insular definition of the nation (Mandler 2006). Discussions of national identity and national character began to centre on a country of darts players and pigeon fanciers, rather than explorers and statesmen, more comfortable in smoky towns and winding roads than in the palace of Westminster or the fields of the Veldt (Orwell 1953). Within this introspective national turn of mind, the British countryside took on renewed importance. Already evident in the prewar years in the works of William Morris and G. K. Chesterton, and the growing suburbanization of the British middle-classes, the interwar period saw a resurgence in the romantic belief that the countryside was the authentic repository of all that was good and true in Britain (Mandler 2006). Particularly strong amongst the middle classes, this 'ruralization' of British national identity, seen in the craze in the period for rambling, camping, touring, and other escapades into the countryside, had a powerful behavioural and attitudinal impact. In politics, for example, the Conservative party under Stanley Baldwin used this organic connection between the countryside and the nation to boost its popular support and to marginalize the Labour party and its overtly urban and industrial constituency (Jarvis 1996; Mandler 1997; McKibbin 1990). In appropriating these powerful conceptual and national sentiments to its own brand through its depictions of the British countryside and its *County Road Guides*, Shell was doing something very similar.

As we survey these strategies, we need to keep in mind that the position of the oil industry in Britain was not immune from criticism during this period. A speech by Adrian Corbett of the American Department of the Anglo-Saxon Petroleum Company to the members of the Oil Industries Club in 1935 emphasizes this point.[32] Corbett argued that the oil industry had become a reviled sector that attracted unfair and undue criticism from authors and journalists alike. He pointed to 14 books that, over the previous 10 years, had attacked the sector. These criticisms, not unlike those today, argued that the industry was global, gigantic, secretive, sinister, and dangerous. It interfered with governments, created wars for its own gain, corrupted money markets, and ruthlessly pursued its own interest.

The development of Shell's corporate brand during this period must be seen in the light of such criticisms. Starting in the late 1930s, Shell-Mex began a series of publications emphasizing its contribution to the economy and welfare of those regions of Britain in which it operated. In 1939, it brought out a series of short pamphlets, dedicated to a number of localities,

entitled *Facts Relating to Shell-Mex and BP Ltd.*[33] These books emphasized, like the campaign in the North-East, the contribution of the company to the local economy. The pamphlet for Merseyside, for example,
stated that the company employed 800 people in the area, paid major taxes
to local government, ordered ships from the Mersey shipbuilding industry,
operated a huge refinery in the area, and ran a fleet of boats and trains that
were all built in Britain.[34]

CONCLUSION

Between 1918 and 1939, Shell-Mex systematically and comprehensively built
up its brand in the UK. It first developed a strong corporate brand, which
then provided powerful marketing externalities for its individual products
and services. In the process, it used highly innovative techniques, strategies,
and market communications. The company was, for example, among only
a handful in the United Kingdom to use art to build up and embellish its
corporate image (Hewitt 1992; Marchand 1998; Saler 1999).[35] Although
the advertising of its competitor, BP, focused on its product, Shell-Mex
emphasized its corporate image. As Vernon Nye remarked, Shell's publicity was much more focused on marketing and public relations.[36] So, as we
have seen, Shell's brand did not concern itself directly with petrol, oil, and
other hydrocarbon products. Rather, it promulgated an image of the benefits that accrued from these. Individual freedom, self-actualization, speed,
modernity, progress, authenticity, and exploration were but some of the
many benefits that Shell offered to purveyors of its products and services.
Shell was not about product, *per se*, but rather about a way of life that this
product facilitated. Equally important was the way in which it wrapped
this in an image of both nation and empire.

Many so-called modern marketing stratagems can be seen in these
brand-building exercises. The company internally marketed to its staff,
developed programmes of corporate social responsibility and cause-related
marketing in its alliances with the CPRE, and developed powerful associations that distinguished its brand from rival offerings; through its sponsorship of pilots, explorers, drivers, artists and critics, it received powerful
endorsement for the brand. The company was also highly creative in its
use of media—print, film, and visual—which were used in an integrated
manner to maximize its brand benefits. Since the company emphasized its
corporate image in its publicity, it made active use of public relations that
supported the reputation and image of the organization (LeMahieu 1988;
Marchand 1998).

For too long, the gaze of British business historians have been myopic,
taken in too much by the allure of brands while remaining blind to the
larger organization that created them. As the case of Shell suggests, historical accounts of corporate image building and public relations have to be

integrated in the accounts of the emergence of the modern brand for a more comprehensive and analytical picture to emerge. They need to acknowledge that the growth of the large-scale organization and the growth of modern marketing and development of consumer markets did not take place uncontested. There was often an imperative for the former to engage with its publics to legitimize itself, both in terms of its size, its scope, and the products and services that it provided. Such awareness and research is crucial if the history of the brand in Britain is to develop and progress.

NOTES

1. BP Archive, BP PLC., Ref. 77958, 'Marketing Agreements Between Anglo-American Oil Co. and SMBP'.
2. Ibid.
3. Ibid., Ref. 102388, 'Shell-Mex and BP Ltd Annual Reports 1932–1936'.
4. Ibid., Ref. 64905, 'Advertising—Continental General Racing Agreements', Ref. 77958, 'Marketing Agreements Between Anglo-American Oil Co. and SMBP', Ref. 64900, 'Advertising—Continental. General'.
5. *Industrial Welfare and Personnel Management*, Nov. 1932, 'Magazines for Staff, Shareholders and Customers': 529.
6. *St. Helen's Court Bulletin*, 21 Nov. 1914: 1.
7. *The Pipeline*, 18 March 1931, 'Shell Journalism': 99.
8. *The Shell Magazine*, March 1934: 95.
9. Ibid., Jan. 1937: 4.
10. Ibid., Oct. 1938: 235.
11. See article, 'Staff Magazines' in *The Pipeline*, July 1933: 353.
12. *The Pipeline*, 21 Dec. 1932: 534.
13. Ibid., 27 May 1931.
14. *The Pipeline*, 2 March 1932, 'The British Industries Fair', 94–95, *The Pipeline*, 12 Oct. 1932, 'Shell-Mex and B.P. News The Charing Cross Exhibition': 415–416.
15. *The Shell Magazine*, Oct. 1934, 'Aviation and the Shell Company': 454–8.
16. See *The Pipeline*, 16 March 1932, 'Shell Shots by G.F.H. Nearly Thirty Years Ago': 113. See also the magazine, *The Motor*, 7 Oct. 1924 for the close association between Malcolm Campbell's land speed record and Shell Motor Oil.
17. Shell Group Archives, London, Photograph Albums, Marchese de Pinedo, 1925.
18. Ibid.
19. *Shell Aviation News*, May 1937: 7.
20. Ibid., July, 1931 (first issue): 1. See also *The Shell Magazine*, January 1934, 'Shell Aviation News': 7–8.
21. *Shell Aviation News*, May 1937: 7.
22. *The Times*, 4 May 1937: 16; and 6 May 1937: 16. *The Daily Telegraph*, 4 May 1937: 14; and 6 May 1937: 18.
23. The *Daily Mail*, 4 May 1937: 13–14; and 6 May 1937: 13. The *Daily Express*, 4 May 1937: 13; and 6 May 1937: 13.
24. Ibid., Oct. 1934, 'Aviation and the Shell Company': 454–58.
25. Ibid.: 457.
26. For a history of Shell's involvement in film over this period, see Shell Group Archives London, Norman Vigars, March 1984, 'A Short History of the Shell Film Unit, 1934–1984'.

27. Both films are available at The British Film Institute Library, London.
28. *The Pipeline*, 24 June 1931: 248.
29. See *The Times*, 15 June 1931, 'Art Exhibition Shell Advertising': 12; and *The Pipeline*, 3 Feb. 1932, 'High Praise': 56; and Paul Nash's article in *The Listener* published 20 Jan. 1932 entitled 'The Artist and The Community'.
30. For Sir Kenneth Clark see *The Shell Magazine*, July 1934, 'Art and Advertising in Alliance': 313–14.
31. *The Pipeline*, 20 Jan. 1932, 'Shell-Mex and B.P. News Publicity Department': 35.
32. *The Shell Magazine*, May 1935, 'Oil Policy and Publicity': 213–16.
33. BP Archives, BP Plc, Ref. 45174, 'Advertising—British Isles Shell-Mex and BP'.
34. Ibid.
35. *The Pipeline*, 3 Feb. 1932, 'High Praise': 56.
36. Shell Art Collection, Beaulieu, 'Recollections of Shell and BP Advertising By Vernon Nye'.

BIBLIOGRAPHY

Aitken, I. (1990) *Film and Reform, John Grierson and the Documentary Film Movement*, London: Routledge.
Artmonsky, R. (2006) *Jack Beddington the Footnote Man*, London: Ruth Artmonsky.
Betjeman, J. (1934) *Cornwall Illustrated, in a Series of Views*, London: Architectural Press.
Betjeman, J. (1936) *Devon Shell Guide*, London: The Architectural Press.
Bird, W. L. (1999) *Advertising, Media, and the New Vocabulary of Business Leadership, 1935–1955*, Illinois: Northwestern University Press.
Connolly, C. (1934) 'The new Medici', *Architectural Review*, 76: 2–5.
Ellis, C. W. (1928) *England and the Octopus*, London: Geoffrey Bles.
Ferrier, R. W. (1986) 'Petrol advertising in the twenties and thirties: The case of the British Petroleum Company', *European Journal of Marketing*, 20 (5): 29–51.
Gospel, H. F. (1992) *Markets, Firms and the Management of Labour in Modern Britain*, Cambridge, UK: Cambridge University Press.
Green, C. L. (ed.) (1994) *John Betjeman Letters, Vol. 1: 1926 to 1951*, London: Methuen.
Hampton, M. (2004) *Visions of the Press in Britain, 1850–1950*, Urbana and Chicago: University of Illinois Press.
Harp, S. L. (2001) *Marketing Michelin: Advertising & Cultural Identity in Twentieth-Century France*, London: The Johns Hopkins University Press.
Heller, M. (2007) 'The National Insurance Acts 1911–1947, the Approved Societies and the Prudential Assurance Company', *Twentieth Century British History*, 19 (1): 1–28.
———. (2008), 'Sport, bureaucracies and London clerks 1880–1939', *The International Journal of the History of Sport*, 35 (5): 579–614.
Hewitt, J. (1992) 'The "nature" and "art" of Shell advertising in the early 1930s', *Journal of Design History*, 5 (2): 121–139.
Howarth, S. (1997) *A Century in Oil*, London: Weidenfeld & Nicolson.
Howarth, S., J. Jonker and J. Luiten van Zanden (2007) *A History of Royal Dutch Shell*, Vols. I–III, Oxford: Oxford University Press.
Jarvis, D. (1996) 'British conservatism and class politics in the 1920s', *English Historical Review*, 61 (440): 59–84.

LeMahieu, D. L. (1988) *A Culture for Democracy: Mass Communication and the Cultivated Mind in Britain Between the Wars*, Oxford: Clarendon.

Lipartito, K. and D. Sicilia (eds.) (2004) *Constructing Corporate America: History, Politics, Culture*, Oxford; Oxford University Press.

Mandler, P. (1997) 'Against "Englishness": English culture and the limits to rural nostalgia 1850–1940', *Transactions of the Royal Historical Society*, 6th Series, 7: 155–175.

Mandler, P. (2006) *The English National Character: The History of an Idea from Edmund Burke to Tony Blair*, London: Yale University Press.

Marchand, R. (1998) *Creating the Corporate Soul: The Rise of Public Relations and Corporate Imagery in American Big Business*, London: University of California Press.

McKibbin, R. (1990) *The Ideologies of Class: Social Relations in Britain, 1880–1950*, Oxford: Clarendon Press.

Nash, J. (1937) *Bucks Shell Guide*, London: The Architectural Press.

Orwell, G. (1953) *England, Your England, and Other Essays*, London: Secker & Warburg.

Rotha, P. (1973) *Documentary Diary: An Informal History of the British Documentary Film, 1928–1939*, London: Secker & Warburg.

Saler, M. T. (1999) *The Avant-Garde in Interwar England: Medieval Modernism and the London Underground*, Oxford: Oxford University Press.

Scannell, P. and D. Cardiff (1991) *A Social History of British Broadcasting*, Vol. 1: *1922–39—Serving the Nation*, Oxford: Basil Blackwell.

Sharp, T. (1937) *Northumberland and Durham Shell Guide*, London: The Architectural Press.

Shell-Mex Ltd. (1931) *An Exhibition of Modern Pictorial Advertising by Shell*, London: Curwen Press.

Shell UK Ltd. (1992) *The Shell Poster Book Oil and Petrol*, London: Hamish Hamilton.

———. (1998) *The Shell Poster Book*, London: Profile Books Limited.

Varey, R. J. and B. R. Lewis (eds.) (2000) *Internal Marketing: Directions of Management*, London: Routledge.

Whyte, W. H. (1956) *Organization Man*, New York: Touchstone.

Zunz, O. (1990) *Making America Corporate, 1870–1920*, Chicago: University of Chicago Press.

10 Unilever's (Other) Brand Wars
Retailers, Private Labels, and Struggles for Supremacy within Product Supply Chains[1]

Peter Miskell

Brand wars are a familiar feature of the fast-moving consumer goods sector. For Unilever, success (indeed, survival) has depended upon an ability to create and maintain strong brands which is why, by the 1980s, it was spending four times as much on marketing as on R&D (Jones 2005). At a global level, Unilever's brands compete head-to-head against those of other multinationals, such as Procter and Gamble, Colgate-Palmolive, Nestlé, and L'Oreal. The ongoing competition provided by these rival brand manufacturers as they expanded aggressively beyond their home territories in the post-war decades undoubtedly shaped the development of Unilever's international business strategy—as has been well documented (Jones 2005; Jones and Miskell 2005). Rival manufacturers, however, did not constitute the only competitive influence on the development of Unilever's brands. Within most developed industrial markets, the past half-century has also witnessed the rapid growth of supermarket retailing (Seth and Randall 2001). The firms responsible for delivering Unilever's brands to consumers are, in some cases, now much larger than Unilever itself. These firms have developed strong brand identities of their own, as recognizable to consumers as the brand names of manufacturers' products. This chapter examines the development of Unilever's brand strategy in the context of this increasingly important form of vertical competition.

'Brand wars', as Paul Duguid's chapter in this volume demonstrates, do not just happen between firms offering competing products, but also between firms in competition for control of a particular supply chain. From publishing in the sixteenth century to the computer industry in the twenty-first, trademarks and brands have played a crucial role in determining which firms were able to dominate and control any particular supply chain, and thus capture the majority of profits in any given industry (Duguid 2003; this volume). Up until the 1960s, Unilever's brands were largely unchallenged in this respect. In seeking reassurance about the quality and reliability of products in their grocery baskets, consumers relied on names such as Omo, Lux, Sunsilk, Rama, or Birds Eye. These were the brands in which consumers placed their trust—where they happened to buy them from was a secondary consideration. The reputation of the retailer (like that of the supplier of raw materials) was subservient to that of the manufacturer. From the 1960s onwards, however, this began to change. Just as Unilever was becoming embroiled in conventional brand wars with rival manufacturers (Omo *v.* Ariel; Signal *v.* Crest), the firm was becoming increasingly concerned about its relationship with its direct customers. The types of brand wars that Duguid describes were all too familiar to Unilever's managers, who appeared to regard the growing power of retailers as at least as great a threat to profitability as competition from rival producers such as Procter and Gamble.

The chapter is divided into three sections. It begins by demonstrating that within Unilever's head office, marketing managers did perceive the growing power of retailers as a threat. As fewer supermarket groups accounted for a growing share of grocery sales in western European markets in the 1960s and '70s, Unilever found it increasingly difficult to control the downstream part of its supply chain. This was reflected in internal reports and memoranda, in which some anxiety and sense of disempowerment was expressed. The second section explores, in more detail, the role played by private labels in the competitive struggle between retailers and brand manufacturers. It argues that as retailers invested more heavily in private labels, these came to compete with more established brands in terms of quality, as well as price, and in so doing provided retailers with a more powerful bargaining tool. The final section explores the various strategies at Unilever's disposal for responding to this threat, and argues that the development of the firm's brand strategies should be seen in the context of vertical as well as horizontal competition.

INDUSTRY STRUCTURE AND MARKET POWER: 'RETAIL POWER WEAKENS OUR BRANDS'

As the retail trade became more concentrated in the hands of fewer large firms, so Unilever became increasingly challenged by the retail end of its supply chain. A committee was set up, chaired by Unilever's most senior marketing manager, to investigate the changing nature of the firm's relationship with the retail trade. It reported in 1968, and its findings were unambiguous. The trend towards concentration in retailing was unmistakable, and it was evident across Western Europe. The increasing prominence of large supermarket chains in national markets meant that they were beginning to dictate terms to manufacturers. For Unilever, this meant that:

> Operating companies have been under constant pressure for special discounts, excessive quality rebates, more credit, more rigorous delivery conditions, limitation of salesman's callage, special packing and pricing and co-operative advertising. The trend to concentration means that the pressure becomes daily more difficult to resist.[2]

Unused to conducting business with partners (or customers) as strong as itself, the members of Unilever's retailing committee found the situation very difficult to accept:

> On balance, however, we judge that many Unilever companies have paid and are still paying too much for nothing other than a concession to power (so-called Mafia money) and we believe that we should try to find means of adopting a firmer attitude, difficult though this will be, before the situation gets worse in the larger European countries.[3]

The shifting balance of power between manufacturers and retailers was a reality that Unilever's senior executives had come to accept by the 1970s, but the implications for profitability remained a real concern. The head of one of Unilever's three major foods divisions described the problem quite directly to the company's three-man Special Committee (its chief executive body) in 1971:

> I believe it can be demonstrated that profitability is fairly closely correlated with power. The proprietary brand manufacturer, when I joined Unilever, had the majority of the power in relation to consumer goods. It is at least arguable that power is now equally between retailers and manufacturers, and may move predominantly to retailers. Store image may become more important than brand image.[4]

Unilever's chairmen were receiving a similar message from the Financial Group and Accounts Department.[5] By the end of the 1970s, Unilever's Marketing Division was in a position to confirm that the concerns it had expressed a decade earlier were well founded:

> In nearly all [West European] countries the top ten customers represented a very large proportion of turnover and a handful of buyers could now decide whether or not our products were stocked. They were not yet fully organised to use their power but its consequences were all pervading. It was weakening our brands and we were now spending less on franchise billing and more on price dealing ... more of our money was getting into the hands of the trade.[6]

A 1979 report entitled 'Retailing in Europe' put it bluntly: 'Retail power weakens our brands'.[7] A key problem was that Unilever found itself being forced to spend an increasing proportion of its marketing budget on special discounts or incentives (so-called 'scheme' marketing), rather than offering more 'theme' support for its brands in the form of advertising. 'Each year in the Annual Plan a determined effort is made to restore theme support—but with varying degrees of success.' In 1978, for example, Unilever planned to spend 57 per cent of its budget on scheme promotions, but by the following year it was estimated that the proportion spent in this area was actually 64 per cent. Moreover:

> Of this scheme money a smaller proportion (6% in 1979) is planned in trial inducing techniques—samples and coupons. 80% is planned to go into price marked packs and trade stimulants—activities which either increase trade income or reduce consumer price. This trend to price-dealing has developed consistently over the last 10 years from just over 50% in 1969.[8]

Far from concentrating resources on building up a strong image or identity for their brands, which was essential if Unilever were to maintain a strong bargaining position against the superstores, increasing amounts of money were, instead, being directed into areas that either strengthened the hand of the retailers or reduced prices. By the mid-1980s, Unilever's Special Committee was being informed that 'there is at this moment a greater general uneasiness about the large retailer's power and the way he uses it (or might use it) than we have ever seen before'.[9]

The simplest explanation for the growing market power of supermarket retailers was their size. As the leading retail chains expanded their reach, the sector became increasingly concentrated, with just a few firms accounting for a large proportion of grocery sales in many countries. The strength of the large supermarkets in European markets by the early 1980s is illustrated in table 10.1. Although the size and buying power of these large organizations undoubtedly did improve their bargaining position with manufacturers, there were other reasons why marketing managers at Unilever were becoming concerned. As supermarkets became larger, they began to tighten their grip over not just retailing, but also distribution (Senker 1988: 31–32).

Unilever had moved into distribution, owning fleets of vehicles that shipped these products from factories to retailers. The ability to distribute its branded packaged products to a multitude of small retailers on a nationwide scale had long been a key competitive advantage for the company in its major European markets. Its extensive distribution network not only gave Unilever direct access to a larger share of the market than its competitors, it also meant that many small retailers relied heavily on Unilever for a regular supply of branded products. Furthermore, it opened up potential economies of scope, with Unilever able to supply retailers with a range of new product types (from ice cream to iced tea) in addition to its traditional staples of soap and edible fats (Jones and Miskell 2007). As the retail trade became more concentrated, however, with the largest supermarkets taking control of their own distribution (or supply) systems, what had once been a key competitive advantage for Unilever was increasingly becoming a burden. Smaller producers were able to access the most important retail outlets (accounting for an increasing

Table 10.1   Concentration of European Grocery Trade: Top 5 Organizations

Country	Share (%)
Austria	59
Belgium	30
Finland	91
France	53
Germany	36
Italy	44*
Netherlands	46
Sweden	95
Switzerland	73**
United Kingdom	46

*Top 10.   **Excluding Migros.
Source: Memo to Special Committee, 13 July 1984, appendix I, Unilever Archives, London [UAL].

proportion of the total market) without having to maintain any distribution network at all. Unilever's distribution system did put it in a position to dominate smaller independent retailers, but these accounted for a declining percentage of total sales. By the 1980s, Unilever managers were beginning to question whether the costs of its distribution network might outweigh the benefits. As one board member explained to his fellow directors in 1983: 'It was right to focus now on the distribution decision because it was very important to recognize the precise moment at which the advantage became a penalty'.[10] Two years later, it was agreed that the line had been crossed:

> For years the company had had a totally integrated distribution system for grocery and traditional trade but this was increasingly becoming a disadvantage to them. It was therefore planned to transfer the whole of the grocery distribution to third parties . . . [11]

Unilever's decision to outsource its distribution activities serves as an indication that it was losing direct control of its downstream supply chain. As the firm's vertically integrated structures broke down, so the strength of its brands took on added significance in the struggle to maintain (indirect) control over downstream links in the chain. For Unilever's brands, the journey from factory floor to grocery store was no longer safely managed and controlled by the vertically integrated parent company. Increasingly. these brands had to prove their value in a more competitive supply chain. As a Marketing Division report from the early 1980s put it:

> In the end the manufacturer will have to decide whether his brands can perform in today's competitive world. If they can, he should not fear DoBs [distributors own brands].[12]

Increased competition here was clearly conceived in vertical rather than horizontal terms. The challenge did not just come from rival manufacturers' own brands (MoBs), but from distributors' own brands (DoBs). Well before the likes of Wal-Mart in the United States or Tesco in the United Kingdom had grown into giant corporations, Unilever recognized that firms such a Carrefour, Sainsbury's, and Albert Heijn posed a potential threat at least as great as that from Nestlé or P&G. The key weapon in the hands of the retailer, as Unilever's managers saw it, was not their size, but their 'own brand' private labels.

BRAND IMAGE AND MARKET POWER

The trend to concentration in grocery retailing and the growing power and industry presence of supermarket groups clearly gave these multiple retailers a strengthened bargaining position against manufacturers within their shared supply chains. Yet, as various Unilever reports in the 1960s and '70s pointed out, retailers were not at this stage felt to be exploiting their market power to the full. A potentially much more worrying development for firms like Unilever, however, was the increasing prominence of alternative product supply chains that supermarket retailers were able to completely dominate. Through their control of private labels, retailers have been able to use classic forms of horizontal competition against established brands as a means of strengthening their position against manufacturers within their shared vertical structures (Mills 1995). The stronger the brand image and appeal of the private label, the more powerful the position of the retailer in this regard. As supermarket groups have developed stronger corporate brand identities since the 1980s, and as their private labels have become more prevalent, their ability to exploit their market power has been enhanced.

Manufacturers like Unilever, it should be stressed, have long faced competition from private labels. Retailers have been selling products under their own brand names in Unilever's major markets since the nineteenth century (Senker 1988). Until the latter part of the twentieth century, however, such private labels tended to compete against manufacturers' brands on the basis of price, rather than quality. In some markets, their existence was a means of getting around retail price maintenance, which prevented retailers selling branded goods at reduced prices. For as long as private labels were widely regarded as a cheap, but inferior, substitute for manufacturers' brands, their threat was a limited one, affecting only the weakest and most vulnerable brand producers. As one Unilever manager put it in the early 1960s: 'Whilst we see little reason to believe that private labels are likely to replace manufacturers' brands, it seems highly possible that the mice are going to nibble away substantial fragments of some manufacturers' cakes'.[13] By the end of the 1960s, Unilever's marketing division appeared to regard private labels as an increasing irritant (a 'hard fact of life'), rather than a major strategic threat:

> Retailers will usually readily admit that most DoBs are technically parasitic in that they follow manufacturers' innovations and benefit by their investments in consumer and technical research and development work generally. This is simply one of the hard facts of life, however, and the public at large are certain to believe that on balance they benefit by having DoBs added to their range of choice. . . . We must, where DoBs are important, treat them as full and worthy competitors and enquire into their physical composition and image as much as we do in the case of competing MoBs.[14]

By the early 1970s, however, Unilever recognized that its brands were becoming increasingly susceptible to the threat from cheaper private labels. As a memo from the firm's Financial Group put it in 1971: 'The threat of [private labels] is a much more potent argument in the hands of a major multiple than in those of a smaller concern'.[15]

The problem, however, appeared to be more acute in some product categories than others. The market shares attained by private labels in personal care categories such as toothpaste, shampoos, or cosmetics, and, indeed, in detergents sectors such as fabric conditioners, remained very modest (typically less than 5 per cent by the early 1970s), but the figure was over 10 per cent for margarine and over 20 per cent for canned fruit and vegetables (Jones 2005). Another sector where Unilever was concerned about the impact of private labels was quick frozen foods (QFF), particularly frozen vegetables:

> The major competitive threats are not from the large national brand competitors but from DoBs and from smaller companies categorized under the heading of 'other' producers. Their major competitive advantages are price [they undercut Unilever by as much as 30 per cent on price] and the market structure which is moving in their favour. . . . The increasing power of large retailers *vis-a-vis* manufacturers (and the growing percentage of QFF sold through such outlets) facilitates DoB growth and hence new entry into the industry and the expansion of smaller producers.[16]

As table 10.2 illustrates, the speed with which private labels had grown in the late 1960s and early '70s varied significantly from country to country. In almost all major markets in Western Europe, however, the share held by retailers' own brands was growing while that held by Unilever was in decline. The countries where Unilever's frozen foods businesses were most under threat were its home markets of the United Kingdom and the Netherlands. In the latter case, the competitive challenge came entirely from retailers' own brands. In the UK market, the growth of private labels was less pronounced, but the emergence of a new retail format (the home freezer centre) had opened the way for a host of smaller producers to enter the market. The brands of these smaller 'other' producers were not to become Unilever's key competitors; in some cases these producers eventually became the suppliers of private labels for the major supermarkets. Their sudden growth in the United Kingdom in the early 1970s, however, serves as a useful illustration of how innovations in retailing could affect the market position of Unilever's brands.

Up to this point, the threat to Unilever from private labels and other cut-price competitors, though recognized as a real challenge, was containable. Private labels may have eroded Unilever's market share in certain product categories, but they were not typically regarded as being equivalent to Unilever's brands in terms of quality or reputation. As supermarkets grew in size and importance, however, they were able to invest more in the advertising of their corporate (brand) identities, and in the development and merchandizing of their own label products.

Table 10.2   Quick Frozen Food Market, Distributors' Own Brands, and Unilever's Share

	Consumption Per Head:Lb.	Market Growth P.A.	Unilever's Share		DOBs		'Others'	
	1972	1969–72	1969	1972	1969	1972	1969	1972
UK	18.6	4.2	65	54	5	8.5	6.5	19.5
Netherlands	9.6	12.2	52.5	41	9	25	31.5	28
Germany	8.8	8.2	61.8	58.3	1	4	26.1	23.6
Austria	6.5	9.3	88*	83	—	—	6*	9
Belgium	5.6	12.5	76	71	1	6	6	5
France	5.6	17.3	0	6	—	3	30	25
Italy	2.1	35.0	75*	74	0	2	17*	15

*1970 figures.
Source: Economics Department, 'Competition in Quick Frozen Foods in Europe' (July 1973), Unilever Archives Rotterdam [UAR].

Such investments helped to improve consumer perceptions of the quality of 'own label' brands (Senker 1988). As supermarkets were able to exert considerable power over the suppliers of these products, private labels could generate higher margins for retailers than more conventional branded products (Dawson 2004). With this being the case, manufacturers like Unilever found that competition for shelf space intensified. Far from being seen as low-cost imitators of more established brands, by the 1980s private labels had become much more serious competitors in a range of product categories.

As some of the previous quotations from internal documents have shown, there was a tendency within Unilever in the 1970s to regard retailers' own brands as 'parasitic'. By imitating and undercutting the manufacturers' brands, they weakened the position of firms such as Unilever, and it was generally felt that manufacturers, rather than retailers, would be at the forefront of innovation and new product development. By the end of the 1980s, however, this was no longer so apparent. From their position further downstream in the supply chain, retailers had much more direct contact with consumers, and were in a position to collect much more detailed and sophisticated data about their shopping patterns. As advances in information technology made the collection and processing of such data much easier, so retailers were in a position to identify opportunities and respond to changes in consumer demand more quickly than manufacturers. Far from being parasites, supermarkets' private labels were able to act as pioneers in some areas.

Chilled ready meals have been described as one such product category 'spawned by the information age' (Cox, Mowatt and Prevezer 1999). The short shelf life of these products 'necessitated a reversion to forms of manufacturing based on batch rather than continuous process methods' (Cox, Mowatt and Prevezer 1999: 1–2). Success in this market depended on the ability to match supply and demand over short periods of time. The availability of electronic point of sale (EPOS) barcode scanning technologies gave supermarkets sufficiently detailed information to identify consumer buying patterns over short time scales. This information could then be used to determine the quantities of any given product being ordered from third party suppliers. The pioneers in the development of this market were not manufacturers (who did not have sufficiently detailed knowledge of consumer behaviour to match supply and demand), but retailers. In the United Kingdom, firms such as Marks and Spencer and Sainsbury, who (using their own brands) were able to monitor and control supply chains far more closely than manufacturers, pioneered this market sector (Cox, Mowatt and Prevezer 2002; 2003).

The development of barcode scanning technologies benefited supermarkets beyond just the chilled ready meals sector. As a Unilever report of 1988 pointed out, it gave retailers a more general advantage in deciding where to invest in future product innovation:

One major impetus: the use of electronic sales data. Retailers can now work out the profitability of each square metre of shelf space, and every product that takes it up; hence their increasing involvement in new product development.[17]

The introduction of supermarket loyalty cards in the 1990s provided retailers with detailed data not just about products, but on individual consumers, enabling them to develop much more focused and personalized marketing strategies than brand manufacturers. As retailers' corporate brands became more familiar (and trusted) in the minds of consumers, and as private labels shed their reputation for inferior quality, the price differential between retailers and manufacturers' brands narrowed substantially. Various studies have found that in those categories where private labels held their highest market shares, the price differential with manufacturers' brands was smallest—suggesting strongly that the appeal of private labels was based on perceived quality as much as price (Cotterill, Putsis and Dhar 2000). In keeping with this, the range of product sectors in which private labels compete has expanded since the 1970s. No longer restricted to commodity groups such as tinned fruit or frozen vegetables, private labels have become increasingly competitive in categories such as toiletries. In the British market, the percentage share of retailer brands in the packaged grocery and toiletries categories increased from little more than 20 per cent in 1980 to almost 40 per cent by the end of the 1990s (Dawson 2004).

Far from being 'parasites', by the 1990s, supermarkets (and their 'own label' brands) were recognized as powerful competitors capable of competing with Unilever's brands in terms of technical quality and brand image as well as price. How could manufacturers like Unilever respond to such formidable competition?

RESPONDING TO THE CHALLENGE

We can begin to answer this question by observing that, at the most general level, managers within Unilever's marketing division realized that the growing power of retailers did constitute a strategic threat, which merited a strategic response. It was not enough for individual operating companies (or the managers of individual brands) to devise their own response to the changing market conditions. As a 1979 report put it:

> The main consequence for Unilever of the growing power of the trade is the need to change our mental approach to marketing. Too many decisions about our business with major customers are still taken tactically, rather than strategically, in an organization which the breakdown of Retail Price Maintenance and the growth of Discounting have rendered old-fashioned.[18]

Unilever knew that its response to the growing power of retailers needed to be reflected in its broader corporate strategy, but what would such a strategy entail? Several strategic options were available.

One possibility, raised in a report by Unilever's retailing committee and subsequently considered at the very highest levels, was for Unilever to significantly expand its activities in the retailing sector itself. The firm already had some retailing operations (in the form of the MacFisheries fish shops in Britain and the Frowein and Nolden chain of self-service stores and supermarkets in Germany). Towards the end of the 1960s, there were suggestions at Board level that further investment in retail could provide the company with a valuable body of knowledge and experience.

Investment in retail, it should be stressed, was never seriously considered as a type of forward vertical integration. Unilever was perfectly aware that it would never be able to directly control a large enough segment of the retailing sector in any one country to be able to guarantee protection (or preferential treatment) for its brands. Even if Unilever did have the financial skills and resources to acquire a leading supermarket chain (which it almost certainly lacked in the late 1960s), such a merger would almost certainly have been ruled out by antimonopoly regulators.

> To buy the biggest multiple in the UK, which does less than 7% of retail grocery business, would cost about £300,000,000—a sum roughly equivalent to Unilever's capital employed in the UK. . . . Public opinion would be likely to react adversely and result in government invoking anti-monopoly legislation.[19]

Even a series of smaller investments providing Unilever with a minority interest in a range of retailers would not, in itself, have done much to bolster the position of Unilever's brands.

> We are seeking to increase Unilever's profits, not fritter them away. For this reason also we are unlikely unduly to press our brands upon our retailers to the extent that we distort their range of goods and so prejudice their performance. If we did, of course, we would merely play into the hands of their competitors.[20]

The rationale behind further entry into retailing was not that it would provide Unilever with market power, so much as market knowledge.

> A deeper understanding of retailing, and the latest developments within retailing, than might be obtained from observation from the outside world would improve our marketing decisions. We need much more precise knowledge of the costs and the effects of such activities as price mark-downs, multi-unit pricing, the way in which price should be presented, space allocation, shelf position and special displays. There

is no doubt that both retailers and manufacturers would benefit by a determined effort to learn from one another. Joint training of buyers and key sales managers would be particularly valuable. Further entry into retailing would widen these opportunities.[21]

The US consultancy firm McKinsey was brought in to advise Unilever on the merits of diversifying further into the retailing sector. Their report, produced in 1971, though acknowledging the possible benefits of such a move, effectively killed the proposal. It pointed out that 'the key factors for success in retailing are not only effective merchandising but shrewd financing and real estate management'. Unilever would 'probably be called upon . . . to provide large amounts of capital' and it 'should expect to achieve only a marginal return on its investment in the initial, volume-building years'. Unilever lacked not only the financial and real estate resources during this period: even in the area of merchandizing it lagged behind these. 'Unilever should anticipate being deeply involved in the sale of toasters, furniture and auto parts—if it wants to maintain a successful position in retailing.'[22]

The McKinsey position was shared by Unilever's finance director, who remained highly sceptical of the benefits to be derived from any investment in retailing.

> I have always had considerable doubts about the way this argument was developed in the Retail Committee's report and, if we are to retain Frowein & Nolden and MacFisheries in their existing form merely to 'deepen our understanding of the food retailing industry', it is a jolly expensive way of doing it.[23]

Diversification into retailing proved too radical a departure. Although Mac-Fisheries did make some attempt to move into more general food retailing in the 1970s, by the end of the decade both this and Frowein and Nolden had been sold off.

In 1984, a marketing division report suggested 'three possible routes' for containing the threat posed by supermarkets and DoBs. The first of these was to 'develop such strong manufacturer brands that even the biggest retailers have to take them'. The second route was to convince the retailers that they were at risk of attracting the attention of monopolies investigators and therefore that 'a jointly agreed code of conduct would be desirable'. The third option was 'to admit to ourselves that one and two above are unachievable and to support as quickly as possible legislation "to protect smaller and medium sized retailers and manufacturers in the interest of the consumer long term"'.[24] The first route was deemed much the most desirable, but the report's author, at least, felt that 'there should be a greater awareness at government level of the power of the trade and the way in which they sometimes abused it'. The Special Committee, for their part, 'agreed that there was a problem and were not averse to some sort of action being taken to strengthen our position *vis-a-vis* the retailer'. However, 'The one point on which they were adamant was that we must not be seen to be leading the attack against the retailer'.[25] The reason that the Special Committee were so adamant on this point is explained in the minutes of a subsequent meeting of the two Unilever chairmen:

> It was thought we should not be seen as being at the forefront of an attack upon retailers for two principal reasons. Firstly, they were our customers. Secondly, we should not be a party to pressing for the introduction of legislation to curb the dominance of the trade as we were fairly dominant in a number of market sectors ourselves.[26]

That Unilever should have contemplated exerting some form of political pressure to strengthen its position may come as little surprise to those who study corporate political activities (Hillman and Keim 1995; Hillman and Hitt 1999). However, the firm's reluctance to act independently, and its preference for using political influence discreetly, are perhaps characteristics more commonly associated with European, rather than US, multinationals (Li 2006).

DIVERSIFICATION AND ACQUISITION

As mentioned, the product categories where private labels posed the greatest threat to Unilever's brands in the 1960s and '70s were typically those closest to basic commodities (such as tinned fruit). These were often large markets (in terms of volume), but they were not necessarily fast growing ones. As consumers became increasingly affluent in post-war Western societies, they did not choose to spend their additional disposable income on ever greater quantities of frozen broccoli. The types of products on which consumers did spend more money as their incomes increased were ones that helped them to express their personality or enhance their self-esteem—such as beauty products or fashion labels (Jones 2008). In such product categories, brand image was particularly important, and the role of supermarket private labels was a marginal one.

As early as the 1950s, Unilever had realized that it needed to develop successful businesses in product markets where both sales growth and profit margins were expected to be high. To this end, it sought to significantly expand its range of food products in areas other than edible fats and margarine, such tea and ice cream (Jones and Miskell 2007). It also began to build a very large and successful personal care business, which included toothpaste, shampoo, deodorants, skin care products, and some cosmetics (Miskell 2004). The strategic decision to diversify into these product areas was not originally taken in response to the growing power of supermarket retailers. As many of Unilever's more traditional branded products came under greater pressure from supermarkets in the 1970s and '80s, however, these areas of its business took on added significance.

There were constraints to Unilever's ability to sidestep the problem of competition from supermarkets' own label brands simply by diversifying into new product categories. Unilever's core competence remained the production and marketing of mass market, fast moving consumer products. The firm's attempt to develop or acquire new brands tended to be less successful the further it strayed from this familiar territory. In the personal care market, for example, Unilever was able to develop strong brands in areas such as toothpaste (Mentadent, Signal), shampoo (Timotei, Sunsilk), and deodorants (Impulse, Lynx), but its acquisitions of more exclusive brands of fragrances (Elizabeth Arden, Calvin Klein) proved less successful and were later sold off (Jones 2005).

Unilever was aware that it needed to concentrate more of its marketing efforts on building and supporting brands that represented far more than just product quality or reliability. In order to retain consumer loyalty in the face of competition from private labels, Unilever's brands needed to hold an emotional appeal, as well as a functional one. As a report in 1970 put it, Unilever (and its brands) needed to become 'more beautiful':

> The future . . . lies in the satisfaction of the higher order needs, with the development of products that fit into the consumer's view of her total personality.[27]

This particular report argued that Unilever needed to become far more involved in beauty products, such as fragrances and cosmetics. Although diversification into such areas proved less than successful, the firm was still able to apply the techniques of 'lifestyle' marketing to mass market products. The company's accumulated knowledge and culture may have made it ill-suited to running an exclusive fashion label or cosmetic brand, but it knew how to appeal to consumers' 'higher order needs' when selling its more traditional product ranges.

One such example is ice cream, where Unilever had established (mainly through acquisitions) a leading international presence by the 1970s. The fastest growing sector of this market, and the one that accounted for the majority of sales volume in many markets by the 1980s, was the 'take-home' sector—large packs (or tubs) of ice cream, bought in supermarkets and stored at home in the freezer. Though Unilever held a strong position in this market in many countries, this was also an area where Unilever's brands faced increasing competition from supermarket private labels, and where profit margins were being squeezed. The firm's response to this situation was to concentrate its resources on developing branded ice cream products that supermarkets could not easily imitate. New ice cream dessert brands were created such as Carte D'or (initially sold only through restaurants) and Viennetta—the design of which (an ice cream version of the millefeuille cake) was protected by patent.[28] The Viennetta brand proved particularly successful in the United Kingdom, and in this case it was retailers, rather than the manufacturer, who saw their profit margins eroded:

> Having been launched at a good value for money price in 1982, the price *to* the retailer for Viennetta has been increased steadily on an annual basis. However, as the brand has become stronger, retailers have felt the need to *be seen* to be competitive with Viennetta with the result that pricing has remained at key levels (eg: 89p and 99p) and retailers have become unhappy with the consequent low margins. In 1986, grocery pricing has moved over the £1 barrier (to £1.09). Again for Christmas, a key retailer cut the price to 89p which stimulated all the major national accounts to do the same, despite the extremely low cash margin to the trade which results.[29]

As well as developing new ice cream dessert brands for the 'take-home' sector of the market, Unilever also sought to develop new brands in the smaller, but more profitable, 'impulse' sector. 'Impulse' ice cream products, typically sold from vans or small kiosks and designed to be consumed at the point of purchase, were an important market for Unilever. Its Cornetto brand was a market leader in many European countries in the 1960s and '70s, and with no pressure from supermarket retailers, margins were very healthy. The seasonality of this market, however, and the fact that it was dependent, to a large extent, on children (a sector of the population in demographic decline) presented a problem. Unilever addressed this by developing an 'impulse' ice cream brand, aimed specifically at adults, which could be sold throughout the year.[30] The marketing of the resulting Magnum brand emphasized not just the product itself, but the sensual and emotional experiences associated with it. As the marketing guidelines for the brand put it: 'Eating a Magnum should be a very personal ritual, implying considerable sensual pleasure'.[31]

In a number of product categories (including margarine and tea, as well as ice cream) Unilever proved to be successful in differentiating its brands from private labels and maintaining healthy profit margins. In the case of margarine, it did this by pioneering a market segmentation strategy in which different brands were developed to meet different consumer tastes or desires—such as low fat, buttery taste, or cholesterol reduction (Jones 2005). In ice cream, the example of Viennetta demonstrated that where Unilever was able to support its brands with other forms of intellectual property protection (such as patents) their position with retailers was strengthened yet further. Unilever, however, was more successful at protecting its position in some product categories than others. The managers of one of the main foods divisions made this assessment to the Special Committee in 1975: 'Looking at the figures for quick frozen foods and ice cream, the uninformed observer could be forgiven for asking why we did not concentrate on ice cream and forget about all the rest'.[32] As sales of frozen ready meals came under increasing pressure from chilled foods (which were predominantly private labels), even informed observers began to ask the same question. In 2006, Unilever did eventually sell off its Birds Eye and Iglo frozen foods brands (while retaining its ice cream business).

CONCLUSIONS

As one of the largest multinational producers of branded packaged consumer products through the twentieth century, Unilever provides an important case study in any historical study of modern branding. The firm's rich archival sources reveal that even this powerful manufacturer of some of Europe's most widely recognized brands was concerned about the increasing threat of vertical competition from retailers from the 1960s. Marketing managers frequently commented in the 1960s and '70s that retailers were not yet exploiting their market power to the full, but as supermarket groups developed more sophisticated store formats and marketing strategies in the 1980s and '90s, as they invested more heavily in IT systems and new product development, their brand image was enhanced significantly. This, in turn, meant that private labels became much more serious competitors to manufacturer's brands in an increasing number of product categories. Rather than imposing their own brand image onto manufacturers' products, retailers had successfully managed to create their own alternative branded product ranges based on supply chains that they were able to dominate.

In the face of this challenge, Unilever's senior management contemplated several strategic options ranging from investment into retailing themselves to the application of political pressure. There were also moves to diversify into new product categories where there was less competition from private labels, though there appeared to be constraints on how far Unilever could venture from its core business of mass market, fast moving consumer products. Ultimately, Unilever's strategic priority was to support and strengthen the identity and appeal of its leading brands. Managers were under continuous pressure to do this from both horizontal and vertical competitors.

The development of Unilever's market segmentation and product differentiation strategies were not simply direct responses to the growing power of supermarket groups. Such strategies were in keeping with post-war developments in consumer product marketing, typified by the creation of a so-called 'Pepsi generation' (Tedlow 1990; Hollander and Germain 1992). The idea of developing brands with strong characteristics that could be associated with, and targeted at, clearly defined sections of the population enabled firms like Unilever to move its brands further up the value chain, and thus generate higher profit margins. This was a strategic path that many brand manufacturers followed, irrespective of their market position in relation to retailers. For Unilever, however, the growing power of super-markets, and increasing competition from private labels, made this type of brand strategy not just attractive, but necessary. Under increasing pressure from retailers, Unilever had to rely far more heavily on the distinctive appeal of its brands, rather than its control over distribution networks, to retain its market position. As such, the firm found it necessary to make adjustments to both the range of products it sold and the way it went about marketing and advertising them. The shifting balance of power between manufacturers and retailers may not have significantly altered the direction in which Unilever's strategy was moving, but it almost certainly did influence the extent to which this strategic path was followed.

NOTES

1. I thank Unilever PLC and Unilever NV for permission to consult Unilever Archives, London [UAL] and Unilever Archives, Rotterdam [UAR].
2. 'Report of the Retailing Committee', (December 1968: 9), UAL, PS, MD, 1995/17.
3. *Ibid.*: 10.
4. Memo to Special Committee (28 May 1971), UAL.
5. 'Margins in the retail trade', (29 March 1971), UAL.
6. Special Committee with Marketing Division, (8 May 1979), UAL.
7. Marketing Division, 'Retailing in Europe' (May 1979), UAL.
8. Marketing Division, 'Retailing in Europe': 7.
9. Memo to Special Committee, (13 July 1984), UAL.
10. Extract from Directors' Conference, (20 October 1983), UAL.
11. Special Committee with Frozen Products Co-ordination (26 November 1985), UAL.
12. Marketing Division, 'MoBs, DoBs and generics: "The divine right" (1982): 1, UAL.
13. D. B. Lewis, 'Covering letter for own label brands', see report by Marketing Division and Economics and Statistics Department (1961), [UAR] OS 61 010.
14. 'Report of the Retailing Committee': 22.
15. J. D. Cormie to D. A. Orr, 'Margins in the retail trade' (29 March 1971), UAL.
16. Economics Department, 'Competition in quick frozen foods in Europe' (July 1973: 1), UAR.
17. Economics Dept., 'Dealer own brands and producer strategies: A note': 3, UAR, ES 88 071.
18. Marketing Division, 'Retailing in Europe' (May 1979: 14), UAL.
19. 'Report of the Retailing Committee', (December 1968: 23–27), UAL.
20. Ibid.
21. Ibid.
22. McKinsey and Company Inc., 'Implications of further entry into food rre-tailing: Unilever', (March 1971: 4, 5, 7), UAL.
23. Memo from Finance Director (26 April 1971), UAL.
24. 'Concentration in the retail trade' (August 1984: 8–9), UAL.
25. Special Committee with Marketing Division (29 August 1984), UAL.
26. Extract from 'Sitting together' (29 August 1984), UAL.

27. Economics and Statistics Dept., 'Towards a more beautiful Unilever' (December 1970), UAR, TR 70 006.
28. 'Co-ordination marketing and technical guidelines for Viennetta' (24 February 1987: 4), UAL.
29. Ibid.
30. 'Project Renaissance qualitative research: Final report', (January 1986), UAR.
31. 'Magnum brand history', p. 4. UAR, ICG 104 19.4.
32. Special Committee with Food & Drinks Co-ordination (7 August 1975), UAL.

BIBLIOGRAPHY

Cotterill, R. W., W. P. Putsis and R. Dhar (2000) 'Assessing the competitive interaction between private labels and national brands', *Journal of Business*, 73(1): 109–37.
Cox, H., S. Mowatt and M. Prevezer (1999) 'From frozen fish fingers to chilled chicken tikka: Organizational responses to technical change in the late twentieth century', *Centre for International Business Studies: Research Papers in International Business*, London, No. 18–99.
———. (2002) 'The firm in the information age: Organizational responses to technological change in the processed foods sector' *Industrial and Corporate Change*, 11(1): 135–58.
———. (2003) 'New product development and product supply within a network setting: The case of chilled ready-meal industry in the UK', *Industry and Innovation*, 10(2): 197–217.
Dawson, J. (2004) 'Food retailing, wholesaling and catering' in M. A. Bourlakis and P. W. H. Weightman (eds.) *Food Supply Chain Management*, Oxford: Blackwell: 116–35.
Duguid, P. (2003) 'Developing the brand: The case of alcohol, 1800–1880', *Enterprise and Society*, 4(3): 405–41.
———. (2008) 'Brands in chains', this volume.
Hillman, A. and G. Keim (1995) 'International variation in the business–government interface: Institutional and organizational considerations', *Academy of Management Review*, 20(1): 193–214.
Hillman, A. and M. Hitt (1999) 'Corporate political strategy formulation: A model of approach, participation and strategy decisions', *Academy of Management Review*, 24(4): 825–42.
Hollander, S. and R. Germain (1992) *Was There a Pepsi Generation Before Pepsi Invented It?*, Lincolnwood, IL: NTC Business Books.
Jones, G. (2005) *Renewing Unilever: Transformation and Tradition*, Oxford: Oxford University Press.
Jones, G. (2008) 'Blonde and blue-eyed? Globalising beauty, c.1945–1980', *Economic History Review*, 61(1): 125–54.
Jones, G. and P. Miskell (2005) 'European integration and corporate restructuring: The strategy of Unilever c.1957–c.1990', *Economic History Review*, 58(1): 113–39.
———. (2007) 'Acquisitions and firm growth: Creating Unilever's ice cream and tea business', *Business History*, 49(1): 8–28.
Li, L. (2006) 'Understanding corporate political activities: A comparative study of 16 firms of different sizes across industries and countries', PhD Thesis, University of Reading, UK.

Mills, D. E. (1995) 'Why retailers sell private labels', *Journal of Economics and Management Strategy*, 4(3): 509–28.

Miskell, P. (2004) 'Cavity protection or cosmetic perfection? Innovation and marketing of toothpaste brands in the United States and Western Europe, 1955–1985', *Business History Review*, 78(1): 29–60.

Senker, J. (1988) *A Taste for Innovation: British Supermarkets' Influence on Food Manufacturers*, Bradford: Horton.

Seth, A. and G. Randall (2001) *The Grocers: The Rise and Rise of the Supermarket Chains*, London: Kogan Page.

Tedlow, R. (1990) *New and Improved: The Story of Mass Marketing in America*, Oxford: Heinemann.

Contributors

Mark Casson is Professor of Economics at the University of Reading and Director of the Centre for Institutional Performance, also at Reading. He has published widely on the economics of the multinational enterprise, entrepreneurship, and business culture. He is coeditor of the *Oxford Handbook of Entrepreneurship* (2006) and currently holds a Leverhulme Major Research Fellowship for the study of the economics of social networks. Casson is also a consultant for the DTI (Central Evaluation Team), Trade Partners UK. Previously he has acted as a consultant to the European Commission (Social Affairs), New Zealand Treasury, UNCTAD (Transnational Corporations), and World Bank (various projects), as well as private companies such as BT and DTZ.

Jennifer Davis is the Herchel Smith College Lecturer in Intellectual Property Law in the Law Faculty, University of Cambridge and a Fellow of Wolfson College. She has a particular interest in trademark law and unfair competition and has published extensively on these topics, including *Intellectual Property Law* in Butterworth's Core Text series, third edition. Before joining the Faculty, Dr. Davis practised as a lawyer in the area of intellectual property litigation.

Paul Duguid is Adjunct Professor in the School of Information at the University of California, Berkeley and Research Professor in the School of Business and Management at Queen Mary, University of London. He is interested in issues of quality, particularly in the 'information age', and this has led him to investigate methods of warranting, including trademarks. He is author (with John Seely Brown) of *The Social Life of Information* and of essays that range from wine history to organizational knowledge.

Per H. Hansen is Professor of Business History at the Centre for Business History, Copenhagen Business School. He has published books and articles on topics as diverse as financial and banking history (including financial crises and central banking), the history of Danish Modern

Furniture Design, and organizational culture and change. He is also interested in branding and consumer culture in a historical and narrative perspective. He has spent two years in the USA, at Rutgers University (1997), UC Berkeley (2004–2005), and was recently Alfred D. Chandler Jr. International Visiting Scholar at Harvard Business School (2005).

Michael Heller is a teaching fellow at the School of Management, Royal Holloway, University of London. His research focuses on the history of corporate communications, such as company magazines, and is increasingly engaging with marketing and organization theory. He is particularly interested in how large-scale organizations built up legitimacy and fostered relationships with their publics through the development and use of media. Heller completed his PhD on the history of clerical employees in London and the development of work in large scale organizations between 1880 and 1914.

Christian Helmers is a DPhil student at the Department of Economics at Oxford University and a member of Wolfson College. He is also a Research Fellow at the Kiel Institute in Germany. His research focuses on the link between innovation, networks, and firm performance. He is also engaged in research on international trade and economic development. Helmers studied at the Catholic Universities of Rio de Janeiro and Eichstaett-Ingolstadt before earning his first degree in Economics from the University of Lausanne. He also holds an MSc from Oxford University and a postgraduate degree from the Kiel Institute.

David M. Higgins is the 40th Anniversary Reader in Business and Economic History at the University of York. His major research interests are the UK textile industry; aspects of corporate governance and industrial performance, including mergers and acquisitions; and the protection of intellectual property. He has received grants from the ESRC, Leverhulme Trust, and the Nuffield Foundation. He is a Fellow of the Royal Historical Society.

Jack Keenan has managed great global trademarks throughout his business career. He is the former CEO of Diageo's wine and spirits business, with leading worldwide brands such as Smirnoff Vodka, Johnnie Walker Scotch whisky, Baileys Irish Cream, Tanqueray, and Gordon's Gin, and so many more. Diageo is the leading premium drinks company in the world, and was formed when Jack merged Grand Metropolitan's International Distillers and Vintners with Guinness's United Distillers in 1997. Jack then led the acquisition of Seagram's wine and spirits, which completed the initial consolidation of the industry. Prior to joining the wine and spirits industry, Jack worked for 33 years for the leading food company in the USA, General Foods, and its successor company, Kraft Foods. Ultimately, Jack was CEO, and then Chairman, of Kraft Foods International. Among the brands he nurtured were Maxwell House Coffee, Jacobs Suchard, and, of course, Kraft Cheese. In 2001, Jack founded Grand Cru Consulting Ltd., and in that capacity chairs the Stock Spirits Group and is a nonexecutive director of Synergy Group (Moscow) and Revolymer Ltd. Jack graduated with honors from Tufts University in Boston and earned an MBA from Harvard University.

Teresa da Silva Lopes is Professor of International Business at the University of York. Her research interests range from globalization, the evolution of international business and the multinational enterprise, to international strategy and marketing, the role of brands in the creation of global capitalism and corporate governance. She is the author of numerous books and articles on brands and trademarks and the growth of firms, including *Global Brands and the Evolution of Multinationals in Alcoholic Beverages* (2007) and *Internationalisation and Concentration in Port Wine* (1998). She is completing a ESRC-funded project on the history of brands and trademarks, jointly, with Paul Duguid and John Mercer. She has held visiting research fellowships at the University of California Berkeley, and École Polytechnique, and a postdoctoral position at Said Business School, Oxford University. She is currently a Council Member and Webmaster of the British Association of Business Historians, a member of the Newcomen Prize Committee of the journal *Enterprise & Society*, a fellow of the Network on Dynamics of Institutions and Markets in Europe (DIME), codirector of the Centre for Globalisation Research (QMUL), a visiting research fellow at Universidade Católica Portuguesa, and a research associate of the Centre for International Business History and Centre for Institutional Performance at the University of Reading. She is former Reviews Editor for the journal *Business History*, and Trustee of the American Business History Conference.

Spyros Maniatis is Professor in Intellectual Property Law, Queen Mary, University of London. His research interests are in the history and economics of trademark law and innovation theories. Selected books include *Trade Marks in Europe: A Practical Jurisprudence* (Sweet and Maxwell 2006); *Perspectives on Intellectual Property* (Vol. 4): *Intellectual Property and Ethics*, with L. Bently (eds.) (Sweet & Maxwell 1998); *Trade Marks, Trade Names, and Unfair Competition World Law and Practice*, with J.R. Olsen and C. Garrigues (Sweet & Maxwell; FT Law & Tax 1996).

John Mercer is Postdoctoral Research Assistant in the School of Business and Management at Queen Mary, University of London, investigating the history of trademarks. He has published on propaganda and politicized consumption in the votes-for-women movement in Britain, as well as on the history of brands and trademarking. He received his PhD in History from the University of Portsmouth.

Peter Miskell is a Senior Lecturer in Business History at the University of Reading Business School. His main research interests are in the history of the international film industry and the evolution of multinationals in the fast moving consumer products sector. He has recently published articles in both areas in journals such as *Business History Review, Business History, Economic History Review*, and *Enterprise and Society*.

Mark Rogers is Economics Fellow at Harris Manchester College, which is Oxford University's mature student college. His research encompasses economic growth, intellectual property, and innovation. He analyses country-level data to understand how technology, education, and communications interact to yield economic growth. He also uses firm-level data to investigate the impact of innovation and intellectual property, with a specific focus on SMEs. He received his PhD in Economics from the Australian National University in 1997, after studying at Warwick University and the London School of Economics.

Stefan Schwarzkopf is Lecturer in Global Marketing in the School of Business and Management at Queen Mary, University of London. His research interests are in the history of advertising, market research and public relations in the twentieth century. Schwarzkopf is a graduate of the University of Jena (Germany). His PhD at Birkbeck College is on the institutional and cultural history of the advertising industry in Great Britain from 1900 to 1950. He has work experience in the advertising and PR industry, where he worked for Philip Morris brands (Marlboro) and Absolut Vodka.

Nigel Wadeson is Lecturer in Economics at the University of Reading. His main research interests lie in information processes, decision making, the internal organization of the firm, contracting relationships, and entrepreneurship. A natural application of his expertise is to the role of reputation in trade. He has also been involved in a number of projects providing high-level policy advice on export promotion. He is co-editor of the Oxford Handbook of Entrepreneurship (2006)

Index

Page numbers in *italics* denotes an illustration/table

211, 217; country 3, 4, 45, 50, 77–99; industry 45, 50; product 46
imitation 105, 108, 112, *see also* counterfeiting
individual brands xv, 5, 28, 32, 194, 224
Industrial Welfare Society 198
industry-level trademarking 69–72
information asymmetry: and trademarks 57
infringement, trademark (Britain) 102–14, 184; definition 102; evolution of trademark law following Trade Marks Act (1875) 106–10; and Lancashire cotton textile industry 111–12; law and trademark registration 104–6
injunction 112, 113
intellectual property 9, 10, 16, 56–58, 65, 73, 114, 127, 131, 153, 155, 165, 166, 229
Inn Crystal v. Waterford Wedgewood Plc (2005) 102, 114n4
innovation: as 'creative destruction' 69, 71, 73; definition 129; and trademarks 3, 57, 119, 120, 122–4, 127–30, 131
intangible assets 61, 62, 125, 187
Intel 46, 133n15, 138, 140, 141, 152, 153, 154–5, 156–7
'Intel Inside' campaign 46, 154, 155, 157, 161n27
intellectual property rights 127
Interbrand 167
intermediation: and export promotion 47–8, 48; and reputation 37–9
internal marketing: and Shell-Mex 197–200, 211
internal reputation 42–3
International Air Traffic Association 203
International Standards Organization 44
International Trademark Association (INTA) 120
Inwood Laboratories Inc. v. Ives Laboratories 129

J
J. Walter Thompson *see* JWT
Jaffe, E.D. 81, 84
James, Henry 145
Japan 44; trademark applications 56

Johns, A. 142
journals, in-house 198–9
Juhl, Finn 87
JWT (J. Walter Thompson) 167, 169, 173–6, *174*, 184, 187, 188; advertisement *185*; conducting of research surveys 180; founding 173; Lux campaign in America 178–9; Lux campaign in Britain 180–3, *182*; services provided 173, *175*; use of market research 181–2

K
Kahn, B.Z. 16 [or Khan?]
Kaye, Danny 92
Kennedy, John F. 95
Kenney, M. 140
King's Patent Agency 170
Koehn, N. 140; *Brand New* 16
Kotler and Gertner 78 [not in bib]

L
Lancashire cotton textile industry 4, 111–12, 116n39
Landes, N. 5, 123
Landor 167
Langdale, Lord 105
Langlois, R. 139
Lanham Act (1946) 13, 28n11 15
law 4–5; evolution of trademark 106–10; formalization of brand management in 183–7; trademark registration and 11–14, 104–6; *see also* Common Law
Leaf, Son & Co. 116n34
legal issues 105, 108; *see also* law
LeMahieu, D.L. 208
Lever Brothers 6, 167, 168, 178, 179, 195 *see also* Lux
Lever v. Goodwin (1886) 112
Lever, William Hesketh 170
Levy, Sidney 188
Licencing Act (1662) 143
lifestyle brand 168, 182–3
lifestyle research 168
Lindemann, J. 134n37
line extension xiv, xv, 125, 168, 178
linear regression model 29n15 69
Linux 154
Litman, Jessica 123–4
logo 36
London Press Exchange: trade advertisements *186*

For Product Safety Concerns and Information please contact our EU
representative GPSR@taylorandfrancis.com
Taylor & Francis Verlag GmbH, Kaufingerstraße 24, 80331 München, Germany